The Mystery of the Mayan Hieroglyphs

The Vision of an Ancient Tradition

Richard Luxton with Pablo Balam

The Mystery
of the
Mayan Hieroglyphs

The Mystery
of the
Mayan Hieroglyphs

The Vision of an Ancient Tradition

*Richard Luxton
with Pablo Balam*

1817

HARPER & ROW, PUBLISHERS, San Francisco
Cambridge, Hagerstown, Philadelphia, New York,
London, Mexico City, São Paulo, Sydney

F1435.3
R3
L89
1981

Originally published in Great Britain by Rider & Company, Hutchinson Publishing Group, London, under the title *Mayan Dream Walk*, 1981.

FIRST U.S. EDITION

Library of Congress
Cataloging in Publication Data

Luxton, Richard.
   The mystery of the Mayan hieroglyphs.

   Bibliography: p. 245.
   1. Mayas—Religion and mythology. 2. Mayas—Writing. 3. Indians of Mexico—Religion and mythology. 4. Indians of Mexico—Writing.
I. Balam, Pablo. II. Title.
F1435.3.R3L89 1982   972′.01   81-48211
ISBN 0-06-065315-9   AACR2

82 83 84 85 86 10 9 8 7 6 5 4 3 2 1

I saw in the night visions, and behold, *one* like the Son of man came with the clouds of heaven, and came to the Ancient of Days, and they brought him near before him. . . .

I came near unto one of them that stood by, and asked him the truth of all this. So he told me, and made me know the interpretation of the things.

Daniel vii 13–16

Contents

Illustrations

Acknowledgements

I am particularly grateful to my father and mother for their help and encouragement – moral, intellectual, and material. They placed this work within its Biblical quotations, beginning and end. To my brothers John and Robert for their time and inventiveness on my behalf. To Daphne Mango and Roger Brammer for some now dusty but not forgotten conversations. To Ray and Sandra Sentis, Rob and Kathy Sinclair, Joe and Hilary Swartz. To Kennan Bowden, Richard Poole, and Jimmy Tranks for some high altitude, wild days in Mexico City. To Ingrid von Essen and Kevin McDermott at Hutchinson for their early interest and careful editing of the text. To Sylvia and Richard and Professor S. Henry Wassén. I am grateful to Federico Copé at Conacyt, Mexico, and to Michael Lane, Dawn Ades, and Munro S. Edmonson for their genuine professional support. I would like to acknowledge the fundamental support of the Mexican National Council of Science and Technology (Conacyt) for their original invitation to come to Mexico and, equally, the British Academy for a timely and crucial Research Award which made the definitive writing of this work with don Pablo a possibility. I wish also to thank Caroline Pirie for her painstaking corrections, criticisms and encouragement – and for her excellent illustrations of the text.

There were unforgettable days during the research and exploration which went into this work. I am especially grateful to my brother Robert Edward for his acute observation of the Maya, for the photographs which accompany the text, and for the laughter and shared times in the Yucatan.

Finally, I am especially beholden to the villagers of Tulum and to don Pablo and his family for 'causing me to learn' this walk.

The quotations from Mircea Eliade's *Myths, Dreams and Mysteries* on pages 32–33 and 227 are reprinted with the permission of the publishers – the Fontana Library of Theology and Philosophy, Collins, London, 1968. The lines from the Quiche Maya Book of Counsel, *The Popol Vuh*, translated by Munro S. Edmonson (1971) and quoted on pages 192–197, and 226, are by permission of the publishers, the Middle American Research Institute, Tulane University, New Orleans, USA.

Preface

Don Pablo Balam's knowledge of his forefathers' history, thought and custom is extremely pure despite over four hundred years of Mayan contact with Spanish European ways. How can this be so?

In conversation don Pablo told me of his family origins. In pre-Columbian times over four hundred years ago they resided near the town of Ebtun, ten miles east of the famed ruins of Chichén Itza. From such times until the early nineteenth century, don Pablo recalled, his family had occupied lands within the jurisdiction of Ebtun. Later I was able to check the colonial Spanish records of this town and confirmed that a branch of the Balam lineage did indeed reside there, the records going back to the pre-Columbian name of Ah Cot Balam.

In the early part of the nineteenth century, during the upheavals which marked the independence of Mexico from the Spanish Crown and, for a time, of Yucatan from Mexico itself, don Pablo's forefathers migrated from Ebtun deep into the independent Mayan lands south of Valladolid in search of peace, an absence of quarrelsome provincial politicians, and a consequent freedom of thought and movement. Here the family settled until the 1940s, when famine pushed don Pablo's grandparents to the east coast and the village of Tulum, where I was to meet him thirty years later.

Glancing back along the trail his family had walked in the

preceding 150 years and more, from the shadows of the ruined city of Chichén Itza, where doubtless his earlier ancestors had attended resplendent festivals and market days, don Pablo could note the way in which succeeding generations had avoided the more exploitative, enslaving Spanish ways, keeping well out of the way of the New World and time that had come to the Yucatan in the sixteenth century. He could see how, under the guidance of learned Mayan shamans such as his grandfather, don Dolores Balam, his people had succeeded in 'bringing the Great Idea' as he called it. This 'Great Idea' was the ancient covenant given to the Mayan people in Classic times over a thousand years ago. It was for them to remember, to carry forward, a sign, an essence, a 'Shrouded Glory' as it is called in their sacred Books of Counsel.

It is said of traditional peoples such as the Mayas that contact with progress, with science, with modernity, inevitably brings the collapse and destruction of their beliefs, culture and civilization. And yet for over four hundred years these apparently nondescript Mayans have withstood such a fate. They are still there – nearly a million of them in the Yucatan peninsula alone. They have held their ancestral lands, they have held the rhythms and dignity of their ancient walk without loss of step, humour, or faith in One True God, known to them long before the arrival of the white man. They have overcome and they have overcome and they have overcome.

Still, if the Mayan vision retains its purity it is not because it has been remembered and repeated parrot fashion – without understanding, without renewed awareness of its continuing value in each succeeding generation. If the Mayan vision is pure today it survives because the people have repeatedly seen deep into our social order, have seen far into our disoriented ways and know that the vision of their forefathers cannot be ignored and scorned for ever by recent arrivals who have made this continent their domain.

The Shrouded Glory cannot eternally be obscured by the seemingly all-encompassing material cloud of unknowing that has surrounded and blinded us since our arrival. This New World is new only to us; to the Mayans it is as ancient and sacred as the Promised Land. They know we have no meanings in our scientific repertory which can rival or surpass what has been revealed to them in their mysterious scripture. We have no great teachers who can replace the learning way they have inherited, a way which reveals the innermost mysteries of this time and world we arrogantly call 'new'.

The living Maya retain a clear vision of their ancient way because, practically speaking, it answers profound human questions in ways science cannot. It is shamanic in essence, God-given in its Shrouded Glory. We may work with these friendly, loving people as they have always desired we should do: we may learn with them, exchanging that which is of value in our world of thought and practice for that which is of value in theirs. We will never dissolve their vision of everything Mayan.

The conversations in this book between don Pablo and myself were recorded on cassettes and subsequently transcribed and edited by both of us into the form in which they appear. They are examples of the dialogue possible across cultural boundaries. Most often they were the spontaneous product of being there. The conversations with don Miguel in the state penitentiary were, naturally enough, not recorded. They are based on memory and notes taken at the time.

The ultimate authenticity of the material presented here will be confirmed when other Mayans are given the opportunity to talk their books and when the ancient Mayan texts are transcribed and deciphered by scholars other than the two of us. Mayan civilisation has been literate since time immemorial. Learning to understand this literacy with the living people brings out not only the mistaken conclusions of our history and anthropology of the New World but also its progressive disintegration. What is offered here by don Pablo Balam and myself is a first counsel only, an opening of the step.

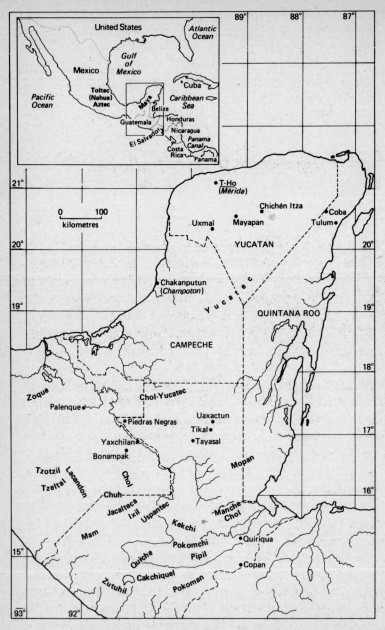

1 *Map of the Mayan area Central America: Location of Mayan area*

•

1

The Realm of Shadows

 Over by the market the *jarana* bands were preparing their performance, the sound of saxophone and clarinet echoing clearly, the drum lost in the loud rumble of traffic. There were fruit sellers, ironmongers, tinkers and haberdashers on the sunny streets of Mérida. It was carnival time in the capital of the Mexican state of Yucatan, the beginning of the dry season. Shy and beautiful Mayan women were dressed in their finest *huipil* dresses, the borders embroidered with multicoloured flowers. Freshly bathed, with hair carefully combed and tied back, gold earrings and necklaces displayed, they waited in the shade for the dancing to begin.

There was an air of excitement as the weeks of work approached their culmination. Thousands of Indians had journeyed from their outlying towns and villages to the capital, to the site of the ancient Mayan city of T-Ho, the 'place of five' within the jurisdiction of the Xiu lineage. There were to be bullfights and dancing, processions and religious pilgrimages. Along the streets there were bright banners and bunting, and temporary stalls selling pottery and cloth, herbal medicines, native sweets and foodstuffs. There were penny-traders selling popcorn and crushed calabash seeds mixed with honey, walnuts and prunes. There were people selling hand mirrors in plastic frames, cheap rings and necklaces, toys and whistles. A

Mayan Indian was carefully examining the intricate Eastern design on a cotton scarf, a new hat on his head.

I strolled from stall to stall, trying to take it all in. There were families with babes in arms, children walking beside them fascinated by the noise, the crowding of people and the tall buildings. There were Spanish and Indian Mexicans and a scattering of tourists. All were being pulled towards the distant music and clamour of a fairground.

In the shadows of the market there were bars and restaurants, while crouched on the pavements Indian women sold neat piles of fruit and vegetables; tomatoes, peppers, mangoes and oranges. A middle-aged woman, jovial and healthy, offered me sweet potatoes and *tamales*, ground maize and chicken wrapped and cooked in fresh banana leaves. It was food as ancient in recipe as Mayan civilization itself, I thought, settling down to unwrap two *tamales*. The woman nodded with approval at my appetite and watched me slowly eat the sacred golden grace of the Mayan Indians.

When a Spanish army first stepped into the Mayan world in 1527 they were astonished at the size of the towns they found. 'It seemed as if the entire land was one vast town,' they recounted later. The Spanish noted that around large *cenotes*, which were deep natural waterholes revealed by a collapse in the soft porous limestone plateau of the Yucatan, there were often as many as ten thousand dwellings. These towns were 'well arranged and they kept the land clean, free of weeds and planted with good trees. The houses were arranged in this way: in the middle of the towns were the temples with handsome plazas, and around these temples were the houses of the rulers and priests, and after these came those of the principal people.' The Spanish marvelled at the good order of the land, the degree of urbanization and the obvious sophistication of the civilization before them. Within a hundred years of the Spaniards' arrival, these towns were reduced and often ruined, the people scattered in the forests for ever.

At the time of that first forceful Spanish entry the whole of the Yucatan peninsula, the southern thumb of Mexico adjacent to Belize and opposite Florida, was divided by the Indians into seventeen jurisdictions, ruled over by specific lineages – the Xius, the Cocoms, the Canuls, the Chels – a litany of privileged and proud Indian families. At the head of each ruling lineage was the *halach uinic*, the 'True Man'. The title was handed down from father to eldest son, providing the latter showed himself worthy both in personal qualities and in application. Each *halach uinic* directed the government of the capital of his jurisdiction and formulated foreign policy. Quite often the area he governed was hardly larger than an English county. Nevertheless the civil bureaucracy at his disposal was complex and advanced, the Mayan body politic sensitive to just statecraft.

The *halach uinic* appointed *batab(ob)* to govern satellite towns within his domain. These officials were responsible for legal matters, for public administration, for good government. Each *batab* could appoint other officials, to keep order at public *fiestas* and to supervise civic projects. The *yalba uinicob*, the Mayan commoners – farmers, hunters, and fishermen – exerted a strong democratic influence over this administration. They set up councils in charge of subdivisions of each town. They collected tribute of maize, cotton cloth, native poultry, vegetables and fruit, and supervised communal food stores. The tribute given to the lords was not onerous and the *yalba uinicob* expected much in return. They examined and criticized their leaders and addressed them face to face. They expected good government and they balanced private ownership of the fruits of their labour, the products of forest and cultivated *milpa*, with public ownership of the land and with cooperative projects such as the building of roads and the care of the old and infirm.

The Spanish army of 1527, under the command of Francisco Montejo, had cause for wonder and awe as they surveyed Yucalpeten, the 'land of the deer' which supported a population of perhaps six million Indians. Although it was a new and frightening world for the Europeans, it was an old, old world to the Mayans. They had already lived several millennia on this continent, the path they had walked trailing back visibly at least two thousand years and much earlier in a now invisible manner. Their civilization was older, by hundreds of years, than the Aztec of central Mexico, older than the Inca to the south in Peru, older than the Iroquois and their nations in North America.

Until the close of the first millennium AD the Mayans had existed as a complex urban society inhabiting the present-day area encompassed by all of Guatemala and Belize, parts of Honduras and El Salvador, and the southern Mexican states of Yucatan and Chiapas. In these seemingly inhospitable jungle and mountain regions the Mayans had created miracles in Stone-Age engineering. They had built religious centres like Tikal, Palenque, Quirigua, Piedras Negras and hundreds of others, each covering many square miles with temples, high mounds and plazas, ballcourts, market places and centres of learning. They dug canals, reservoirs, irrigation networks and terraces and they raised causeways or *sac be* (white roads), linking centres hundreds of miles apart. All this was accomplished without metal tools.

These 'Classic' Maya were divided by lowland and highland ecologies and, most significantly, by the many forms of the Mayan word which they had evolved in earlier stages of their civilization. Yucatec Mayan is one of twenty-four Mayan languages surviving to this day, mostly incomprehensible to one another. Yet the Classic Maya had all shared and been defined by a deep and penetrating vision which they left enshrined and immortalized in hieroglyphic writings carved upon stone stelae, temple walls and stairways. These are scattered now in jungle and mountain regions, in museums and private collections.

For me the most compelling qualities of this Classic vision are its extensiveness, from the Guatemalan highlands to the Yucatec lowlands, and the cohesion of purpose which its development and expression implied over at least a thousand year period. Though I had yet to understand any of the intricacies of this ancient written vision, I was astonished at the hidden power in the now fragmented scale and design of its architectural and hieroglyphic expression.

During the five hundred years preceding the arrival of the Spanish, Mayan unity had fractured and been overlaid by new cultures emanating from central Mexico. New lords came to rule in some Mayan areas, disassembling and obscuring the Classic body of their civilization. There were Aztec warrior groups who subjugated some Mayan nations, notably in highland Guatemala; there were Toltec scholars who listened, learnt and taught; there were Itza who resettled Chichén Itza and devoted themselves, brokenly, to the ancient Mayan ways of knowledge. These incursive dynasties built architectural showplaces which greatly exaggerated their spiritual and intellectual domination of the Maya.

The strongest indigenous resistance to this descent of aggressive, predominantly central Mexican lineages was maintained by the Yucatec Maya, throughout the five hundred years of the post-Classic era. Here in Yucatan the ancient hieroglyphic vision was remembered in its fullest form, here the literature of the Classic Mayan spirit lords continued to be studied. When the Spanish touched this world in 1527 and definitively occupied it in 1541, with the foundation of Mérida, they were just one more destructive ruling class to be suffered and won over by the Mayas, one more foreign minority deluded and enchanted by a world which remained, somehow, unquestionably Mayan.

I wandered away from the market, back to the main plaza of Mérida, dominated by the cathedral fortress of the early Franciscan priests. In the less than four hundred yards which separated this square from the market I entered a Spanish world, erudite and cosmopolitan. The gardens and trees set before the cathedral were well tended. Stone seats and wooden benches in the shade were occupied by people reading newspapers, resting, talking or eating, while shoeshine boys and hammock sellers hovered and hustled nearby.

On the other side of the plaza there was a row of cafés and shops, newsstands and restaurants inside a colonnaded arch shading tables and chairs upon the pavement. The palace of the conqueror of the Yucatan, Francisco Montejo, faced the cafés. In a large carved relief over the main doorway the point was made without delicacy – two conquistadores stood on the heads of downcast Indians while malign medieval dwarfs acted as custodians.

Beyond the main plaza numerous small colonial inns were tucked obscurely into the narrow streets, reflecting a growing tourism by Mexicans and Americans, yet there was a sense of a rapidly fading era here. Dark foyers gave way to tiled patios, interior gardens, fountains and tall narrow windows barred on the outside. Under the high ceilings of the rooms fans turned lazily, while decrepit plumbing knocked and tumbled around the buildings. There was something of Cordoba here, and of Seville, but it was rapidly being superseded by the air-conditioned sameness of half-hearted travellers.

I ate in a small restaurant bar in the back streets. There was cold Montejo beer and a frosted glass, oyster cocktails, and white fish marinated in lime juice, tomato, chilli and chopped onion. The people of Mérida were subdued and polite drinkers, talking in low tones, addressing each other as don Antonio, don Enrique and so forth, briefly embracing upon first meeting, shaking hands with friends they saw every day. Yucatecans, they dressed in *guayaberas*, light cotton shirts worn outside their trousers, embroidered delicately and decorated with a surfeit of buttons. They wore loose-fitting cotton trousers, sandals and panama hats. They spoke Mayan as casually as Spanish, a remarkable bilingualism I had never encountered elsewhere in America, where Indian languages are usually dismissed as mere dialects.

The federal police agent who arrested me outside wore a *guayabera*, dark glasses, polyester trousers and pinched Italian shoes. He showed me his credentials and asked to see my papers. I showed him my passport and official visa. He scowled at my youthful appearance and examined the impressive visa stamped in my passport.

'There is something wrong here, señor', he said after a while, without a trace of real politeness in his voice. 'You will have to accompany me.'

I began to argue in Spanish. The man was angry and antagonistic. My fluency distressed him further and he grabbed my arm tightly and began pulling me along the pavement. Only in Mexico, I thought, still in good humour, could an official visa get you into trouble rather than protect you from it. This gorilla had never seen a 'tourist' with one of these and he thought there was something wrong with the paper rather than with his perception of it. But I went along, still under the illusion that things would be quickly straightened out and I could get back to the carnival.

A maximum security cell in the state penitentiary was my destination. Unwillingly I stepped into the underworld capital of the Yucatan, fearing Dickensian nightmare visions of dribbling psychosis, rats and darkness. A solid, one-hundred-year-old prison, painted yellow, it stood by the railway tracks leading from the town. It was guarded by the Mexican army and run by a civilian governor. In the main gaol there were several hundred prisoners. In the maximum security cells of la Redonda, the hub of the penitentiary, I counted a further 130.

Around me there were high walls and bored sentries gazing down. In this prison within a prison there were four main cells, fifty feet by thirty, set along the lengths of a courtyard. The far wall of this contained two smaller cells. The *federal* had handed me over to the prison authorities after a night in a downtown precinct. We were not on good terms when we parted. Most of my belongings were missing, bounty collected by the police, but my rucksack, sleeping-bag, books, letters, pen and toothbrush had been returned. I had not been physically abused and I was now, temporarily, out of the clutches of the police.

There were no guards inside la Redonda. I was safely behind

several locked gates. Leaning back against the wall I waited for something to happen. A prisoner explained where I was to leave my rucksack, the floorspace I was to occupy, the first rules of the game. I was free to move from cell to cell, to sit in the courtyard and to associate with the others from dawn to dusk. At first my mind, numbed by fear, was incapable of registering names or faces.

Slowly I began to realize that this was not the ordinary Mexican prison I had imagined it to be. The cell was spotless, including the solitary toilet and shower used by thirty people or more. However poor, all those around me wore their own clothes and kept themselves immaculately clean. I began to notice that nearly half of the prisoners were distinctively Indian. This did not surprise me, since I had read somewhere that there were nearly a million Indians in the peninsula, some 50 per cent of its overall population. The Mayans inside la Redonda seemed to exert a considerable control over it. The place played to a distinct rhythm, calmed down, meditative, relaxed. It lacked the *macho* violence I had expected and heard about elsewhere in Mexico. The mood here had to be coming from the Mayans.

Covertly I glanced at an old Indian who had been watching me from across the cell. He had come in a few moments before, looking around for me, cautious but interested. Now he beckoned me over. He was taller and thinner than most Mayans, normally as stocky as boxers. His face was dark and gaunt, Aztec in its sobriety, weathered with deep wrinkles recording the hardships of agricultural life in the Yucatan. I could not judge his age. His eyes were so bright and penetrating that his glance was hard to meet and hold. I knew immediately that he was a spiritual leader of some sort amongst his people, and I wondered at his interest in me. We shook hands and he patted me on the shoulder, examining my face closely.

'I am don Miguel Caamal,' he said, more to himself than to me.

I introduced myself. I noted that his shirt was faded and

patched. He wore a pair of cotton trousers, the traditional Mayan *culex*, which reached only as far as his knees. On his feet he had a pair of leather *huaraches*, the soles cut from the rubber of old car tyres. He was bareheaded, a straw hat in his hand, his grey hair trimmed short. While he was evidently very poor, there was a self-respect here which greatly attracted me.

'Did they allow you to keep the books?' don Miguel asked, feigning casualness.

Momentarily taken aback at his first question, I paused for an answer. Before leaving Mexico City I had bought a couple of books on the Mayans. Each was extensively illustrated with examples of ancient Mayan hieroglyphs and photographs of various sacred Indian cities in the Yucatan and Guatemala. I assumed don Miguel was referring to these.

'Yes. Do you want to see them?' I motioned vaguely towards where I had left my few belongings.

'Perhaps they can wait until tomorrow,' don Miguel answered, reassured. 'You speak the language of Castille well. We can talk first. Many times I have wondered what you, the English, are thinking when you come to Yucatan with your books and the writings of the old ones, the *abuelos*.' After a few seconds he added, 'I have never known one of you able to speak to us. Now then is the time.'

Rather lamely I remarked that his Spanish was excellent. He shrugged indifferently, seeing it as an enforced necessity. I realized then that he was only revealing that he knew Spanish at all because he wanted to examine my books on the Mayas and ask me questions. The language of Castille was the common ground between us.

We moved to settle by the barred windows overlooking the courtyard. Cigarettes were offered and we squatted on our heels, Indian fashion. I had overcome the initial discomfort of this custom in the past and now found it natural and comfortable. Moreover I had previously noted that both *campesinos* and Indians alike quickly perceive the implications of such gestures on our part. In Mexico it is enough to begin establishing you as being more than a *gringo*.

In low tones don Miguel asked me where I came from and what I was doing wandering so far from home.

'Is there trouble in those places,' he wondered aloud, 'that you come here looking for another life? How is it that you have so much money that you don't need to keep *milpa*? I have seen you here in T-Ho with your money. You go into the bank and they give you money right away. How can this be? I ask myself. What do they do when there is a drought and they can't buy food with their money? Do they eat it as we eat the bark of the *cocol* tree when there is no maize?'

As we talked people approached to listen. Their initial reticence had restrained their now evident curiosity in me and I had been too distracted and withdrawn to look very closely at the men around me. They were aged eighteen upwards, of all shapes and origins. Half a dozen men were busy making hammocks. The frames were lined up across the cell. The bands of brightly coloured strings on each frame formed an everchanging wave pattern of primary colours as they wove hour into day, and days into months and years. In the far corner a couple of people were brewing coffee on a small primus. Others lay in their hammocks, sleeping, talking and reading. Outside in the courtyard people played handball while others came and went from a small store by the main gate of the Redonda.

Don Miguel was a true man from the forest, utterly absorbed by the ancient Mayan way of life. I began explaining that, unlike the Mayas, not everyone was a farmer keeping *milpa* out in the forest, relying on maize as a staple food, self-sufficient from a monetary economy.

'When is the latest it has rained here?' I asked.

'One time, I think it was in 1950, there was a great drought here. It just did not rain. Even when the *h-menob*, the shamans, made the *chai-chac* ceremony it did not rain. May was when we expected it and it did not arrive until October. The *chacs*, the spirits who make it rain, deserted us.'

'And what did the people eat?' I asked, after I had absorbed his reference to the Mayan rain-making ceremony. It was an ancient ritual which had survived for thousands of years because, normally, it worked.

'At that time there was a lot of maize stored from the year before. People worked their *milpas* hard in those days. There was an abundance of maize. Each family had a store in reserve, out on their *milpas*. But who does that now? There is money but no maize. In those days the people survived because they were prepared. But not now, not any more. Now there is only money . . . paper. What are they going to do when there is nothing to buy with it?'

'Then we will all be finished,' I eventually answered. I could see that the world we found so real, a world in which we could instantly put a monetary price on everything, a number on a piece of paper, was as mysterious and incomprehensible to don Miguel as Mayan hieroglyphs were to me.

Don Miguel nodded and carried on. 'Those who see, who know, are in a hurry to plant as much as possible. The Earth King will always provide. Not like those other kings who walk the world saying to us "It is all mine, give it to me".'

There was a general murmur of agreement from the people around us. Don Miguel was beginning to overcome an initial shyness and warm to his theme.

'How many generations have there been of this Spanish descendancy?' he asked rhetorically. 'They say thirteen generations of these rulers, these Castillian kings have been upon us. Now it is finishing, now is the reversal. When that descendancy began, when this generation in which we find ourselves began, in that time each people had their king. Each one over there, a king,' don Miguel said, pointing to the corner of the cell, 'and over there, a king, and over there another and another.' He marked the four quarters of his world. 'Our king was Xiu . . . I don't remember his first name, his surname was Xiu. That finished. Then came . . . well, egoism, slavery. When the Spanish came to control the Americas they put slavery here. That is what they came to give us'. He was silent for a while, his thoughts here and at the end of a past world.

I waited, wanting to hear more. No one said anything. After

a while I asked, 'Do you think the Mayans are going to disappear now?'

'We only remain from the slavery,' don Miguel said, 'the power of the Mayans is going to come with the ending of this world. There is too much evil. Where is there going to be salvation? Who will be saved? The *abuelos* had this written, the ending of this world. So they say. Soon we will be able to see if it is true. They say that we are going to see the final justice . . . to see who has won and who has lost.'

All the while he was speaking don Miguel was watching my reactions carefully. His tone was not angry or bitter. He was offering counsel and seeking discussion. From my expression he could see that I was somewhat sceptical about the final justice and the return of what I took to be the spiritual power of the Mayans. I realized that my scepticism, if necessary, was also superficial and born of my European point of view. Don Miguel had made a point of ascribing his words to the writings of the Mayan *abuelos*, the ancient hieroglyphs still largely undeciphered by outsiders. To doubt his words without knowing the old Indian writing was a sign of ignorance rather than enlightenment. I felt that don Miguel was watching for this.

Sensing my hesitancy, don Miguel suggested that we leave further conversation until the next day. The meeting broke up gradually and I bade him goodbye. I hadn't risen to a certain challenge put to me, I knew, but I wanted to proceed with a degree of caution. My immediate predicament loomed larger in my mind than a mysterious and hypothetical ending of the world. I was still expecting someone to come and pull me out of this shadow realm. I had to come to terms with the unlikelihood of immediate release. My tension was like a physical force pressing down on me.

2

The Whispering of Ancient Voices

The Mayas were expecting the beginning of another era when Francisco Montejo and his army arrived in 1527. In the preceding hundred years five of their spiritual leaders had spoken of the coming of a new word and one of them, Chilam Balam, had been very specific, as reported in the *Relación de la Ciudad de Mérida*, dated 1579 and compiled by various authors. It records that there were some provinces which never warred but rather received the Spanish in peace.

This was particularly the case with the province of Tutul Xiu whose capital was and is the town of Maní, fourteen leagues southeast of this city [Mérida]. A few years before the Spanish came to conquer there was an Indian leader here, who was a priest called Chilam Balam. They had him as a great prophet and diviner and he said that within a short time a white and bearded people would come from the East carrying a sign like this ✝ on high. Their gods would not reach [this sign] and would flee. These people were to rule the land and those people who received them in peace would not be harmed and those who warred would be killed. The people of this land would leave their idols and worship only one god, which [the Spaniards] worshipped and had to preach, and they would become tributaries. He had a cotton cloth woven and he said that this was to be the tribute they paid, and he ordered the lord of Maní, who was called Mochan Xiu, to offer the cloth to the idols so that it be kept as a memory. The sign of the cross which he had drawn was carved on numerous stones which were put in the patios of the temples where everyone could see them and he said that it was the green tree of the world. Many people were to see it as something new and it seemed that they worshipped it from that time. Later when the Spanish came and they saw that they brought with them the sign of the Holy Cross, which was like the one their prophet Chilam Balam had drawn, they knew that what he had said was true. They decided to receive the Spaniards in peace and not to make war, but be their friends, as they have been after they populated these provinces, and they helped them with supplies and mercenaries to conquer and pacify other provinces.

The counsels of the future given by Chilam Balam and by other Mayan priests, Napuc Tun, Ah Kuil Chel, Ahau Pech, and Natzin Abun Chan amongst them, were completely pessimistic. Only the Christian Word was to have meaning in a world of suffering never experienced before in such degree or intensity. Theft, murder, systematic injustice and general enslavement were to be the bowl of bitter fruit placed before them. It was not surprising then that other Mayan priests and the people under their jurisdictions took to flight or suicidal war as alternative policies. They also knew it was the end of one world and the beginning of another, disordered and unfavourable.

Historians and scholars, writing Mayan history from Spanish sources, have found Chilam Balam's prophecy an uncomfortable fact. Some say it was uttered in hindsight or after reports of the Spanish arrival in Cuba and Haiti had reached nearby Yucatan. Others have interpreted his words as a *post facto* Christianized account of native legends concerning the return of their culture heroes. They say they might even had been written by Spanish priests to trick the Mayans into conversion. In this way Mayan thought and history have been obscured rather than explained.

The words of Chilam Balam arose out of shamanic practices more ancient than Christianity. The Balam lineage extended back to the very dawn of Mayan civilization, to 300 BC and earlier. Other Mayans saw them as being possessed of particularly acute shamanic powers. Indeed they spoke of the *balams* as the original shamans amongst the people. The prophet, speaking in the early part of the 1500s, was the spokesman, the *chilam*, of this most ancient Indian family. His words were uttered in trance, his vision received from the spirits of the *abuelos* and from God, a dream induced by chant, drum and dance.

Wisdom or vision given this way, and brought to the visible world in the subsequent counsel of the shaman, contains distinctive traces of its supernatural origins. The shaman is able to 'see' the causes of an illness and to cure by explanation alone. He or she is able to retrieve lost souls and read people's thoughts. He has powers of clairvoyance and telepathy; he can see the future. These are paranormal abilities which demonstrate, in a practical manner, that the shaman has temporarily suppressed or abolished his normal sensibility. He has entered through the paradoxical gateway to the spirit world where past and future are one and the rules of secular time and space no longer hold true.

A shaman's powers may be directed towards remedying individual circumstances. He might use them to cure one sick person, or to divine an individual's future, or to fend off sorcery. Equally these powers might express themselves as a counsel for an entire community, as a remedy for disorders in the body politic as a whole. Chilam Balam's counsel was of this order, preparing the people for the disease and oppression to come. When the Spanish arrived, confirming Chilam Balam's words, they strengthened the Mayan faith in their ancient shamanic wisdom. The Christian Word reaffirmed, rather than undermined, their shamanic vision. In fact the Mayans believed that it had come from within this very way of learning.

A shaman's way consists of very specific techniques of learning. He is initiated by spontaneous vision often brought about by an accident or serious illness, an involuntary 'death' which pushes him, unwillingly and temporarily, through the gateway between worlds. A first vision derived from this journey to the realm of shadows, the land of the dead, is often puzzling, sometimes frightening, always paranormally powerful. It is a communication with the spirits of the ancients, a direct experience of God, which leaves the novice profoundly shaken, his previous sensibility irredeemably shattered.

The first vision establishes the novice on the path to illumination, to engendered inner light. Once he has begun and has been 'elected' by a first vision, the novice cannot defy the spirits of the *abuelos* and return to his previous sensibility. For years now he must engage upon a disciplined, systematic learning under the guidance of an established shaman. The learning way is twofold. He must acquire techniques for communicating, at will, with the spirit world. He must learn to induce trances and visions in himself and to interpret his dreams. Simultaneously he learns the traditions and songs of the people, the names and qualities of the spirits, ancient myths and rituals, curing practices and herbal medicine. The visionary powers he gradually acquires must be tempered by extraordinary knowledge of his culture and its ways.

A shaman's techniques for inducing visions might make use of alcohol, tobacco, or various plants with recognized hallucinogenic properties. He may employ meditative practices and long periods of fasting. The actual catalyst for the journey to the spirit world is not as important as being able to arrive at a genuine contemplation of one's own skeleton, to 'die' at will. It is in this intense contemplation that the shaman abolishes his normal existence and the rules of reality which govern it. A leading scholar and historian of shamanism, Mircea Eliade, has written:

such a spiritual exercise implies the 'exit from time' for not only is the shaman, by means of an interior vision, anticipating his physical death, but he is finding again what one might call the non-temporal source of life, the *bone*. Indeed for the hunting peoples the bone symbolises the ultimate root of animal life, the matrix from which the flesh is continually renewed. It is starting with the *bones* that animals and men are reborn; they maintain themselves a while in carnal existence, and when they die their 'life' is reduced to the essence concentrated in the skeleton, whence they will be born anew according to an uninterrupted cycle that constitutes an eternal return. It is duration alone, *time*, which breaks and separates, by the intervals of carnal existence, the timeless unity represented by the quintessence of life concentrated in the bones. By contemplating himself as a skeleton, the shaman does away with time and stands in the presence of the eternal source of life. (Mircea Eliade, *Myths, Dreams and Mysteries*, pp. 82–3)

In the case of the Yucatec Mayan shamans, and Chilam Balam in particular, this contemplation of their skeletons was intimately linked to the ancient hieroglyphic writing. Within these signs, carved in immortal stone and incised upon bone, their *abuelos*, most powerful shamans of Classic antiquity, had left a record of their 'skeleton'. The skeleton of Mayan writing was, and is, the immutable chronology it records. This system, utterly Mayan in its overall design, consists of a series of time cycles beginning with a twenty-day cycle known as the Uinal but expanding to cycles of tens of thousands, even millions of days. At the time of the Spanish arrival it was the Yucatec Maya who had continued the ancient count of time without error, retaining the unity of the skeleton of Classic Mayan wisdom. Chilam Balam's counsel of the future was the renewed flesh on this skeleton. According to the unbroken sequence of the count a new cycle of 256 years, a new 'world', was due to begin with the next Katun XI Ahau, the traditional twenty-'year' period (360 × 20 days) opening a cycle of thirteen *katuns*.*

The counsels of the shamans in the hundred years preceding the arrival of Francisco Montejo in 1527 were based upon far-seeing the nature of the forthcoming world which had been written into their chronological skeleton perhaps 1500 years before, perhaps earlier. While shamans might have

* Recorded by Bishop Landa in his *Relación de las Cosas de Yucatan*.

visions of varying intensities and detail, while they might even offer alternative counsels of action, the fact of a forthcoming new cycle had been built into their chronology when it was first designed. When the Christian Word arrived, it was, in consequence, seen as born of ancient Indian bones, a renewal of ancient shamanic understanding. And amongst this distinguished company Chilam Balam demonstrated, once again, the acute special powers of his lineage.

For his part Francisco Montejo left the Yucatan, after he had spied out the land over a six-month period. An army under the command of his son returned in 1539 and the Spanish capital of Mérida was established two years later in the very jurisdiction where Chilam Balam's counsel had been first published. The Mayas pointed out that 'the Spaniards finally reached the city of T-Ho in the year of Our Lord 1541, which was exactly at the first year of the era of Buluc (XI) Ahau.' They added, 'they also arrived in the month Pop which is the first month of our year.'

Francisco Montejo may have made judicious use of the Mayan counsels of the future in the instructions he gave his son. He had spent long enough in the Yucatan in 1527 to learn of them and to be told of the most propitious time and place for a definitive occupation. But neither he nor the Mayans he encountered could have rewritten the ancient count of time. In their respective ways both he and they were bowing to a Power superior to that which either commanded.

I was awakened by the loud ringing of a bell. I had slept fitfully on the hard floor. The initial adrenalin rush of my arrest and preliminary interrogation had worn off, but the coughs and conversation throughout the night, the lights left burning, and fear, had kept me alert until almost dawn. Now I awoke suddenly, my heart full of apprehension. I washed and nervously rolled up my sleeping bag.

The night before I had learnt a little about don Miguel. Talking with some of the Mayans who had been listening to his words, I discovered that he was considered to be a

powerful *h-men*, the Yucatec Maya word for a shaman. I had
asked a young Mayan, lying in a hammock in the corner of the
cell, what this meant to him.

'One who knows the secrets of the *abuelos*', he answered
without hesitation. 'He knows how to pray, he knows the
costumbre, the old traditions and customs. He guides us, he
gives us counsel.'

'But what are these traditions and secrets?' I asked. 'Are they
really the old, old secrets from before the Spanish?'

'I can't tell you that because I don't know,' the young man
said unperturbed. 'We listen to his words, his stories of the
abuelos, because there is power in them. Some say that they
have lost this power today and have no meaning. But you
must ask don Miguel about this. They say that you must study
hard, to see the power that is there. And then it is not certain
that you will see. Talk with don Miguel about this,' he
repeated.

'But why is a man like that, a great *h-men*, in here?' I pressed
him.

'Who knows? I have never asked him. Perhaps it is because
he is a *h-men* and has seen things invisible to us. But only God
knows, really, why he is here. Perhaps there is something he
must do here, and he came for that, and then he will just
disappear. The *h-menob*, the really powerful ones, are spirits
only and they do that sometimes.' He shrugged and began
asking me to teach him some English.

At seven o'clock the cells were unlocked and all the prisoners filed out into the yard for morning roll call. There were
two of these every day, early morning and an hour before
sunset. After the first we were free to move around within the
confines of la Redonda; after the second we were locked into
the cells for the night. Sometimes, I was to learn, there were
roll calls at random intervals during the day. This first day, the
freshness of the morning lifted my spirits momentarily, the
clear sunlight illuminating the darkness I was in. I was raven-
ously hungry and impatient with the seemingly interminable
delays and lumbering movements of prison life.

We lined up, finally, in two columns along the length of the courtyard. A soldier marched in smartly with the lists, and the whispering, backchat and intermittent laughter ceased. The columns turned and faced each other across the yard – a half-asleep rag-tag army of malcontents and unfortunates. As the names were called the prisoners answered, '*Presó*', defiantly, as if to shrug it off for the day. The roll proceeded slowly, with frequent double checks and matching of faces to names. I realize that the prisoners knew just how far they could play with the soldier calling the roll before he became uncontrollably infuriated. They edged him, by guile and delay, closer and closer towards this breaking point. Then he would receive a stream of instant responses which brought him back to momentary good humour. The game was repeated until each prisoner was suppressing a smile, feeling that he still had some tricks up his non-existent sleeve to show the world. The soldier marched out briskly and we were left alone for the day.

Most of the prisoners spent the day working. They could make hammocks, leather sandals and belts, or work as tailors and even jewellers in supervised workshops outside la Redonda. There was a genuine programme of rehabilitation underpinning prison life. The incentive to work was provided by the contrast between the awfulness of the weevil-infested government food and the small store at the gate where people could buy soft drinks, cigarettes, tinned milk, coffee and basic foods like beans, maize flour, eggs and chillis. Wages were low, 20 pesos (a dollar) a day at most, but the prisoners managed. Fortunately I had 400 pesos sewn into my trousers and could fend for myself. Twice a week a prisoner's family was allowed to visit inside the cells, staying several hours with minimal supervision. They would bring food and clean laundry. Fathers had the opportunity of playing with their children as well as enjoying a more intimate relation with their wives. I decided that if it had to be my fate to be in prison for a while, then this Mexican penitentiary was preferable to Brixton prison or some other cold Victorian monstrosity back in England.

I went in search of don Miguel. He was in one of the large cells across the yard pumping a small primus stove in preparation for his morning coffee. His hammock had been unhooked for the day and he sat on a small wooden trunk, which, painted in bright colours, contained his few belongings. From this position he could survey the activities in the courtyard through the barred window, and he could also watch the entrance to the cell. All around people were organizing themselves for the day. Some were working on hammock frames, others were heading off to the workshops outside la Redonda. A young Mayan was going from one person to another requesting laundry. Another, seeing me, wandered over to ask if I wanted *frijoles* and *tortillas* with coffee for breakfast. I nodded and asked don Miguel to join me.

I had made a point of bringing the two books on the Mayas and I held these out to don Miguel. He took them and motioned for me to settle down. He shut off the stove and then held the books lightly in his hand, turning them over and examining the bindings and their workmanship. In silence he began to turn the pages of *The Ancient Maya*, written by the great Mayanist Sylvanus G. Morley. Every time don Miguel came across a photograph of one of the Classic Mayan sites, or the portrait of an Indian family outside a traditional Mayan house, he paused to read the names underneath. When he came to illustrations of Mayan hieroglyphs he studied them intently, eyes half closed, index finger moving from one glyph to another as he pronounced their Mayan names.

After a few moments our breakfast arrived and I handed over 10 pesos, thanking the cook with a grin across the cell to where he was working. The warm *tortillas* were wrapped in a clean white cloth embroidered along its edges with birds and flowers. This had been placed in a *lec*, a small round gourd used by the Mayas for this purpose. Two smaller gourds contained the beans in a rich, heavily spiced sauce. A small dish of coarse-grain salt, chopped chilli peppers, onions and tomato and a sliced lemon was placed on the floor beside us. The coffee would be ready when we had eaten. There was no cutlery, the *tortillas* serving as the Indian equivalent of a spoon.

I waited for don Miguel. Carefully marking his place in *The Ancient Maya*, he laid it on the ledge by the barred window. He surveyed the food before him nodding with approval. He opened up the bundle of *tortillas* and took one out. Tearing off a piece he rolled it into a cone, dipped it into the gourd of beans and then took a bite. He chewed slowly, adding a little salt and chilli to the beans, some chopped onion and a pinch of lemon. He motioned for me to follow his example. Although the few spoonfuls of beans in each gourd would have appeared as a mere side dish to a European, it was a filling, leisurely meal for us. There was a good supply of *tortillas* and don Miguel ate very slowly. It was nearly an hour before we had finished.

Our coffee, flavoured with cinnamon and native honey, arrived as we completed the meal. Don Miguel wiped his hands and mouth on a handkerchief and returned to the book.

'What are they saying about us here?' He pointed to a page near the front. I shifted my position so that I could read a few paragraphs.

'It is about the old Mayan writing and its meanings. It says that your people were great mathematicians and astronomers. It says that you were great scholars and that what is written in your writings is so complicated and mysterious that we can only understand a little of it.'

'But can they read what was written so long ago? What is it that you understand of our secrets?' don Miguel asked, a look of deep inquiry on his face.

'Not exactly. These archaeologists can understand something of how . . . the way the *abuelos* explored the mysteries of time . . . the calendar that the Mayas used before the coming of the Spanish.' I was fumbling for some brief encapsulation of our studies of the Maya. 'They say that you knew exactly the movement of the sun, the moon, the stars and the planets. The *abuelos*, they say, could predict eclipses. But this is only a little of what is written in these characters. We do not know very much, only the mathematics and the count of your old calendar.'

I was not entirely happy about this answer. I thought don Miguel might be bewildered by the subjects I had mentioned. There was a long pause while he thought about my words. He seemed to be searching for more precise questions to ask, questions that would tell him in more detail what outsiders knew about ancient Mayan hieroglyphs. He began to re-examine the illustrations as if it were in these that he would find what he was searching for in his mind.

A quarter of an hour passed. I noticed that don Miguel was now studying the twenty signs of the Uinal, the basic Mayan time cycle of twenty days. Many Mayanist scholars in the last hundred years had puzzled over the meaning of these signs, as don Miguel seemed to be doing now. It is felt that they must contain ideas fundamental to reading the hieroglyphic system as a whole. Something of their meaning had been deciphered, mostly as a result of comparing the enigmatic Mayan glyphs with the twenty pictographs employed by the Aztec and Toltec in central Mexico. They shared a common origin with the glyphs, but their meanings had been more carefully documented by the Spanish priests and, in any case, pictographs are open signs, obvious in their content. As a result the Mayan signs of the Uinal have been partially deciphered and their meanings agreed upon.

I had spent some time reading these decipherments, notably those by Sylvanus Morley and Sir Eric S. Thompson, but also many other contributing scholars. It was this reading and research which had brought me to the Yucatan, and hence to la Redonda and don Miguel. I was profoundly dissatisfied with the decipherments I had studied. It was not that I had found serious error in them or in the methods employed to arrive at them. It was just that they were so obviously incomplete, so lacking in coherence.

The word *uinal*, for example, was evidently derived from *uinic*, the Yucatec Maya for 'man'. It seemed logical to me that *uinal* represented a spirit body, equivalent to the anatomical

Imix

Ik

Akbal

Kan

Chicchán

Cimi

Manik

Lamat

Muluc

Oc

Chuen

Eb

Ben

Ix

Men

Cib

Caban

Etznab

Cauac

Ahau

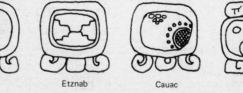

2 *The twenty signs of the Uinal*

body of *homo erectus*. No such *uinal* emerged from the established decipherments. Equally, it seemed an error to me to
subsume Mayan glyph within Aztec pictograph. Granted that
Mayan glyphs, alone, were too enigmatic to yield their meanings and that the Aztec pictographs helped us towards a partial

decipherment. However, glyph and pictograph are intrinsically different, the former *signifying* an idea, the latter *picturing*
an object. This difference had to mean something important,
but what this was I did not know.

The twenty glyphs of the Mayan Uinal were before don
Miguel's eyes, beginning with the first sign Imix.

He was still silently examining them, my presence seemingly forgotten. It was a remarkable fact to me that no Mayan
explanation of their writing, no explanation which actually
allows us to comprehend the meaning of the writing, has ever
been given to us by the Indians. Some of the Spanish priests,
such as fray Diego de Landa, thought that they understood,
but his *Relación* proves the opposite. He thought, for example,
that the system was alphabetical. True, the Spanish priests
were given the basic skeleton, the ancient count of days, which
had been correlated with Christian chronology by Mayan
Indian scholars immediately after first contact with the
Spanish. From the Spanish records of these explanations the
hieroglyphs dealing with time were deciphered four centuries
later. But no more than this has ever been explained.

Mayanist scholars have ignored the significance of this
Indian silence, assuming that the Mayans have simply forgotten how to read the signs. The record makes it appear as if
they, not we, are ignorant, a familiar European tale. But the
Mayas learnt to read and write our Roman script within a
score of years of the Spanish occupation, and they certainly
had not lost interest in their own system. This much I could see
before my very eyes.

'What does it say about these *figuras*?' don Miguel asked
finally, passing the book to me.

'It says that these are very important *figuras* in the writings
of the *abuelos*. You could say that they are the heart of the old
writing.'

'But what does it say about the ideas hidden there?'

'Very little. It is like children learning the alphabet, learning
A, B, C, D . . . . That is where we are with Mayan writing. We
have only learnt a little in all these generations here.'

'The *abuelos* said that one of you who speaks English would come to understand their writing. This was to be one sign of the return of the old Mayan power. So they say,' explained don Miguel in a completely matter of fact tone. 'They said that it would be read there, before the year 2000.'

Now I began to understand his real interest in the books and in me. He wanted to see how far we had progressed in the last four hundred years. I was momentarily puzzled by his reference to the English language and those who spoke it. It could be explained in terms of how such people had appeared to the Mayans in the past. Many early Mayan archaeologists tended to be American or English. The Mayas had seen them digging up bones, examining the sacred places of their *abuelos*, and noting down colonial Mayan texts, if not stealing them away. Archaeology meant nothing to the Mayas as such, but these activities clearly fitted their shamanic vision and, in fact, when viewed from this original perspective, acquired deeper meanings than we have suspected.

Apart from this the English represented the 'enemy of my enemy' to the Maya of colonial times. Many English pirates had raided the Spanish Main from bases on the east coast of the Yucatan peninsula and occasionally had joined forces with rebel Mayas, raiding Spanish towns fifty or sixty miles inland. As late as the turn of this century English merchants in Belize had sold guns to the Mayas during their successful rebellion against the harsh enslavement of Yucatec landowners, *hacendados* and *caciques*. But whilst for me these were historical antecedents which could be seized upon to explain don Miguel's words, for him they were signs of a future.

'Perhaps we will learn to see what is in the writing, don Miguel,' I said. 'Many people are studying these *figuras*. More and more people each year. They feel that a great truth is hidden here, a truth that we have not seen. Only their feelings and intuitions tell them of the power which is behind it all. How else could the *abuelos* have achieved all those things, building those cities, their mathematics and astronomy, all those miracles? Only because the people knew of the true ideas, the power that was there. But we don't see it today, or understand it.'

'It is true, what you say. The *abuelos* had virtues, they could do things that appear to be miracles today. But what they put there in the writing was not obvious. This was how it was meant to be. Only when the time arrives will it become clear. Then someone will see it, simply.'

'But if the *abuelos* could see the future like this, don Miguel, how was it that they disappeared so suddenly? They lost their power just as their wisdom was at its peak.' I expected don Miguel to be stumped by this question about the collapse of the Classic Maya.

'Their gods told them to do that, to hide what they knew and to disappear,' don Miguel answered without hesitation. 'The gods distanced themselves at that time so the lords had to go in search of them. That was how it was . . . so they say.'

He looked to see what my reaction was going to be. Many Mayanists have tried to explain the sudden end of certain Mayan customs in the ninth century AD, such as the carving and erecting of tall stone stelae, and the occupation and construction of large centres of learning and worship like Tikal and Palenque. They speculate in terms of soil exhaustion, overpopulation and political upheaval. I had yet to see an explanation in terms of Mayan gods (and thus their writing) telling the Indians deliberately to cease such practices. I explained our speculations to don Miguel. He looked dumbfounded and exasperated at our rudimentary imagination and shrugged, confident in his own Mayan interpretation.

'But do you really think that the *abuelos* could understand time so clearly, could see what was coming, and that they would even abandon all the work they had done, because of a counsel like that?' I asked.

'They were great *h-menob*. Today there are none like them. We discuss the counsels which they left us as a memory of their wisdom. Some say that the words are not true, others say that what they said came to pass with the arrival of Christianity and will come to pass again. That which happened will happen again,' don Miguel said, repeating a crucial formula of Mayan thought. It was a reference to shamanic time, past and future paradoxically mirroring each other.

'Why did the *abuelos* not leave an explanation of their writing for us, don Miguel? Why did they only give us a part? Why did they keep the rest purely amongst the Mayas?'

'Because the time had not arrived for you to see it. They were just preparing the way a little to begin with. They said that it was there, by the year 2000, that the power to see like that would return. It was remembered only,' don Miguel explained patiently.

He seemed to sense my continuing scepticism of prophecies, of knowing the future in advance. My feelings were complex and hard to unravel. It was one thing for me to have the deepest admiration for the Maya and, in the case of the Yucatec Maya, for their succesful struggle to rid themselves of the Spanish leeches. It was quite another matter for me to place them on pedestals as idols, blindly accepting their words. This to me was to misunderstand their four-hundred-year struggle to show us that there was no such thing as an 'Indian problem' in the New World, but rather a problem in the way we had always treated them either as 'primitives', who had to be integrated and civilized, or as 'noble savages', who were as intellectually capable as we except that, and here was the rub, we alone were scientific in our thinking whilst they remained locked in myth and superstition.

Both of these pedestals, or slaughtering blocks, were, and are, equally uninviting. What I wanted to learn to see in the Mayas was both *uinic* and *uinal* – that is to say their self-definition and explanation as Mayan people, capable of error, but also capable of true vision. Learning to see them as *uinic* and *uinal* meant understanding that their thinking was not just myth but that there was true scientific wisdom, an insight into God, put here and it was we Europeans who were missing it. But don Miguel was emphasizing a shamanic ability, that of far-seeing the future, in his explanations and I knew of the resistance of science to ideas such as this. I was feeling it

myself, even though I could see that don Miguel was completely sincere, a wise shaman with no reason to lie or to
engage in fakery. My feelings, really, could only be unravelled
and resolved by the meanings hidden within the signs. But
neither blind faith nor dogmatic rejection could serve to bring
the *uinal* forth again. Only real dialogue and a careful weighing
of Mayan words could illuminate me here.

Don Miguel had become as withdrawn as I was. He had
closed the book and replaced it on the windowledge and was
now examining his sandalled feet, deep in thought. He glanced
up, finally coming to a decision, and murmured, 'You will be
here for nine nights only. Then you will be gone. There are
things to discuss before then. The *abuelos* said that one of you
would come to understand their writing. I believe them. Here
we shall begin to discuss their words a little'. He paused,
glancing around to make sure that we were not being over-
heard. 'But I see that your mind is in shadow. You have a
different *costumbre*. Thus you cannot see yet. The path we must
follow is not easy. Think carefully whether you truly want to
know, whether you want the walk that is coming.'

He stood up, the counsel at an end.

•••

3

Forward to Sunrise

After driving across Mérida for twenty minutes, the police van stopped. The back doors were unlocked by three *federales* and I was told to get out. We seemed to be near the centre of town for I could hear the bustle of traffic around the main plaza. Glancing up and down the street I hastened to search out some identifying feature. After four days inside la Redonda, incommunicado, I knew that my disappearance could remain indefinite.

I was hustled into an administrative building of some kind. On the ground floor I could see several rooms equipped as offices. A portrait of El Presidente hung on the wall facing the entrance. The air of formality around the place reassured me. I was quickly escorted upstairs.

I was in a bare room with two *federales* facing mc. They had small snub-nose pistols stuck precariously in their belts. One of them, Gonzalo, was the man who had sent me to la Redonda in the first place. He looked as if he had eaten his way into the part he was playing. His fat stomach overhung a pair of tight trousers, light blue in colour. He wore an open-necked white shirt with two breast pockets and the same pinched Italian-style shoes I had seen before. He had a pair of sunglasses on, indoors, but he could not hide the sense of unease and unpleasantness that he communicated to those around him.

'Alright,' he said, addressing me sternly, 'I know that you speak Spanish and can understand me very clearly. You are going to sign this paper. I have had enough of your arrogance.'

He thrust the paper under my nose and held out a ballpoint pen. All I could see was the bottom few lines and the space where I was supposed to sign.

'Can I read it first? What exactly does it say? Anyway, I have not done anything so I fail to see what could be written there,' I said nervously. I was stalling the inevitable, for under no conditions was I going to sign anything.

Gonzalo started to get angry, scowling and shifting his considerable weight from one foot to another. He seemed to be trying to decide whether to hit me or threaten me. He plunged ahead with the second alternative.

'You are going to sign right now,' he menaced, poking me in the chest with the ballpoint. 'We have not even begun to show you what we are capable of doing.'

'I can't sign something without reading it first. Anyway, I would like the British consul to be here.' I hurried to get the refusal out before it died on me.

Gonzalo started shouting at me, 'You will do exactly what I say.' After repeating this a few times he calmed down. I was surprised that he had not hit me. I began to suspect that he had explicit orders not to do so. Possibly only psychological pressure would be applied to me. It was a risk I had to take. Gonzalo nodded towards the other *federal* and said, 'Guard him while I go and get something to persuade this *hijo de la chingada*.' He left, shutting the door behind him.

The new interrogator introduced himself as Felipe. He was in his early thirties, well built, lean and *macho*. He had been sizing me up, looking for a new approach to break down my defenses. There was something to worry about here. He was probably looking to prove himself to Gonzalo. He started out by being friendly.

'This is no good. Why don't you make it easy for yourself? If you sign the paper it is a mere formality. You will be free in a couple of days with no complications. Listen to my advice, my friend, for one way or another you will be signing.' He attempted a genuine smile of encouragement, decided it looked false and forced, and finished up leering at me slightly thin lipped. I was not inclined to believe him and said nothing.

Gonzalo returned with another *federal*. I was relieved to see that he was not carrying anything except the fateful piece of paper which I was supposed to sign. He came over and faced me, close to, while, as if by prearranged signal, Felipe moved around behind me. He ostentatiously made sure that I saw him take out his pistol. The third man tensed. He was not enjoying this and I wondered what was about to happen.

Gonzalo moved even closer, so that I was sandwiched between him and Felipe. The third man stood to one side near the door. I began to tremble slightly, clenching my fists to control it.

'Have you changed your mind yet?' asked Gonzalo.

'No.'

Felipe stuck his pistol into the nape of my neck. 'Come on, enough of this. I am losing my patience with you,' he said, no friendship in his voice now. 'We can hurt you and not leave a mark.' He pushed the gun deep into the back of my head.

I remained silent, checking my reactions. The trembling stopped as suddenly as it had begun. Nothing happened. Seconds and minutes ticked by and I knew that the hardest moment had passed. I refused to believe that Felipe was capable of shooting me under these circumstances. Gonzalo started to speak.

'*Bueno*, we will let you give your statement and then you will sign it. Come with me.'

He moved towards the door and we all trooped out behind him. We went downstairs and Gonzalo led me into one of the offices. I was told to sit in front of a woman whom I took to be a secretary or typist. While Gonzalo explained to her that I was going to make a statement, I gathered my thoughts together, running through the events of the previous two weeks. Since I

had done no wrong, I was not worried about giving a statement. What bothered me was Gonzalo's evident confidence in
this new approach. Did he really think that my story would
serve his purposes? Since I had not been physically abused, I
still had some faith that everything would be resolved and that
I would be released. The flaw in this argument was that
Gonzalo seemed very keen to pin something on me, even if he
had to write it himself.

The secretary was now ready for my statement. I began
talking while the three *federales* stood by, watching. After a
few words Gonzalo interrupted.

'We want you to begin from the time you left Mexico City,
not your arrival in Yucatan.'

I paused for a few seconds, casting back over the journey,
arranging the events into sequence. I wanted there to be no
gaps in the account that could be exploited by Gonzalo. The
secretary selected a clean sheet of paper and we began again. I
decided to be as detailed and long winded as possible for I was
beginning to sense a trick which I could not yet put my finger
on. Gonzalo's confidence bothered me greatly.

I recounted my departure from Mexico City and the bus
journey to the sacred Mayan site of Palenque. I continued with
details of where I had stayed, of side trips to Tenosique, days
spent in different places and a timetable of my movements.
The secretary was very nervous. I watched her young face for
some indication of why this was so. She typed slowly, frequently asking me to repeat my words as if she had only been
half-listening. At first I thought her agitation was over her
typing performance but, moment to moment, it became more
acute. I tried to catch her eye but she was purposefully looking
down at the machine. I paused, giving her an opportunity to
look at me, but she steadfastly kept her eyes lowered.

I continued with my story, talking for forty minutes until
reaching the moment of my arrest. As I was explaining this,
watching the secretary, I sensed the boredom and restlessness
of the two *federales* behind me. They were there but they were
not listening. Only Gonzalo was attentive, hovering close to

the typewriter, ready to pluck the final sheet from the machine. I noticed that he had gathered up the preceding pages out of my line of sight.

As the secretary finished and Gonzalo reached for the final sheet, she blurted out, 'I am only the secretary. It isn't my job to . . .'

Gonzalo interrupted, ordering her to shut up. For the first time she looked at me directly, warning me of something. Gonzalo angrily shuffled the papers and then placed them on the table before me. His hand was covering all but the blank space at the bottom of the top page.

'Sign here,' he said.

I waited. The thought came to me that he could easily have inserted the earlier 'statement' amongst the pages and that it was this that he was tricking me into signing.

'I want to read it first,' I said, 'to make sure that it is all correct and as I explained it.'

Gonzalo lost his temper, pulling the pages away from me, tearing them and hurling the pieces into the wastepaper basket. I ignored him momentarily, looking towards the frightened secretary, thankful for her brave warning. I wanted to say something but I decided that she probably already faced enough problems.

Gonzalo turned to the other *federales* and said, 'Take him back to prison. We'll deal with this case after he has had a few more days in there.' Turning to me he added, 'You will be signing, even if it takes weeks, months for you to see reason.'

'When the Spaniards first arrived here, many of us believed in the power of their words. It was said by our spokesman that a new time was about to begin. This was written in our sacred books. We went to speak with the Spaniards, to know of the word they were bringing. We wanted their counsel for we believed them to be our elder brothers. But they rode in fear of all before them. They were afraid of our numbers and thought we meant to trick them. We offered them a place to live here, we brought them food when they had none, and we taught them to tie houses and to prepare *milpa*. So it was. We thought they were our elder brothers.

'Soon we learnt of their egoism. They trampled our children and stole our women. When we sought to speak with them, they burnt our villages and in fits of anger they killed us. They hunted us with dogs. There was no reason then. There was no respect.

'In the villages we talked amongst ourselves. What were we to do? Some said we should rise up and kill them all. They said our spokesman had betrayed us, they had spoken falsely. Others said that God was revengeful and that we were lost, abandoned orphans.

'Everywhere the Spanish acted in this way. They destroyed our temples and killed our *abuelos*. They trampled everything. We had no recourse. We were divided. There was no agreement amongst us.

'Some went to hide in the forests many leagues from Mérida. They hid the paths to their villages and *ranchos*. They turned their backs. They lived in the shadow of their poverty, hiding in their poverty. Some stayed to fight, wishing to be dead. In this way their souls would return . . . the power of the Mayas.

'But everything was lost, everything was finished. Who could help us? We were children, abandoned, left there at the ruins. So they say. Such is the counsel.'

We were sitting in the courtyard of la Redonda as don Miguel spoke. A few Mayans were squatting in a semicircle around us listening intently. My books were being examined page by page. A couple of the younger Mayans were copying hieroglyphs onto pieces of brown paper. In the five days I had been inside, the books had passed from hand to hand and from cell to cell. Many questions had been asked about our knowledge of Mayan history and wisdom.

'Who knows how many generations of Mayan slaves have lived since those days? In misery we walked, in misery we suffered the insults and blows of the Spaniards. We hid our faces and our thoughts. But little by little we gathered our powers.'

Don Miguel's right hand moved over the ground as if he were counting grains of maize into neat groups.

'We learnt the language of the Spanish, we learnt the word they brought us. We kept *milpa*, hiding in the forests where they would not find us. Our Father, Tata Dios, began to love us again. But how much was already lost! Millions of us died here, in the ruins, in the forest, against sharp rocks. We stumbled at each step under the weight of our loads, under the whips of the Spaniards. There was no recourse.'

Don Miguel spoke in Spanish for my benefit, carefully pronouncing each phrase and sentence. His hands moved in slow rhythmic gestures of punctuation, as if he were reciting a poem. At the end of each long verse he would pause and repeat his words in Mayan. Each time the Indians gathered around us leaned forward at this point. They took in every word don Miguel said, often repeating his words to themselves. I realized that the Spanish account I was hearing was a simplified paraphrasing of an established oral tradition, a Mayan counsel on our occupation of their world.

'We learnt that only our poverty protected us – the mercy of God. The Spanish took everything we had. They took our wealth. They stole our books. They took everything. They left us our poverty and labours. These they did not want.

'So here then was our power and our strength. We could still live hidden in the forests. When Our Lord wanted it there was food.

'We could think and speak amongst ourselves. We hid the paths we walked and waited.

'From amongst us new spokesmen came to give guidance. They were learned people who studied the Book of Our Lord and counselled us. They were very learned. They were *abuelos*, true men.'

There was a murmur of agreement from the gathering. In the few days I had lived with these people they had repeatedly astonished me. The intelligence and openness of their faces, their irrepressible curiosity about our ideas, and the polite way they explored my face and thoughts, all combined to show me the living continuation of the Mayan learning way. These Indians, locked in an urban prison, were evidently well versed in the traditions of their *abuelos*, traditions lodged in language and the formal counsels of their elders. But this traditionalism did not close them off from inquiry into alien, essentially hostile worlds such as ours. If anything their inherited vision seemed to cut the quick deceit of our world and question its very foundations.

'Then the fighting began. We rose against the Spaniards like before. They ran to hide in the towns. They hid their treasures, all the wealth they had stolen. There we found them hiding in the towns. There we finished them in their fear. We burnt their houses, all their haciendas and their towns. We killed them. We left those places to the black buzzards. We only wanted freedom. Respect.

'When we had won all the land, all the lands of our *abuelos*, we retired. We only wanted respect. The Spanish could live over there, where they had run, where they had escaped our justice. Away from us. Only here, where they had no right we killed them. We finished them. We wanted peace. When the Spaniards were here there was no peace. Only theft, only violence. That was what they gave us. That was what they brought us in the villages.

'Here then the power of the Mayas began to return a little, as it was written, as it was promised from before. We walked in freedom, in respect for each one. So it is. We established ourselves in the Territorio, as they say. We became strong again. We became Separate Ones. We walked our own road away from the evil of the Spanish.

'No longer were we hiding in our poverty. We worked and there was an abundance of maize. There was sufficient for each one. We commanded the roads. Only those we wanted came into the Territorio . . . Territorio de Quintana Roo. We lived our freedom.

'Here in Yucatan there were those who forgot the *costumbre* of the *abuelos*. There were those who thought that the *abuelos* had lost their power, that their path was no longer good. What could we do? There was no longer agreement amongst us. We kept our guns prepared. We cultivated our way.

'A certain time arrived for us. Tata Dios punished us. A great death came to us. In the villages and *ranchos* we died. Many, many of us finished there. Whole families finished. So it was. There was no recourse. People spoke without sense.

'Some said it was because of our fight with the Spaniards. Some said it was because we had forgotten our *costumbre* and our *abuelos*. So it was said in counsel. We argued about the meaning of such death. It touched us all. No one escaped. Those who lived according to the old road. Those who lived close to the white road. Each one suffered in his *rancho*, in his family. So it was. We were diminished.

'There was disunity like before. The Word of Tata Dios was doubted by some. The *h-menob* were confused. No longer were we shown a clear path. We were reduced. So it is today. We won our land, our freedom. We remain from the Fight. This is what I have lived.

'What is to become of us? Where are we to see our path? Only Our Lord knows what is to be shown to us. Each year we see the return of the white road. Where before there were only Mayas now there are Spaniards. Again. This will not come to pass. Such are my words to you today.'

The carefully prepared delivery of words ceased. Don Miguel's eyes were downcast, lost in memory. His hands were still, resting lightly on his knees. The other Mayans began asking him questions and I listened to the slow putting together of ideograms, and watched the hands of the speakers design texts in thin air. The conversations were good-humoured and attentive, punctuated by nods, shrugs and laughter. If don Miguel was a great *h-men* amongst these people, they showed their respect and love of him by listening to his words and thinking about them carefully. There are no classrooms here, I thought, and no obligation, just the desire to learn in the fresh air.

The Spanish introduced slavery to the Yucatan because there was no other immediate means of rapid enrichment in a land of turkey and deer rather than gold and silver. In comparison with the rich veins and immediate metallic wealth of Peru and central Mexico, the cotton *mantas* and slight agricultural surplus of the Yucatec Maya were a paltry prize. Mayan lords had been wealthy not so much in material goods, for there were few of these, but in the services they were entitled to receive from the *yalba uinicob*, the farmers and hunters who recognized them as statesmen and political leaders. There are no sumptuous Mayan palaces or pleasure houses at the various ruined sites, only temples and squat stone buildings markedly more uncomfortable, and unhealthy, than the wooden houses which the *yalba uinicob* tied and thatched for themselves. The lords were somewhat better attended than the people of the forests and the *milpas*. But this was a symbolic rather than a substantial difference. They were carried in litters as a mark of respect and esteem, they were provided with foodstuffs, cloth, and services in exchange for their guidance of the overall jurisdiction. They were expected to lead exemplary lives, disciplined, ascetic, astute.

The symmetry and reciprocity of Mayan life hardly suited the Spanish adventurers who, pushed by their own poverty more often than by aristocratic vagabondage, came to extort, plunder and thieve the wealth of Indian America. Each, to a man, had risked all his material wealth, as well as his life, on this wild business venture. Their boats had been figuratively, and sometimes literally, burnt upon landing. They were gamblers and ruthless mercenaries who could not afford to look back. If there was no gold in the Yucatan, then the wealth they sought, maddened by the mere thought of it, would have to come out of the veins and muscles of the Indians. Mayan labour would have to be intensified, reciprocity torn asunder and concentrated towards a single end – the rapid production and expropriation of all tangible wealth.

The Mayas did not work like this amongst themselves. If they recognized a hierarchical order in society, elder and younger brothers, they were also acutely individualistic in their everyday affairs. They hunted in the mornings, harvested maize and calabash in the afternoon, discussed their dreams and the movement of the stars in the evening. Socially they cultivated discretion, tolerance and a discouragement of neighbourhood gossip. Then, as now, they worked at a task while the feeling, the spirit of it, was there. The idea of boundless accumulation of material goods dismayed them. Greed was alien to their nature and to the careful balance of relationships with the spirit world and other people. They fulfilled their spiritual and physical needs day by day and could not abide the avarice and disorder of the universe which the Spanish were trying to impose on them. If they took to the Christian Word as their own, they were not fooled by the bringers of it.

Soon after the Spanish foundation of Mérida in 1541 the Mayas in certain areas rose against those Spaniards who sought to establish themselves outside of the towns such as Mérida, Valladolid and Bacalar which they had been given as places to live. The Mayas rebelled against those individual Spaniards who sought to concentrate them around their towns and haciendas, severing their ties to ancient *costumbre* and sacred places. In 1546 more than 20,000 Indians laid siege to Valladolid, killing eighteen Spanish *encomenderos* in outlying areas and driving Franciscan priests back to the town. The point made, they retired as Spanish reinforcements arrived. Other localized rebellions periodically broke out – in 1548, 1562, 1597, in 1610, 1639 and 1695. Spanish chroniclers recorded that these rebellions were quickly crushed and the leaders hanged.

The European chroniclers did not record that the Mayas succeeded in earning their fearful respect. The Indian heartland south of Valladolid and all the way to Guatemala remained unconquered, the sons and daughters of the ruins living hard by the graveyards of their *abuelos*. Equally, Yucatec Maya came to be reluctantly recognized by the Church as a true liturgical language, the only Indian language so recognized. The Christian Word was to be explained in the language of the Mayas so that they might remain their own interpreters and prayer-makers. The Indians were insistent about this, and these hard-won achievements guaranteed the survival of the ancient Mayan way in reduced but intact form.

More than two centuries after the first Valladolid rebellion in 1546 the continuing Spanish respect and fear of this ancient way was shown again, in their response to a further rebellion in the Mayan heartland. A great Mayan shaman and learned Christian theologian, Jacinto Canek, led a short-lived but carefully planned uprising against the Spanish landowners who had been mistreating the Indians. When the fighting finally stopped in the heart of the forest, Jacinto Canek and many of his followers were brought to Mérida for public punishment. Eight of his closest followers were hanged, their bodies dismembered and the parts sent to numerous outlying villages. Jacinto Canek was publicly tortured in the main plaza of the city, his flesh torn from his bones by red hot pincers, and all his bones broken by metal bars. His dismembered, splintered body was cast upon the city refuse dump. In this way the Spanish unwittingly left historical record of their continuing fear and respect for Mayan shamanism.

Don Miguel's counsel harked back to these days of no quarter, but the events most immediate in his mind were more recent. If the Yucatec Mayas were the Indians who most completely adhered to the dictates of the hieroglyphic count kept since Classic Mayan times a thousand years before, they were also the Indians who most successfully rebelled against the law of the foreigners. In 1847 the 'Fight' don Miguel had spoken about broke out in the vicinity of Valladolid. Those same settlements which had so bravely fought Spanish incursions in the preceding three centuries now rose in masterful coordination.

Throughout the Yucatan peninsula, under numerous leaders drawn from the ancient learned lineages, the Mayan farmers and hacienda workers rebelled simultaneously in their thousands. They quickly cast the Spanish back into their towns. Within a year they controlled all but Mérida and its immediate environs. This, willingly ceded by the Xiu to the Spanish three hundred years before, they left them as a refuge.

The Indian leaders Cecilio Chi and Jacinto Pat wrote to the Yucatec authorities, 'If we are killing you now, you first showed us the way. If we are burning the houses and haciendas of the whites, it is because you first burnt the village of Tepich and all the ranchos where the poor Indians were, and the whites ate all their cattle, and the same whites harvested their *milpas* when they passed through them looking to kill us with gunpowder.'

The Mayas offered peace provided they were granted a part of the peninsula as an independent Mayan territory. They had no objections to the whites living in this territory as long as they would not exercise authority over the Indians. The proposal was rejected and the Fight continued for the next fifty years and more. Although rejected and, for the most part, forgotten by outside historians, the Mayan written missives provide documentary evidence of the real motives for the rebellion. It was not a 'caste war' as it has been portrayed but, as don Miguel said, the fight of an ignored people for freedom and respect, for ancient self-determination. Alongside this they offered the Spanish Yucatecans a reciprocal freedom and respect.

In their thousands the Mayan rebels deserted the Spanish towns they had vanquished. They ducked down secret trails into the Mayan heartland, the vast area south of Valladolid to the Rio Hondo and east to the Caribbean. Here they founded an independent Mayan nation defended by guns bought from the English in Belize. They signed independent contracts with colonial logging companies and recognized only their own laws and leaders. After the Yucatecans rejected their proposals in the 1850s, the Indians of successive generations lived the irrelevance of their broken authority. Soon, very soon, in faraway central Mexico Emiliano Zapata, descended from ancient Nahuatl line and vision, was to begin his fateful emergence from the Indians hills around Mexico City.

In his counsels don Miguel often identified himself with these rebel Maya – the Separate Ones. Although he was always to skirt around his past, I suspected that his perspective and opinions emanated from this adamantly conservative branch of the Yucatec Maya. His explanations to me about the Mayan world and his hints at the survival of the basic ideograms of Mayan writing beckoned me onwards to unknown places and unrecorded histories. I sensed there was something here, in this modest, obscure corner of the hidden continent, which could change everything we knew about Indian America.

'In these few days I have learnt many things I do not understand, don Miguel,' I said after we had finished breakfast. 'I have seen a little way into another world here in la Redonda. The discussions we have had . . . .'

I paused, lost for words, then recovered myself. 'I have found something true and unseen in watching and talking with you, don Miguel. But I do not know much and cannot express to you how intense it all seems. There is a faith amongst you Mayas permanent as the stones you carved a thousand years ago. This is what I see.'

I watched his impassive face for some giveaway sign of approval.

'It is true,' don Miguel said quietly. 'You have your machines and we only have faith in Our Lord to win a living from the earth. Only our *costumbre* teaches us how to live.'

'Do you think that I could learn to understand the *costumbre* of the Mayas? Do you think that an outsider can come to understand the vision of the *abuelos*?'

'The Indians have always been of good heart, don Ricardo.

They always gave place to those who sincerely came to learn. But they were very few people. It is very hard. I don't think ... you need to grow up used to it. This is what I think. To be *milperos* and understand the forest, you need to be born here, to be gradually accustomed from when you learn to walk.'

'How then can I come to understand more?' I asked, foreseeing a difficult path ahead.

'Little by little it would be shown to you. But not in words themselves.' Don Miguel paused to pick up *The Ancient Maya*. He thumbed through it until he came to some hieroglyphs.

'You see here, these are not words as you write them. Here you see a face, an eye, a hand, a foot. These are *figuras* – people. You must learn from the Mayas. In their eyes, in their movement of hand and foot, you can learn our *costumbre*. If you only listen to words you will miss much.'

Don Miguel watched my face to see if his advice had registered.

I realized that whatever don Miguel meant by his words it was evident he was not going to spell out what he knew about the ancient glyphs. True shaman, he was naming parts of the Mayan body in mysterious fashion, turning my attention from verb to still hidden ideogram. I saw that the spirit of his gesture and advice was the same inspiration that had led his *abuelos* to insist on understanding and praying the word in their own language, according to their own learning way. But this insight on my part did not enter and unravel the enigmatic point don Miguel was trying to make.

'If I were to live amongst the Mayas, would I come to understand the ancient writing, don Miguel?' I asked bluntly.

'It is possible. The *abuelos* said this would happen. If you study these matters, if you do not forget what you have seen and heard here, it is possible. But is is not obvious. From what you have told me of these books I think it is still hidden.'

'If I went to live in a Mayan village, do you think the Indians would guide me in these matters?'

'They would think about you. Perhaps they would say

nothing. They would consider many things first. Only if it is your fate . . . I cannot say. They would look into your heart.'

Don Miguel watched the hint of scepticism pass, like a shadow, across my mind. Firmly he added, 'Do not think my silence is ignorance. You should think carefully if this is your road. There is sacrifice there, it is a difficult road. This I know. Look into the *figuras* first. To begin with you will see only questions. They are like mirrors which turn in your mind. You do not know what you are seeing there. Then they become a little clearer, a little brighter. It is as if they are nothing at first. You cannot see them. Then the idea appears.'

Don Miguel chuckled. It reminded me that he often seemed amused at our conversations. I looked at him closely. His age and vigour, his relaxed manner and his prominent Indian features all combined to emphasize the power of his counsels. His very gestures were taken from the portraits of wise men on the ancient temple walls. It must have amused him to see my doubt that the Mayas remembered so much about the past when all around and before my very eyes there was living, conscious evidence that it was so. But, equal to their inherited quiet self-identity as Mayas, the living people were not going to spell themselves out to me. I was going to have to immerse myself in their world and its hidden pathways if I was to learn to see further and, perhaps, begin reading the ancient hiero-glyphs.

Don Miguel was evidently still thinking about my wanting to live in a Mayan village to learn more about the people. He stirred from thought and said, 'The *abuelos* wrote that when the foreigners first descended upon us, when they first arrived, it was there to the east, there at Tulum. They said it was there also that the writing would awaken again, there it would appear again.'

Noticing my continuing scepticism he added, 'It is written that way, that is all. Today we do not know if it is true.'

He shrugged, showing me that my disbelief was not particu-larly important to his faith in the Old Ones and their vision.

'We only see a little way now,' he murmured. 'How can we know for sure if it is to be true as it was written so long ago?'

Early on the tenth day I was told to prepare my belongings. My release from the shadows was as sudden and unexpected as my first entrapment within them. My papers, I was informed, were in order after all. The word had come down from Mexico City by talking wire that I was to be released immediately.

The other prisoners shared in my relief at this welcome change of fate. In spirit they were coming out with me. I began giving away a few things as gifts. After a few minutes I looked up from sorting through my shirts to find don Miguel watching me. He held himself with confidence and reserve, his prediction about my release speaking for itself. Tying up my remaining belongings, I wandered out into the courtyard with him, looking for somewhere quiet to talk. Now that I felt certain of release, there was room and time to feel sad that our conversations were nearly over. I searched for words to express my gratitude to don Miguel as we squatted down in the shade, under the curious glance of a guard on the prison wall. Don Miguel waited a few minutes before producing my books from a *henequen* bag he was carrying.

'So the time has arrived, don Ricardo. I am pleased for you,' he said. 'It will be good to see you gone.'

'Nine nights, don Miguel, as you promised,' I replied, tapping him on the knee in a moment of over-familiarity. 'A pretty good guess, wouldn't you say?'

Don Miguel grinned slightly, nodding to himself. The guard on the wall was even more intrigued. To break his concentration, I got up and wandered over to the gate to buy don Miguel some cigarettes as a parting gift. He preferred the cheapest – Alas (wings). Each packet had a pair of golden wings emblazoned on a blue wrapping.

Wandering back to don Miguel, feigning casualness, I held them out to him.

'*Alas para volar*. Wings to fly away from this place,' he said jokingly, opening up one of the packets and offering me a cigarette.

'I wish there was some way of getting you out of here, don Miguel, back to your village and *milpa*,' I said, realizing he had still not told me which village he was from, or why he was here. His personal biography was invisible, unnecessary to his purpose in talking to me.

'Do not concern yourself, don Ricardo. This is for others to decide. But think upon the counsels you have heard. Do not forget what you have heard here. Do not forget us,' don Miguel said, finality in his voice. After a while he added, 'The *abuelos* say that the *figuras* are like gods – they speak to you in your dreams. They come and explain things to you. When you wake up you know these explanations. Then you remember them. "How did I learn these things?" you ask yourself. "No one showed them to me." That is how it is, don Ricardo. That is when you begin, that is when you learn to see. But do not forget what you have heard here.'

'But can those things be true for a foreigner, don Miguel?' As I understood his words, he was explaining to me that there was a source of learning beyond this *uinic* plane of existence, a learning that came to us in dream. But could an outsider, without the language and with only minimal knowledge of the Mayan way, come to experience this?

'The *abuelos* prepared this path for all those of good heart, those who are sincere, those who respect the greatness of what is hidden there in the writing. It comes from God, don Ricardo. It is for those who want to learn. It doesn't matter that they might not be Mayan.'

Don Miguel finished his counsel here, offering me the books back.

'Don't you want to keep them?' I asked.

'No, no. You might need them later. In any case what is known is here,' don Miguel said, tapping his forehead.

••••

4

The Counsel of the Ruins

 Long deserted, overhung by tropical vine and forest canopy, the ruins of Tulum still maintain an ancestral enchantment over the living Mayas. From beneath the foundations of the walled city, where they are believed to dwell, the spirits of the ancient Mayans speak to the people in their daily movement through the forest, in their hunting and farming, in their dreaming. The ruined city huddles three miles north-east of the present-day village of Tulum, silently defended on three sides by walls, on the fourth by deceptively calm Caribbean waters. In its downfallen, damp and demoted state it still remains a place of signs written on temple walls and inspires thoughts upon its mysterious history.

No one knows when the name Tulum, or 'rotten earth' in Mayan, was given to this, the first city sighted by the Spanish on their early, tentative expeditions to the mainland coast of the New World. 'We followed the shore day and night,' one of them wrote in 1518, 'and the next day toward sunset we perceived a city or town so large that Seville would not have seemed more considerable nor better; one saw there a very large tower; on the shore was a great throng of Indians who bore two standards which they raised and lowered to signal us to approach them; the commander did not wish it.' The size of the city discouraged the outnumbered, peripatetic *conquistadores* from landing.

Nine years later, in 1527, when Francisco Montejo arrived off the coast of Tulum he was careful to land discreetly north of the city – close enough to beg food and information, far enough away not to appear as an immediate threat to the populace. Francisco Montejo was evidently not invited within the city walls for no description beyond the cursory, seaborne glance of 1518 has survived. The city's real name, however, was recorded by Montejo as Zama, 'sunrise' or 'awakening', and the jurisdiction of which it was a part Ekab. No more is revealed. For over three hundred years Zama was forgotten to outsiders. After Francisco Montejo's abortive first landing in 1527, the Spaniards decided that the east coast of the peninsula of Yucatan, in what is now the new Mexican state of Quintana Roo, was not a suitable beachhead for an invading force of armed and greedy Europeans. When Montejo's son, confusingly also called Francisco, returned in 1539, it was to Campeche and northern Yucatan itself, not the dense jungle fastness around Zama. Even after the definitive occupation of Yucatan and the foundation of Mérida in 1541, this Mayan jurisdiction remained free territory, an eastern heartland where the Mayas sought freedom to practice their ancient customs, language, and independent economic life.

When the next foreign explorer of these parts, John Stephens, wrote of his and Frederick Catherwood's rediscovery of Zama in 1842, referring to it as Tulum for the first time, they spoke of the complete absence of roads or even well-trodden paths connecting Yucatan to this east-coast territory. Their plans for walking from the last Yucatecan outpost, at Chemax, to Tulum were described by the locals in the former village as impossible, a seventy-mile scramble through tangled, uncharted forest, over sharp limestone rock. Intimidated, lacking a trusted Mayan guide, they abandoned the overland expedition. When Stephens and Catherwood finally journeyed forth to the city of the east they followed the original Spanish seaborne approach.

I wandered through a gateway in the city wall, the high temple – the Castillo – facing me. I was trying to bring together the spectacle before my eyes with Stephens's exuberant description and the even earlier Spanish reference to a large city. It was difficult. Where the latter described a city the equal of Seville, there now appeared only the reduced foundations of past splendour. Where Stephens spoke of the 'wildest scenery yet found in Yucatan' and of the 'magnificence of nature', there was now only low shrubbery, clear ground, a ticket office, and many stores selling Indian blankets, jewellery and dresses. The ruins stood mute, mesmerizing in their white reflection of the midday sun.

The most impressive building was the Castillo set on limestone cliffs above the clearest aquamarine ocean I had ever seen. The building consisted of a temple crowning a steep limestone mound. The base of this manmade mound extended a hundred feet, its front a stairway, wide and dangerously steep, balustrades and two lower chambers on each side. Climbing the stairway diagonally, due to the sharp incline, I came to the high temple itself – the summit, thirty feet above the city. The doorway of this temple was supported by two columns, both with a recess above for idols long disappeared. Inside, the temple was divided by two corridors with stone benches at each end. These were cramped, confined quarters, made bearable only by openings in the far wall through which a warm breeze was blowing from the sea. Turning to face inland I sat on the top step and surveyed all that was below me.

The Castillo stairway faced the west, shoulders to the ocean, broad and visible from afar. Its purpose had not been to welcome fishermen and seafaring merchants, but rather, to offer a stairway to the dawn, a vision for those arriving from inland. On my right was a small cove, white coral beach, a cluster of coconut palms swaying in the wind. Numerous minor temples were gathered in groups below, squat, crude buildings, easily dismissed. Where once they had all been brightly painted, both interior and exterior, heightening the tropical colours of sea, beach and forest, now they were crumbled, blank and empty. Upon one there was a carved relief – the figure of a man diving, descending from the sky – a forgotten Indian Icarus.

My eye wandered past the buildings to the wall around the city. It marked off the central, rectangular area, devoted to sacred duties and functions. As high as seventeen feet in places, as low as four feet in others, the wall ran 390 yards along the longer side of the rectangle, and 172 yards inland on its two shorter sides. Beyond this wall the endless forest canopy began. I could hear the incessant calling of tropical birds amongst the trees, their songs the same as they had been in the sixth century AD, when Mayan stonemasons first disturbed their dominion of the site.

Within the city walls, where Stephens once noted deep green foliage and a profusion of *ramon* trees growing from the very ruins, there was no trace of nature's magnificence now. I recalled the early Spanish description of a Mayan town. 'In the middle of the towns were their temples, with beautiful plazas and all around the temples stood the houses of the lords and priests and then of the most important people. Then came the houses of the richest, and of those held in the highest estimation. Nearest to these, and at the outskirts of the town, were the houses of the lower class.'

I could see no residential building within the walls of Tulum. On my left there were more temples too uncomfortable to have been dwelling places. They had been sanctuaries, resting-places for the great number of idols which the Indians had employed to symbolize diverse elements of their intricate theology. No more than fifty yards from where I sat I could see the Temple of the Frescoes. So thick were the trees and secondary growth here when Stephens and his party arrived that this temple had remained obscured from their view, sitting where I was now. I climbed down the Castillo steps and crossed the clear ground.

The temple seemed a haphazard amalgam of building stages. It consisted of two levels. The lower of these was divided by four columns which gave onto a narrow corridor.

The walls of the corridor and the central chamber were once covered with paintings of Mayan gods, the moon goddess Ixchel still discernible within a woven vine border. The Mayan rain god Chac could be seen astride a four-legged animal – a horse. It seemed, then, that the murals were painted after the arrival of the Spanish.

The outside of this lower level of the Temple of the Frescoes had once been elaborately ornamented with stucco and regular design. Three niches above contained further examples of the diving Icarus figure I had seen from the Castillo. The corners of the temple were elaborate face masks, Chac rain gods with 180° vision.

The upper level of the temple represented a later addition, perhaps 1200–1300 AD. It lacked all paintings or decoration, although a niche over its sole doorway had evidently contained a figure at one time. The whole level seemed an afterthought, a crude weight upon the artistry of painted murals below. The distinct levels gave some clue to Tulum's history for they combined Mayan and central Mexican characteristics, late memory of past occupations.

Wandering about for a further hour I concluded that these ruins were the inner sanctum to a much more widespread city. If Francisco Montejo, 400 soldiers, and 150 horses, uninvited, had been provided for by this community, it was once of considerably greater size and sophistication than these rain and time-washed remains suggested. Much use must have been made of the good cedar, mahogany and rosewood which abounded in the forest around. With this wood, and palm thatch, the Mayans built houses more comfortable and ventilated than the small damp stone buildings I was seeing here in the inner city. Quite probably the populace had been widely and agreeably dispersed along the coast, north and south, in family cantons, *ranchos*, and only ventured to Tulum for festivals, markets and religious duties. Fishermen and spirit-lords, craftsmen and ladies had walked and died here. Perhaps a mysterious, geomantic sense of their presence was possible, intuited from high on the Castillo stairway. Perhaps when the temples had been coloured red, yellow, blue and green, translucent as the plumage on the tropical birds, this city of dawn, of awakening, had presented a breathtaking vision and adoration of the ancient gods. Perhaps, I thought half-heartedly, but the colour and movement were gone now, only white stuccoed stone left as grave memory of it all, five hundred years later.

I stumbled along the beach in the intense heat, half-blinded by the reflection from the white coral sand and limestone rock, perspiring heavily under the weight of my rucksack. The beach was deserted, save for two iguanas sunning themselves on nearby rocks and innumerable crabs which scattered at the sound of my approach. To my right were coconut palms set on a bank a few yards back from the calm and inviting Caribbean. A few parakeets called loudly in the shaded groves formed by the palms and I longed to take a rest. But I had walked a mere half mile south of the ruins, expecting to find some type of shelter, a fishing community, a scattering of Mayan houses, something to justify my impulse to leave the ruins. I walked on, mouth parched, until I arrived at a coastal *rancho*. A solitary Mayan fisherman was squatting in the shade, sipping on a cold Bohemia beer. Glancing at my exhausted, overloaded condition, he laughed a pleasant welcome, motioning for me to take my rucksack off and rest. He sorted amongst fish, lobster and ice to find me a beer from a cheap styrofoam icebox.

'In ancient times our *abuelos* said you could hear music there at the ruins at night. There at Coba also,' don Pablo said, mentioning a large Classic Mayan ceremonial centre thirty miles north-west of Tulum.

'Those who had just left the ruins, those who lost their lives when it was discovered by the Spaniards, they say it is they who try to hear the music at the end of the year. It is to celebrate their name, a festival of birth such as those of previous times.'

Don Pablo looked at me intently as he spoke, watching for something I could not discover.

'The lords of the ruins knew of their existence for many years. They made *milpa* there, working the land. There were two of them – friends. One day one of them returned to his village. The other one heard the music as it had been heard before – beautiful music. He became frightened, lying there in his hammock at night. He did not know what to do except listen. He knew there was no one there.'

We were squatting outside the doorway of don Pablo's house, backs resting against the wall, the Caribbean coral coast a mere twenty yards away. Ostensibly don Pablo was watching the dusk sky to see if El Norte was arriving. This was a strong cold front that approached from the north-west, bringing rain and high winds. It was coming in above the prevailing south-eastern warm sea breeze. His chances of a calm sea and clear water, the prerequisites for his diving, were receding. But now he was absorbed in giving the counsel of the ruins.

'The souls of the ancient people live under the ruins. They have their homes prepared there. Yes, their souls went there. It is they who play and hold their *fiestas* there.'

He sought for a different way to explain his vision to me. 'It is as if the world is reversed. The world turns over and those who lived here,' he motioned around us, 'passed below. Those below came here. It was a change of generations. When the hour arrives again, the power of the ancient souls will return. There at the ruins you can see the figure, the King of the Poor. There you see him upside down. But when the hour arrives he will be turned over again. But who can know when that will be? The example is given that way, that is all.'

He nodded, affirming the sincerity of his words, watching me take notes, squatting casually in the shade.

After a while I asked him whether Tulum held any special religious power as the eastern-most mainland city of the Mayas. I had read that many pilgrimages were made here in pre-Columbian times and that Tulum was still considered one of five Mayan sacred villages amongst the contemporary people. This fact had been registered as a mere footnote in anthropological work thirty-five years ago. I suspected that it was a sign to a sacred Mayan topography of their world.

'The ruins have lost their power now,' don Pablo explained sadly. 'My *abuelos* told me it that way. Before, they said, there was a road to the sky which went from Tulum to Coba, and from Chichén Itza to Uxmal. Here in Quintana Roo, and there in Yucatan, in each place, the great centres, the most powerful places, were joined by a road to the sky. They called this road "Kuxan Suum". It was a large cord which had blood in its centre, it was alive, it had life in its centre. The blood was sent along this cord to the kings, the lords of old. The cord maintained them so that they could live. They say they cut the cord and that was when it ceased. Too much blood was lost. The blood became weak.'

Don Pablo opened ancient time and mystery in his naming of the cord. The Kuxan Suum existed in a primordial world where the umbilical cord of the universe still held earth and sky together. In that distant first world there was no need of shamanism for there was instant and direct communication between the heart of the sky and mankind. After the Kuxan Suum was cut, man could only intermittently restore this communication through shamanic vision journeys, perilous and exhausting. In the Mayan sacred Books of Counsel the sky is spoken of as a womb, the first age a time of whole blood. In naming the Kuxan Suum, mysterious part of the Mayan body, don Pablo was beginning his counsel for me at the beginning, with the first birth of the world. He was also saying that Tulum had indeed been a place of special power, one of several places where earth and sky were joined in legendary times.

'The *sac be*, the white roads which the *abuelos* prepared, were different – they were here on earth. You can still see those in the forest. The Kuxan Suum was another thing. This is how I heard it. The cord began here in Tulum. My *abuelos* also said that an animal like a squirrel ran along the cord. Before, when the cord was working, they would send a squirrel along it to another ruin, another lord – to Chichén, to Coba – wherever

the cord was placed, there it would go, and very quickly too.
The lords only had to send it to the chief of the others. Directly
it would arrive there with urgent messages. But that is lost
now, the power of how that was done.'

There was a respectable silence as we thought about the
counsel. Tulum to the east had evidently been an arterial city
of primary importance. Don Pablo had begun to show me a
little of the Mayan map of their world upon which I could
catch a glimpse of a first time and space, and a sight of the
invisible shamanic hand which had formed and shaped it. I
continued to take notes, my mind quickly seeking new questions and simultaneously trying to absorb a vision entirely
unlike that which I had read in Spanish chronicles or
archaeological reports.

'But is it possible that the cutting of the Kuxan Suum meant
that everything, all the festivals, the histories, the legends and
music which the people prepared, were forgotten, don Pablo?'

He thought this question over carefully, perhaps only
half-willing to continue explaining a further dimension of
Mayan time and thought.

'The *abuelos* have passed. Those who remain here are their
grandchildren. Then they also had sons. But it was the *abuelos*
who learnt more. The older they were the more they knew.
All the children of these *abuelos* made festivals for them, there
in the ruins. Even in my lifetime this was so. But if they came
now to ask for permission, to arrive at the ruins, well, there is
no permission. Now someone else rules. The Spaniard has
taken it, to exploit it in a different way. Our way, you could
say, has been forgotten. The Spaniard did not want it to be.
That, anyway, is how it *appears* to be now,' don Pablo added
cryptically.

'Who amongst their chiefs will say, "Let us make a festival
here in the ruins for the poor who live nearby, those who have
looked after the ruins, those who have thought of God and all
the spirits, those who have done these works?" They do not
think of that. Now all they do is charge you your entrance fee.'

Don Pablo laughed loudly at the irony of this, paradise and a parking lot. Then, more seriously, he said, 'Where is their right to do this? That is what has changed a great deal. We should look after the work of our *abuelos* so that we can hear their way, their path.'

His perception of the changes around ancient sites in Quintana Roo and the Yucatan, their development for the clear sight of tourists, was that these ran counter to Mayan beliefs. If Mayans were allowed to pass freely, to remember their forefathers' work, then there would be no problem. The way things were now he shrugged off as alien in spirit.

Don Pablo was much younger than don Miguel. I judged him to be in his early forties, his body not yet tired, his hair and face unmarked by signs of time. He was strong, muscular, well-proportioned. He stood and moved with the confidence of an ancient Olmec ballplayer. Even at first glance he seemed warrior and wise man – utterly Mayan in his generous friendship, his deep devotion to God, his wealth of spirit and wisdom amidst material poverty. I knew I was talking with a very ancient, very pure Mayan – his thoughts came from the depths of the Petén forest.

We were a long mile south of the ruins of Tulum on don Pablo's coastal *rancho*, DzibAktun – the 'cave with writing'. Somewhere in these parts, don Pablo told me, there was a cave with ancient writing in it. He claimed he had never found it but that was how the *rancho* had been named. Here on the coast he employed snorkel and fin, speargun hunting for lobster and fish on the coral reef a half mile offshore.

It was late afternoon, the sky golden-red, heavy-tempered and unsettled. Early November and the beach was still deserted, seasonal rains keeping outsiders away. For the past few days I had been staying on the *rancho* in a Mayan house rented from don Pablo. Initially I had hoped to learn a few phrases of Yucatec Mayan from this fisherman. Already I was having to revise my plan. As don Miguel had done before, this Mayan Indian *campesino* was showing me a world unknown to outsiders, a world superb and ancient as the cities hidden in the dense forest behind us.

We spoke on, in unhurried rhythms, our words turning to the arrival of the Spanish and the departure of the Mayan *abuelos*. All around us the animals don Pablo kept on the *rancho* were searching out their final feed before nightfall. Pigs scuffed the earth, seeking a cool placc to lic; a half dozen Indian hunting dogs barked at noises and shadows in the gathering darkness; and the finely bred chickens and turkeys clucked and pecked amongst a pile of coconuts drying in the sun.

'When the Spaniards first arrived our king was don Juan Tutul Xiu. He lived at T-Ho; he only came here to pray. In those days Tulum still had power. It was here also that the Spaniards first arrived. When don Juan Tutul Xiu saw why they came, he decided right away to leave this land. He left from here, from Tulum. His path leads from under the ruins to the sea. When you arrive there at the ruins you can see the door under the largest ruin. There, right in the middle of the Castillo, down below, there it is.'

Don Pablo drew a diagram in the earth, showing me how to enter by the wing of the Castillo, along a corridor to a spot immediately under the temple crowning the mound.

'There was a man who lived in Tulum village,' he continued, 'he entered that doorway and went down under the sea. As he walked he saw the footprints of the Mayas who had passed before. He arrived at a place where there was a large stone table. There were some well-made plates on the table. When he tried to pick them up, to take them away, the earth trembled. He only had time to return to safety before the path was covered up. There at the ruins you can see the doorway facing the sea, covered up as it should be, until the return of don Juan Tutul Xiu.'

'When will that be?' I asked.

Again I could sense a very careful examination of the question. Don Pablo reviewed his library and found what he wanted. He began explaining to me how the Mayas believed that God had created pairs of the different races on earth. Each pair was given a part of the world where they 'could look for life, where they could live.'

'What the Mayas say is not right, that which according to God's work is not correct, is that one should leave one's place and come somewhere without permission, without treaty. Each one has his place where he can find his life. The Spaniards saw that where they were was not very productive. So they came here.'

He stopped. Before I could grasp what he was trying to make clear he would have to explain something about traditional Mayan economics to me.

'You could say that in ancient times the Mayas had an agreement whereby if anything happened to one community, if another saw that it was not very productive where they were, then they would invite their friends to come and live with them. As long as everyone was content, and no one was fighting, that was fine. That is what they wanted.

'So if the Spaniards had arrived here, poor, bringing only tools, let us say, as carpenters, or to clear the forest and plant *milpa* . . . a little apart but on a par with those already here, then the Indians would have helped them. They would have been of good heart, and would have helped them really establish themselves. Whoever arrived could help us also, with new knowledge and new tools. But when the Spaniards arrived, it was only to persecute us, to take away our titles to the land. That is how the example we have explains it.

'First they arrived and we did nothing to stop them. But it was not what they wanted. We always gave them freedom to live here. We taught them the work of how to live here. It was not what they wanted. They did not appreciate this, they did not come for this, they did not think this. Because if they had learnt to work together, with us, if they had learnt more, then maybe . . . .'

Don Pablo's face hardly manifested the intense feeling behind his words. It was as if he wanted them to stand alone, in the failing light, while he stepped back, effacing himself.

'They showed us that they came to rob. That was when everything was cut off.' He echoed the legend of the Kuxan

Suum. 'They could have learnt some virtues here, but they never gave them place.'

Pablo fell silent, watching his words tumble into my mind, transforming my perception of the way things were when the Spaniards first arrived. I could not fault the historical accuracy of his words. Francisco Montejo was initially greeted in decidedly friendly fashion by the Indians of Tulum. What I had not understood previously, because it was not explained in the Spanish chronicles, was that the greeting was inspired not only by prophecy drawn from the ancient count of time but by the traditional cooperative ethos of Mayan civilization. As this realization came to me, don Pablo added, 'Who then would not become annoyed? One wasp arrives, two wasps, three wasps, only to prejudice you. Then more arrived and more. They did not come here to live with the poor.'

The final sentence seemed to be the deepest of accusations, made by generations of Indians, *campesinos*, towards outsiders. It was a statement which summed up our entry into their world. Don Pablo had said much, in answer to my question, without answering it. When I asked again about the return of the power of the *abuelos,* he shrugged noncommittally.

'How can our power return if such a spirit rules the land?'

We moved inside, darkness upon us. The wind was still blowing from the sea. I wanted this since it kept the mosquitoes in the forest. 'It will change,' don Pablo said, and later it did. He stoked up the fire and lit a candle. He found an empty bottle to hold this and placed it over in the far corner of the house. He motioned towards a small wooden seat, a *kanché*, a carved half-trunk of wood which rose a mere four inches off the ground. I sat down while don Pablo prepared some hot chocolate, ancient Mayan beverage and currency.

Caught between the light of the fire and the distant candle, don Pablo's features and manners were even more discreet and shaded in expression than before. A slight frown of concentration crossed his face as he sought to hook a pan of milk over the fire. What he was thinking and whether he was often as forthcoming as he had been over the past hour remained hidden from me. No matter, for his words had confirmed in new ways the strength and continuity of the Mayan way.

For an hour or so we talked of practical matters, of the sea and of the forest. I mentioned to him that John Stephens had left Tulum, in the 1840s, with the distinct impression that it remained occupied long after the conquest. Stephens wrote, 'In fact I conceive it to be not impossible that within this secluded region may exist at this day, unknown to white men, a living aboriginal city occupied by relics [*sic*] of the ancient race who still worship in the temples of their fathers.'

Don Pablo commented, 'That would be too obvious, living in the ancient city. It would attract too much attention. And what if the land around the city was good for *milpas* and for hunting? The Indians would lose the titles to it. It would be better to change your clothes. Like these,' he added, pinching the cloth of his trousers between thumb and index finger.

This gesture reminded me of something I had seen in the Yucatan and I said, 'The first time I went to Chichén I was standing there, looking at all the buildings. The first person I saw was a Mayan carrying a great load on his back, held up with a tumpline. He had his water-gourd at his side and a *machete*. He looked like one of the Mayan *abuelos*. It was like an apparition from the past. He had his *milpa* there, he said, in the middle of old Chichén. And all around him were the on-lookers who had come from another world to see the ruins of this one, who had come by bus to take pictures of it.'

Don Pablo hesitated before answering. He chose his words with great care, one by one, turned them over, and said, 'They carry a Great Idea. It is they who are bringing it out.'

He would say no more that night. He had offered a first enigmatic sign at the end of his counsel. I wondered if he knew of the central place that the image of the walker with his load occupied in Mayan hieroglyphic writing. Time itself, the central obsession of the Mayan *abuelos*, was depicted as such a walker. Don Pablo's statement was cryptic as a hieroglyph, a riddle to catch my thought and sustain it.

'What do the Mayans call these counsels, don Pablo?'

'They call them *almaxikin*'. He pronounced the 'sh' sound of the Mayan 'x'. 'They are the examples a father leaves his children.'

5

The Cave with Writing

 If I had been an anthropologist I would have been seriously concerned about my chosen *pied à terre*. It was almost too tropical and easy. The same gnawing doubt would have encircled my relationship with don Pablo, the 'informant' as anthropologists say in an unusually insulting lapse of expression. Don Pablo's presence and importance in the walk to come was immediate, prescient. At the same time the place and person were too obvious for the kind of research that seeks a 'traditional' community and inaccessibility, as if these euphemisms for extreme deprivation are prerequisites for authenticity.

Tulum would have suited the clichés of anthropology perfectly until 1968, the year the 'white road' arrived in the village, linking it to the Yucatan and to Chetumal, the capital of Quintana Roo, 150 miles to the south on the borders with Belize. The last decade had finally and irrevocably changed the Mayan world here, a change which reached into every Indian heart. I was to discover that it was precisely this jeopardy which inspired don Pablo's counsels to me and led, eventually, to the first real Mayan explanation of their writing given to us. For the time being I only knew that here in the shadows of the ruined City of Dawn I had heard a clear Mayan voice speaking. I understood that I had come to a place of learning, here to the east, a cave with a rich store of writing.

DzibAktun, the 'cave with writing', covered about five acres of limestone rock interspersed, as the entire peninsula of Yucatan is, by pockets of fertile earth. Much of the *rancho's* acreage formed a promontory, jutting out into the Caribbean. Upon this, wherever there was sufficient earth to do so, don Pablo had planted coconut palms for copra, shade and food. He had also built five Mayan houses, each distinctive, balanced, well-proportioned – each thatched with *guano* palm. The houses were cut and tied with a skill inherited from countless generations of Mayan carpenters. The houses were secluded with the forest just behind their shoulders, the shade of the coconut grove beyond their doorways. The gaps in the wooden palisade walls kept them cool and ventilated. Bright shafts of sunlight pierced these walls, an ever-shifting play of light and shadow. They kept your vision outdoors, the walls a mere screen to the outside world.

Northwards of DzibAktun there was a cove, a further promontory of sharp limestone escarpment, and then a seemingly endless, white-sanded beach which curved a mile away to the ruined city. Most days waves swept lazily up the idyllic shore and the clear celestial blue sea seemed placid and inviting. Sometimes, though, tropical squalls, sharks and moray eels made it more dangerous than the jungle. In the distance a line of white, low breakers washed over the coral reef, the sea wall of Tulum. In this location, I thought, there can hardly be distinction between dream and reality.

Don Pablo told me that he had begun to develop DzibAktun in 1953. A coconut ranch of that name had existed here from years before, but in the early 1940s it had been abandoned, only its name surviving. The rest of the absent owner's efforts had been quickly swallowed by forest and storm. Don Pablo cleared the forest anew and broke limestone to make the *rancho* I saw now. As a young boy he had fished from the rocks here using hook and line. He knew of a trail which ran from DzibAktun through the forest, past *cenote* and hidden ruin, to the village three miles inland. He learnt of the bounty of the sea in those early years, and the relative ease of the harvest. He enjoyed the solitude, the sounds and colours of the coast, the movement of the sea, the distant line of the horizon.

In those days Tulum village and all the forest for endless miles around was entirely isolated from the Yucatan and the outside world. Only an occasional boat from the offshore island of Cozumel, or from Chetumal and Belize, landed at the ruins on the coast. Through the forest there were trails south to the next Mayan village, Chumpon, to Tancah on the coast to the north, and a *Noh Be*, or 'great road', which ran just south of Tulum village north-west into the Yucatan, to Saci – seventy miles through dense jungle, a two-day walk for a Mayan. Each year, in those days, many of the villagers made at least one journey to Saci to buy cloth, pots and pans, pepper and other necessities. Money for these trips was earned by working the *chicle* season, taping the *zapote* trees for their resin, instantly convertible into cash, or by selling copra to passing boats. A hundred dollars a year, in today's terms, was a good income then. The village was small, perhaps 150 people, and there was hunting and fishing, fruit, honey, and reasonable land for *milpas*. The outside world was a mysterious and frightening place notable most of all for its past enslavement and exploitation of the Indians.

Don Pablo told me that until the 1930s the Mayas considered that the Fight continued between Mayan *campesinos* and federal soldiers. The law of Mexico did not rule then. The rebel Maya of Tulum, Chumpon, Chanka Veracruz, San Antonio and Xcacal Guardia listened to the counsels of a prophetic Oracular Cross guarded by armed Indians in the sacred centre of Xcacal. These Cruzob villages were scattered throughout present-day Quintana Roo and their spiritual cohesion, military independence and accentuated traditionalism emphasized their victorious and adamant claim to an independent territory – to being Separate Ones.

From the mid-1930s there had been a growing cooperation between the rebel Cruzob Maya and the central Mexican federal authorities. Tulum and all the other Cruzob villages had accepted legal titles as *ejidos*. This meant that ownership of a generous, valuable acreage of forest passed into the collective hands of the villagers. Each would own the fruits of his or her labours. The entire central Quintana Roo area had been pacified in this way. In addition, don Pablo told me, the Mexican government had begun to subsidize medicine for the Mayans here and had been responsive to other needs, too. They had left the resources of the forest, notably *chicle* and its ready conversion into money, in the hands of those who worked it. The Mayas also retained rights over the valuable wood in the forest – mahogany, rosewood, cedar. While not a perfect arrangement, it had rid the Indians of more onerous, whip-in-hand exploitation.

The cooperative terms offered by the Mexican authorities were considered acceptable to the majority of rebel Maya. The President of Mexico, Lazaro Cardenas, personally confirmed a negotiated settlement on a visit to the Territorio in 1939. Ever since that year this hinterland area gradually came under Mexican law. At least one Mayan chief and rebel general had been made an honorary general in the Mexican army. Equally, the terms of the agreement between Mayan and Mexican chiefs were startingly reminiscent of those practiced by the Mayan *abuelos*. It was hardly surprising then that don Pablo's voice never carried trace or hint of conquest and humiliation. The Mayan example he had grown up with said that the Indians had won their land and complete freedom as a result of the Fight.

From 1940 to the present day, for nearly forty years, there had been peace and obscurity in the village and in Quintana Roo as a whole. From time to time archaeologists such as J. Eric S. Thompson and Sylvanus Morley had come by boat, and later by small plane, to see the ruins on the coast. They did not bother with the village. The land, according to Mayan tradition, belonged to God, the fruits of one's labour belonging to the individual. A person earned the right to occupy land according to necessity, not because of privilege or a spurious sense of property.

What don Pablo was beginning to see now was a new law which exploited the land in a different way. A person was said to own the actual earth. It was this way which the white road was bringing to the Mayas. I asked him if he thought the white road was viewed negatively by the people of Tulum. He gave this some thought and then said 'progress' was desired. He held onto the word 'progress' as if it were an unfamiliar coin. He quoted the example of his speargun and other equipment, saying that they only arrived with the road and the outsiders that came down it. He had learnt to dive, to hunt beneath the waves, in caves in the coral reef, from Mexicans. I asked him if he was the first villager of Tulum to hunt this way. He said that, coincidentally, he was. Now a few dozen fishermen worked the coast here for lobster, conch and fish.

'Everything is changing,' don Pablo said. The government planned a new town of Tulum, hotels and restaurants, sailing and diving. Someone had decided that east-coast Quintana Roo was plump for exploitation. The combination of ruined cities, tropical flowers and birds, magnificent Caribbean waters, pure crystalline sunlight, and mildly mannered Mayan Indians, was hard to resist. Already the forest around the ruins was being divided into blocks, 'parcels', and secondary roads were under construction. 'It is like a nightmare,' don Pablo said.

I could see that this was so. His coconut ranch, DzibAktun, with its rudimentary but real hospitality, would soon appear as a mirage, a distant oasis surrounded by a desert of air-conditioned bungalows, beach chalets and studios, *taco* stands and diving shops. I asked him if the coastal land had been included in the *ejido* title of 1939, signed with the President of Mexico. He said it had not but that it had been 'requested' a little later. I could see then that DzibAktun might not even survive as a waking dream. Don Pablo, in spite of his twenty years of working here, was technically a squatter on titled but long-abandoned land. 'When they came to count noses, that was when all this began,' he finally said.

This conversation was very different from the *almaxikin*, the counsel of the ruins. There, don Pablo had recreated a set piece, a discourse defined closely by tradition. There had been verse, original perception and legend in that counsel – a drawing up of hidden, timeless resources from underground depths. There was time set apart for me to hear this performance. The conversation about DzibAktun, a subject much more his personal concern, was different. It was given intermittently, during moments of rest between don Pablo's other work. On calm mornings he fished on the distant reef, diving repeatedly for lobster and red snapper. In the afternoons he opened hundreds of coconuts, leaving them to dry in the sun. Our conversations about land and ranch during these activities were somehow marked off as secular, but they conveyed an unspoken feeling of deep and abiding anguish.

Don Pablo was living alone at the ranch during the rains, his house in a state of disarray, his wife doña Ophelia and the seven children preferring the village inland, protected from the wind. Some evenings he would go there, returning in the early dawn. Other times he would stay at DzibAktun. Somewhat eccentrically in Mayan eyes, this was where he lived. We talked briefly on several occasions. I did not want to bother him with a lot of questions about his *abuelos*.

For me, DzibAktun was an unfamiliar, exotic world, marred only by the mosquitoes which proliferated during the rainy season. But they dispersed at first light and the days were hot, the rays of the sun heightening the delicate colours of sea and beach. Cumulus nimbus and fierce, sudden squalls shared the sky, red–gold at dust, rose at dawn. Early morning and evening the surrounding forest was filled with an orchestra of tropical birds, parakeets, *chachalakas*, the solitary *pich*, the sky-blue *che'el*, pairs of pelicans and flocks of pure white igrises calling back and forth. My house was bare, save for my hammock, mosquito net, a few books, paper and pencil, some clothes. Driftwood and stone served as chair and table. The floor was earth, the house facing sunrise over the sea, palm grove and white limestone in the foreground.

At dawn my tasks were clearly defined by need. I collected firewood from the forest, drew water from a well near Pablo's house, caught and cooked fish for breakfast, opened a coconut, made coffee. 'The life of the rich,' don Pablo commented. An hour would pass this way, until at 6 a.m. the sun gradually rose out of the sea in front of me – visible, daily miracle. The day unfolded to meet it.

There were three or four small stores in Tulum, a forty-minute walk away, through the forest along ancient track. The stores were full of tins and boxes. There was Dutch cheese, Danish butter and cream, American chocolate and batteries, cornflakes, peanut butter, candles, rope and corned beef. The shelves were filled in the dark, secure stores. This surprising collection was the legacy of centuries of isolation from Mexico. Before the coming of the white road most goods were imported from Belize by boat, and overland in mule train. The absence of government control made these goods duty free, so to speak, the glittering prizes awarded for a *chicle* season of hard labour. The Indians had grown used to labels written in English.

Gazing at this bizarre display, I had the disturbing feeling of having stumbled across a cargo cult, the Indians acquiring the symbols of our world in the hopes that their power might work for them, too. They never saw a white man work, as they defined this term, yet they always saw us with the power to command these material goods at will. They were trying to do the same for themselves and the secret, somehow, was written on these mysterious labels. They couldn't possibly eat this stuff, I thought in dismay; most likely they just showed it to the neighbours. Disillusioned I stumbled back to the coast, back to hook and line. I had yet to learn that this acquisition of labels was a hobby to them, much like my attempts to read Mayan hieroglyphs were to me.

Wandering about DzibAktun for days on end, my senses became attuned to a different scale of things, a small world seemingly large because of its isolation and the exuberance of the surroundings. Details – rich red, mauve lichen and moss on the limestone, hermit crabs, butterflies, cactus, and iguanas lazing in the sun by the sea – these all invited hours of observation, of magnifying wonder, and a startling sensation of living in a different century unmarked by the passage of Europeans. Though the days lacked visible event, they were filled with thought and simple routine, the boundaries of imagination finally extended beyond urban skylines and induced fantasies.

I knew that don Pablo was thinking of the counsel of the ruins, although for days he made no reference to it, as if it had not been spoken. Then, unprompted, he said, 'The way in which the Kuxan Suum was cut was like this. The lords who knew of the cord's power hid it in a small box, buried in the earth. One day a boy found it. He opened the box and the cord came out. When he realized what he had found, the boy tried to put it back. But it would no longer fit. However hard he tried, however he arranged it, there was always a little of the cord left over. In the end he cut this part and closed the box. The cord was cut and the blood ran out. That was how it was.'

Although I could not understand the hidden significance of this story I could see that the teller of it was inching forward, offering ancient legend in friendship, seeing what I would do with it.

North and south of the *rancho* the beach and coconut groves remained deserted. There was no other *rancho* between here and the ruins, a few palm lean-tos representing the only alternative to don Pablo's place in this direction. To the south there were two or three coconut ranches like DzibAktun, more or less at two mile intervals. Here too there were Mayan houses to rent, a scattering of people working the copra harvest and the sea. In the forest behind DzibAktun there were no houses, only hunters' trails, ruins, the path from beach to village, and the poor earth that gave Tulum its name. People made *milpa* further inland, leaving the coastal forest to wild game and for firewood and house-building materials.

Occasionally at dusk a few fishermen came to DzibAktun. The nights were twelve hours long, mosquito-ridden, candlelit only. Gathering together was a way of passing these long hours. Tulum was recent fishing for these men. Many came from Isla Mujeres, the 'Island of Women', seventy miles to the north. It was said that this island got its name as a pirate's stronghold, where treasures from the Spanish Main were kept, together with mistresses and cooks – the plunder of my English and European ancestors. If apocryphal, the story was suitably sited amidst barnacle-covered cannon dredged from below and hauled to the surface, and it did provide the tourists with a frisson of excitement to take home from an otherwise rather undistinguished, barren island.

The fishermen lived on the island and saw it differently. They fished lobster, turtles and conch, as the season demanded. They were Mexicans who had learnt their skills from generations of Isla fishermen. John Stephens encountered their forefathers in 1842, sailing back from his visit to the ruins of Tulum. In those days they fished with nets and searched for turtles, whose prodigious supply of eggs and meat was a rich prize and their oil the only source of money open to the poor fishermen. Stephens wrote of some of them whom he met at Kan Kune on the mainland opposite Isla Mujeres, 'The fishermen were busy within the hut, mending their nets, and seemed to be leading a hardy, independent, and social life, entirely different from anything encountered in the interior.' Having said this, the intrepid explorer and his grumbling party sailed away.

The men gathered at DzibAktun were the present-day counterparts of the anonymous fishermen of Kan Kune. In the flickering candlelight, holding a bottle of *aguardiente* (firewater), unshaven, wearing only thin cotton trousers, sandals and straw hats, these hardy men seemed like brigands on shore leave from a pirate ship. They were proud, honest, fast talkers; they gambled a week's earnings on a single throw of the dice. They regarded the cold season of El Norte as a vacation, the winds and currents at Isla Mujeres unsuitable for diving. They came here to fish a few lobster for daily living, to get away from the island bars, to meet new people. Although they talked grandly of their earnings, they were poor people, owning a change of clothes, a machete, a speargun, mask and fins. They slept in broken hammocks, drank heavily 'to resist the cold', and were generous to a fault. They were free people living hard, short lives. They were well received at Dzib-Aktun.

A new kind of fisherman was here also – Mayans who had recently emerged from their forest lives, realizing that the coast offered a more lucrative, easier living. The King of the Poor was a diver, the ruins proclaimed. These Mayan divers were young, sixteen and seventeen, already matured and dignified by their work. Don Pablo and the Isla fishermen treated them as adults – equal wage-earners. They were muscular and fit, witty, unaccustomed to alcohol and the fast life of the Mexican fishermen. Pablo told me that ten years before, the Mayans had only used line and hook, and sometimes rudimentary harpoon to fish at Tulum. Now these young men were talking of forming a cooperative to protect the resources off the coast of Tulum and, thus, their work. These young Indians listened intently to their Mexican cousins, respecting their greater experience and skill as divers, fascinated by their tall stories of money, loose women and the sea.

'And who is he?' one of the fishermen asked don Pablo, seeing me sitting there with the rest of the men. He had a long scar from a *machete* cut down his left cheek, his face pock-marked and abused. But his question was not unfriendly. I explained that I had come to the new Mexican state of Quintana Roo to learn of the work people did, and to study *la historia*. He soon settled down.

We began talking of people's work here and the rapid changes that were being wrought by the federal government. There were to be ice factories, and the exporting of lobster to the US was beginning soon. A new Acapulco, built from scratch and showing it, was being prepared at Can Cun, and the tourist industry was rapidly expanding. In the rural areas the government planned cattle cooperatives, beekeepers' cooperatives, and the exploitation of quality wood through saw mills. New colonies of Mexicans were to be funded and established in the forest near the Mayas and the latter were to be progessively brought into the mainstream of Mexican national life. Electricity was coming, the Isla fishermen told me, more roads, more goods. 'People are hopeful,' they said.

All the time we were talking the fishermen were squatting in the shadows, drinking and joking vociferously. Some spoke Mayan, some played cards for pesos. Three Mayans were reading borrowed comics by candlelight, listening to the words of the rest. Don Pablo sat near the fire, occasionally answering questions, taking a swig from a passing bottle, watching the game of cards. I could see that he enjoyed the company of these *amigos*, his mind curious about their lives and thoughts so different from his. They in turn seemed to regard him as a good friend, DzibAktun as a hospitable place to while away the evening.

Don Pablo stirred at our conversation on Tulum's development. Forcefully he said, 'When the *abuelos* signed the *ejido* papers it was the forest which gave them a living. They had *milpas* there and they made a little money from the *chicle* season. The coast was hardly worked in those days – only a little fishing, turtles, a few coconuts. No one was interested in the coast then. They thought it had little value. So when they made the papers for the *ejido* they only asked for the forest. But the *abuelos* signed the papers and the Mexicans have honoured our title, our *ejido* rights over the forest. We can only ask them for a share of the coast. It is their right.'

The Isla fishermen nodded in agreement at this. These men were amongst the few Mexicans accessible to don Pablo. I could see that there had been long hours of discussion over this point on past occasions. To some extent, it seemed to me, don Pablo was repeating an argument only recently learnt. Although, perhaps, he was watching twenty years labour at DzibAktun come to nothing, he felt obliged to concede that the Mayan *abuelos* of fifty years ago bore a great responsibility. If the Mexican government claimed the coast for development, they were acting within the law that the Mayan *abuelos* had accepted. Still, I could feel the convulsion these plans of progress were introducing into Mayan life. Everything was changing and the Mayans were discovering, as they had always found with the outsider, that they were in grave danger of ending up at the bottom of the economic pile. 'We never have gone elsewhere to do that to them,' don Pablo said to me. This was historically true for over two thousand years. The Mayas had never showed an interest in conquering central Mexico. They were confident in themselves, in the secluded life beneath the forest canopy.

They were still quietly sure of themselves, sitting at DzibAktun on the edge of a new world and time, reading comics, talking Mayan, absorbing everything the Isla fishermen said and did in Spanish. They spoke to don Pablo respectfully, as an elder. They seemed to regard him as somewhat mysterious, unfathomable, his words cryptic and important in some undefinable way.

Don Pablo was serious now. He said that the Mayas wanted a part in the development plans of Tulum and Quintana Roo as a whole. He said that when Mexicans came to work on *ejido* land, to tap the *chicle* trees for example, they shared half the proceeds with the Mayas. The same principle should apply on the coast. The Mayan fishermen should be assured of a place here even though the *abuelos* had foolishly given away their right to it. It would be a sign of good faith by the Mexican government to recognize the cruel irony of the Mayan position. In matters of the heart rather than imperfect law, these poor Indian *campesinos* were asking for something irrefutably theirs.

The Isla fishermen agreed with this. They also had lived here for generations, albeit clinging precariously to the peripheral island. They understood the unease of the Mayans. The Mexican government had given them shorefront property on the Isla and they knew how necessary this was for their work. Not knowing if the same generosity on the part of the government was to apply to Tulum was a source of acute suffering and anxiety. A new civilization was approaching. The government planned to settle many thousands of landless Mexican peasants, *campesinos*, in Quintana Roo. The Mayans already living there could not but feel insecure at this veritable onslaught of people.

'The trouble is that you Mayans are still a tribe,' the fishermen with the deep *machete* scar, don Crescencio , said. He had exactly framed Mexican resentments. Here was the particular strength of the Mayans, their resilience through four hundred years of occupation, their secret solidarity, a tribe of one million Yucatec Maya. It was a pragmatic observation that only someone who had worked alongside the Indians could have made. In his generosity this fisherman had been hurt by the Indians' persistent, polite refusal to let him in. He had sensed the power of their customs and obligations to each other, and his exclusion. They were a different people, holding out until they were met halfway, on their own terms.

Another man in the shadows said, 'Yes, the Mayas are uncivilized, they don't know anything. They are very ignorant. Look how poor this man is.'

I looked around the darkened house. By the hearth there were a couple of enamel cups, a saucepan, a frying pan. Hanging above the fire, slightly to one side, there was a *peten,* a circular tray made from vines. There were a few *tortillas* in this, wrapped in an embroidered cloth, out of reach of the dogs and chickens. In one corner of the room there was a bed made from saplings tied evenly across a frame with vines; some thin cotton bedding covered this, a mosquito net was rolled above. There was a hammock also, a couple of *kanché* stools, a rifle hanging in another corner alongside *machete* and fishing equipment. On the crossbeams of the house don Pablo had placed two wooden planks and I could see a wooden trunk resting on this. I realized that it was his lack of manufactured goods which made him 'uncivilized', 'ignorant' and very poor in this Mexican fisherman's eyes. Don Pablo lacked radio, watch, penknife and disposable Bic ligher. He did not lack self-sufficiency, practical skills and vision. These evidently did not count anymore in the modern world coming fleetfoot.

What most amazed me was the way the Mayans responded to these comments. They all carried on as if nothing had been said, showing no trace of the psychic blow delivered. They did not so much as blink at this spoken prejudice, understanding the poverty which had inspired it. The card-playing, joking and drinking continued. Two Mayans talked riddles and laughed at the insight these hid, a memory and rehearsal of the ancient hieroglyphs. Don Pablo sat silent, stamping his feet softly to keep the mosquitoes away from his ankles. He was ahead of the argument, far beyond its hook and bait. In the reversal of his world, suffered by generations of Indians, his traditionalism made him the most radical visionary of us all. These people were arguing over matters he had worked through, here, gazing into the fire night after night, ever since the coming of the white road. He had been the first diver, diviner of the future lives of many of the Mayas, his children amongst them. If he did not rebuke the fisherman's remarks, it was a silence born of knowledge, not emptiness and defeat.

After all the fishermen had gone, don Pablo led me away from the *rancho* into the darkened forest behind. It was a quarter moon, a clear starlit night. I had no idea what he was about to show me. After a few minutes walking along a narrow path we stopped. Don Pablo walked off to the right, to the foot of a tall tree.

He knelt down, his head close to the ground, and listened. He lifted a small stone aside and listened again. There was a quiet, almost inaudible, chirping sound. 'The guardian,' don Pablo announced in a whisper. He lifted another stone and, placing it to one side, pointed to a small recess. The chirping from within continued. I crouched down wondering what on earth was going on. Slowly don Pablo lifted up another stone and searched around in the hole that had now been uncovered. He found what he was looking for and, without showing it to me, stood up and turned aside.

After a few seconds don Pablo faced me, his right hand outstretched. In his palm I saw eight tiny stones. Before I had time to examine these he closed his hand and held his left hand up to the quarter moon. He was holding a small, oval-shaped stone, a stone the colour of the midday Caribbean. He gave it to me to examine more closely by the light of a match. It was a stone from an old Mayan necklace, I quickly concluded, a small hole running through it lengthwise. It was polished, obviously worked by man and, but for Pablo's dramatic introduction, would hardly have struck me as particularly memorable.

'It is all here,' don Pablo said, after I had given it back to him. 'He who knows how to, sees it. Otherwise they cannot even look at it. But it is all here, the power of the *abuelos*. This is a puzzle, Ricardo. What do you see in this stone? How does it speak to you?'

I was more than perplexed at don Pablo's words and mystical gestures. For a moment I thought he was putting me on, playing with my interest in the Mayas. But he was so intent and patient it could not be the case. How could the stone be a puzzle? In order to say something I mumbled that there were thousands of stones like this one in museums and that it came from an old Indian necklace.

'But if you question this powerful stone it will speak a great truth, don Ricardo.'

I examined the stone again. Its power remained opaque and hidden from me. Try as I might, I could not understand what don Pablo was talking about. I could not see how this stone could have much to say to me. I handed it back with a shrug.

'But what question do I ask, Pablo?' I said in final desperation.

Don Pablo hesitated a few seconds, hoping I might have something more intelligent to add. Then he handed me the stone a third time

'You see how this stone is, how there is no other stone in Yucatan as hard as this.'

I looked at it more carefully. He was quite right, the stone was extremely hard. Suddenly, I thought of the question.

'How did the Mayan *abuelos* drill such a tiny hole right through such a hard stone, don Pablo?'

'That is the question, Ricardo. That is the puzzle. The archaeologists say, the great experts say, that the *abuelos* did not have metal tools. How then, did they make these tiny holes?'

He laughed. I could give him no answer. I realized that he had very neatly turned the so-called ignorance of the Stone Age Maya back upon us technological wizards. In all the books I had read on the Mayas, I had never come across the question don Pablo had asked. I doubted very much if we could answer it.

'Who then is ignorant?' the stone said to me.

'Truly you are a powerful stone,' I said, 'more effective in defending those who worked you, those who valued you, those who understood you, than any number of words.'

·

6

Hunter's Walk

 The path don Pablo was leading me along was hardly distinguishable from the thick and tangled undergrowth beneath the forest trees. We had been walking for an hour and must have been three miles north-west of the ruins of Tulum when we made a first stop. Don Pablo was carrying his forest equipment – gun and cartridges, *machete*, hammock, water-gourd, small cooking pot, string, *tortillas*, and a change of clothing. These were packed carefully into a *mecapal*, the Mayan carrying-bag made of *henequen*. This load was carried in the small of his back, sustained by a tumpline passed across his forehead, under his straw hat. His gun and *machete* were slung under his arms, tools from our world.

I carried my own hammock, *machete*, water container, food and clothes in my rucksack. We were on a hunting walk, early morning, and don Pablo was in a talkative, happy mood here in his forest world. He handed me the water-gourd, *chu ha* in Maya, and I took a few sips before handing it back to him. I noticed that he merely refreshed his mouth with water, spitting it out after a few seconds. Squatting down he opened his *mecapal* and took out an especially thick, salted *tortilla* – travelling fare to share with me.

We rested by the side of the path listening to the calling of toucans and the chattering of the blue *che'el* birds. Glancing up, I noticed mauve and red aerial flowers suspended from the branches of the tall trees which surrounded us. It was already hot and humid under forest cover, the ground rocky and overgrown with numerous trees tumbled across our trail. We had opened our way through this jungle, walking towards a *rancho* which was to serve as our base for a day of hunting. We were nearly halfway, don Pablo told me. This walk was my first real experience of the Quintana Roo forest and I felt overwhelmed and ignorant at the end of the first hour. I could not even see the path don Pablo claimed to be following.

'The last hurricane,' he said casually, 'tore up the forest here and the path is a little difficult.'

He showed me how to see the trail by examining the limestone rocks scattered underfoot and all about. Those which were on the path were worn smooth along their edges where countless Mayan feet had trodden. Once I learnt to see this I could pick up the rhythm from rock to rock, heading north-west. In truth I had barely an opportunity to look about me for the walk had involved paying close attention to the few feet immediately ahead of me. For long stretches we had stepped from one rock to another, clambered over and under fallen trees and cut through undergrowth blocking our way. My new *machete* leant against a tree, blunt and initiated.

'After you have practiced, you will learn to walk the Mayan way,' don Pablo assured me, his voice and expression careful to avoid hurting my feelings.

'You need a certain measure to your step,' he added. 'If you look at the rocks you can see where those who have gone before placed their feet. If you measure your step against theirs you will find it easier.'

Looking around us don Pablo began naming the various trees for me. I took out my notebook and began to write. He showed me the *chico zapote* tree with zigzag *machete* cuts in its bark. From this tree, he told me, the Mayans collected the resin which is used for making chewing-gum. It was during the rainy season that the resin ran like milk. Throughout the forest of Quintana Roo hundreds of *chicleros* were hard at work now. We might meet up with some of them on our walk. 'This is how the poor earn a little money for their necessities,' don Pablo said.

He showed me the brown *zapote* fruit scattered under the tree. 'By March these will be much larger and very good for eating.' He handed me one. I held it in the palm of my hand, feeling its protective skin. It was round, the size of a walnut. Taking out my penknife I cut through the skin and peeled it back, exposing a sweet, dark brown meat. It tasted like crystallized fruit and I searched around for a few more.

Don Pablo kept me busy describing the various trees. He showed me a *pom* tree used by the Indians to make incense. He pointed out various trees excellent for house-building, the *yaax ek* for the forked posts of the roof, the *chintok* for the mainposts, and the *xaan*, or low *guano* palm used for the roof thatch. He gestured towards a certain tree, saying that in times of famine the people mixed a little maize with the bark to make their *tortillas*. With his *machete* he cut some of the bark from the *takinché* and showed me its rose inner colouring.

'This bark can be cooked with water to make a drink like hot chocolate. It is very good for dysentery.'

Soon he had named and explained the uses of all the trees in our vicinity. Pausing to let me complete my notes, he started on the plants, picking some leaves from a small bush beside the trail. He asked me to chew one. After a few seconds my mouth went numb and I felt momentarily cold.

'That is good for toothache, the *sisché*,' don Pablo said, 'for headaches also.'

He showed me some of the vines used for tying houses, *ak*, some herbs used in cooking, and medicinal plants used for poultices and in the treatment of fever.

I was impressed by don Pablo's erudition. It seemed there was no plant or tree near us which did not have some use in the Mayan scheme of things. Pablo had pointed out each one to me, reading lucidly the phrases of his forest text. His gestures, his learning way, was open and natural. His enjoyment in sharing his practical mastery of the Mayan way was as great as mine in learning of it.

'How did you come to learn these things, don Pablo?' I asked him eventually.

'My *abuelo* taught me everything about the forest, he taught me hunting.' Don Pablo settled down to sort through the plants he had collected. 'My *abuelo* was a great *h-men*, "one who knows"; he was don Dolores Balam. People would come and ask him where they should go hunting. When they hunted deer, wild boar, or even *chic* (coati), he would see it first. He knew where they would find the animal they wanted. So when they hunted they would give him a leg, a share of the hunt. There in his house there was always meat. I inherited a little from my *abuelo*, Hunter. He was a master of the forest, great herbalist also.'

Don Pablo tied the small bundles of plants with thin vine and put them in his *mecapal*.

'Are you a *h-men*, a shaman like your *abuelo*?' I asked him.

'Well,' he hesitated, 'my *abuelo* died when I was young so I did not learn much. I remember what he told me, what he showed me, that is all. I went with him to collect plants and I listened to his counsels. But I was young when he died. You see, if you want to worship it is always a matter for the *h-menob*. They know everything about how to worship, how to pray. They are the people amongst us who most quickly arrive before God. It is He who gives them power and then they share it with the rest of the people. But I only know a little.'

I thought about his reticent words for a while. Listening to his counsels was enough to tell me of his devotion to the ancient Mayan way. Indeed even his inexplicitness concerning his own shamanic abilities was a traditional dissimulation towards outsiders, a deeply ingrained defence of that area of Mayan scholarship which we had persecuted and rejected the most forcefully. But watching him walk here in the forest, relaxed and completely absorbed, was enough to tell me I had found the dream walk guide I was seeking.

It was not until later that I realized the significance of don Pablo's reference to his grandfather, don Dolores Balam. If Mayan knowledge was handed down within a lineage, I had stumbled across the contemporary continuation of the very traditions from which Chilam Balam had drawn his counsel of the Christian future over four hundred years ago. The ancient sage and prophet may well have been a distant, direct *abuelo* of this man before me now.

'Are there shamans as great in their powers as the *abuelos*, don Pablo?'

'No, not anymore. Well, there may be, but we do not know where to find them. There are still *h-menob*, but not like before, making an idol which moves, which walks, which has power. Not anymore, that virtue is lost now.'

His comment reminded me of a passage in one of the Mayan Books of Counsel, the Quiché *Popol Vuh*. In this passage Former and Shaper attempt to make man from mud. Don Pablo seemed to be taking my question as a reference to these first shamans and their God-given powers. We were in legendary time now and don Pablo was continuing to start my learning at the very beginning, in a first time.

'Could the shamans fly before, changing their bodies into those of birds and animals?' I asked.

'That they say there is, that there are places where that happens, where a sorcerer, a *brujo*, can go as a tiger or as a jaguar.'

'But are these sorcerers the same as shamans?' I was a little confused at the sudden appearance of sorcery in the conversation.

'There are shamans who only learn to help you, don Ricardo,' Pablo explained. 'but there are others who are also sorcerers and practice evil. There are those that turn into cats and go into the house. The food becomes rotten. But there are shamans who don't know about sorcery.'

'But why do some shamans become sorcerers?'

'Because they want to, they learn what they know from the *abuelos*. But that is not what I learnt from my *abuelo*. It is not good what they do. The shamans have the power of God. If anything happens to us we go to them. Sometimes the shaman tells you the truth. If you do as he says you recover. That way, little by little, one notices that they really do have power, a little power of explanation. There are those who speak truths and those who do not. They think they do only.'

I wrote all this down and then, thinking about it, asked, 'How do they learn these truths, don Pablo?'

'In dreams they see things. They also have small crystals, *zastun*, to see what blessing is going to appear in the future. They know it. They learn when they are little. They are given a sign – a dream arrives, or a bird or animal tells them to begin learning. Sometimes an *abuelo* or an uncle shows them and they begin to practice, to learn to see who is going to speak, who is powerful, who is a shaman. Well, he begins to speak, to practise.'

'What do your dreams say to you, don Pablo?' I asked. He did not seem annoyed or impatient with my stream of questions.

'There are dreams which come directly from God. Let us suppose, if you listened well to how our *abuelos* explained it before, there are times when without remembering the explanation, forgotten years later, you dream it. If you notice it, if you see it, then you see it is true as it was explained. Because there are also dreams which are only jokes, only fantasy. But there are dreams which come directly from Heaven. From there you are sent something to see before it happens.'

Don Pablo spoke cautiously as if knowing how alien such a proposition was to our scientific learning way.

I realized that his words to me, here by the side of this obscure trail, were somehow very important, but I could not unravel their significance. I noticed only that for don Pablo the ancient Indian *abuelos* and their words and traditions were synonymous with God himself. After reflection I realized that this was entirely logical within Mayan shamanism. The words and customs of the ancients were visions of Hunab Ku, the pre-Columbian One True God, they were the result of a visit

to Him in the heart of the sky. It made sense to treat those who
had received such vision as mediums only, mirrors for His
reflection.

'Do you mean that the *abuelos* left signs or riddles in their
words which you can only answer in your dreams?'

In truth I felt that don Pablo, like don Miguel before him,
was being purposefully enigmatic and elusive on questions
concerning shamanism and the ancient Mayan signs. Now he
stated clearly, as if cued by the precision of my question, 'Yes,
it is that way. You see, the shamans begin their practice, their
learning that way. First they just hear the words without
understanding them. Then they are sent a sign, sometimes in a
dream, sometimes something happens to them, or a bird
comes and tells them. Then they begin to see, to devote
themselves to studying. But it is always only if God wants
it – to send a sign that way. Then they learn of things that are
to happen.'

'Do you mean *before* they happen?' I repeated, making sure I
understood his point very clearly.

'Yes. You always revise your dreams to see what they are
saying to you. For example, if I dream that I am flying, my
wings outstretched like this,' Pablo said, extending his arms,
'turning and turning in the air, that is a bad sign. It means that
someone close to you is going to die. But there are good
dreams also. Let us say a mother, or a brother is a long way
away. If you dream that they are thin then, in a few days, they
will arrive to see you in good health.'

'But are the shamans better at reading these dreams than an
ordinary person?' I ventured to ask.

'Yes. They can understand more because they have more
wisdom. They know how to work. If someone comes to them
sick they know it. When you arrive with them they already
know you are coming, they already know of your illness.
They know who are the spirits, the owners of illness. They go
in spirit to talk with them, to see which one is causing the
illness. But you have to study hard for many years to know
how to do this, to know where every sickness comes from.

They see the spirits in their crystals. There in the *zastun* they present themselves. But if you don't know it, you don't see it.'

I was reduced to a momentary loss of questioning powers by this highly compressed discussion of Mayan knowledge. I hid away in my notebook, reviewing what Pablo had been saying. It was pure shamanism tied closely to its hunter origins, the restless visionary walker psychically tracking his prey, so closely in communion with nature and the spirit world that he or she could change forms with animals and talk with the birds. Don Pablo's explanation of a shaman as someone who could most quickly arrive with God, be given wisdom and vision, and then share it with the rest of the community was the essential characteristic of shamanism. The shaman restores broken communication between Heaven and earth and his knowledge and curative powers are merely the result of successful trance techniques to accomplish this.

I felt that don Pablo consciously planned to immerse me in these fundamental elements of the Mayan learning way. I sensed that he had clearly measured what he was going to show me on this first walk. In every way he knew how far we were going. He was putting things before me to see, and words were just a part of the vision. Timing, context, gesture, all seem charged with mysterious meaning out here in the forest – a hunter's walk. I felt these things. I did not, as yet, articulate and confirm them with don Pablo. I was also beginning to notice how rarely don Pablo ever asked me a question and I wondered at his patient, thoughtful responses to my naiveté.

'Do you think that in your dreams you can talk to someone a long way away?' I asked, after these few minutes of silent assessment.

'One can pass an idea amongst ideas. You don't know where it comes from, it just appears in your head. You just think that you thought of it yourself. But the shamans know when a spirit has arrived to talk to them. They know what is being said to them. They know how to listen. They can also send a spirit to talk to someone else. They just appear in your mind like an idea. They are very powerful.'

Don Pablo stood up suddenly, restless. I sensed that his counsel was about to end and asked hurriedly, 'Are there women shamans?'

'Women can become prayermakers and *h-menob*, certainly. If they have good intentions, if they know how to pray, no one takes that right from them. It is the same prayer for everyone in the village. It is not important that she is a woman. She can become a prayermaker, a curer, herbalist, a shaman, if she learns it, if it is her fate.'

He was clearly surprised that this was an issue amongst us. I noticed also that there were a series of sub-specialities in Mayan shamanism. The individual chose those he, or she, was attracted to or had a special gift for practising.

'The English word for these people – *h-menob*,' I said to him as I concluded my notes, 'is "shaman".'

'Shaman,' he repeated, obviously enjoying the rich Mayan sound of the word, like *xaman*, the Mayan word for north where shamanism originated.

Our ten minute *lub*, or resting place and interval, had stretched to nearly an hour. Don Pablo balanced his load on his back and hung his gun over his shoulder. It was a quiet gesture which hid much Indian suffering and achievement. A mere eleven years after the Spanish occupation of T-Ho in 1541, a series of laws issued by the new rulers said, 'since the Indians are always wandering the forest to hunt I order that all bows and arrows are to be burned. The Indians must not live off in the forests but must come into the towns together in good strong houses, under pain of whipping or prison.' For good measure these laws added, 'No one shall cast grains of maize for divination, nor tell dreams.' None of this had persuaded or deterred the Mayans. But how many blows had been suffered and delivered to protect this casual, armed walk we were on? In 1761, after the Mayan rebellion led by Jacinto Canek, great

shaman, the Spanish authorities issued a new law. This said
that all Indians who had guns must hand them in, under pain of
death.

Slowly we set off, feeling the growing heat of the day and
the stiffness of too long a respite. We halted after a few minutes
and don Pablo asked me if I found the walking easier than
before. Now that I could discern a path on the rocks my
walking was less hesitant. He took me to one side of the path
and explained that he was going to go on ahead a little
way.

'If God forgives me,' he said, 'I will hunt something.'

He showed me, with the aid of three stones, the signs he
would leave wherever the trail became confusing. This way I
would not get lost. I looked on apprehensively, making sure I
understood. We started off again and within a few seconds he
was gone, silently merging into the forest.

I walked on steadily for forty minutes, my clothes drenched
in perspiration. The forest began to change, shafts of sunlight
penetrating the foliage above, occasional clearings opening to
left and right. At this time of year the vegetation was at its
fullest, the wild game fat, the insects innumerable. It hardly
seemed possible that such exuberant life could thrive on so
scanty a soil as I saw around me. The entire Yucatan peninsula,
I had read, is a flat limestone escarpment hardly rising above
sea level. Limestone is an extremely porous rock which leaves
little surface water. There were small patches of earth in the
rock around me, and occasional low marsh, but this hardly
altered the overriding impression of endless sharp rock
covered, miraculously, by thick tropical savannah forest.
Looking closely at the white rocks I could see some ancient
seashells incrusted in them, a sign that this flat land had once
been seabed. Later don Pablo was to explain to me that after a
flood which ended one of the Indian worlds here, the receding
foam, mixed with shells, had become solid. The rocks around
me were the result of this.

The path became clearer as I walked, my *machete* idle by my
side. I could begin to make out mounds of worked stone,

tumbled-down temples and broken walls with trees growing out of their ruins. I passed some deep, dry pits in the limestone rock, full of centuries of humus and wood. Examining these I realized they had been prepared by man, the sides chipped into near circular form. These pits were *chultunob*, ancient reserves of water and storage pits.

The ancient Maya of Yucatan, much like the Inca in the Andes and deserts of Peru, were great hydraulic engineers. Although there is little surface water in the Yucatan, beneath the limestone rock there are rivers and lakes of the purest and sweetest water. In ancient days the Indians explored this natural, hidden system along miles of underground caverns and channels. They also devised canal systems, terracing and artificial reservoirs to control the rapid flow of rain from the surface to the underground lakes and rivers.

Little of this extraordinary labour is evident on the surface today. The relatively small population of a million Indians makes use of the natural breaks in the surface rock, *cenotes* which expose the watertable, and they sink wells knowing that wherever they choose to do so they must eventually find water. But amongst them there are those who have explored the ancient hydraulic science of their forefathers. They point to its hidden extensiveness as a clear indication of the vastly greater, ten times greater, Mayan population of pre-Columbian times.

As the walking became more and more an unconscious rhythm, I observed my surroundings with more care. I could see that there were hardly any areas where there were no ruins, no signs of Mayan occupation. The forest I was seeing now, seemingly wild and primeval, had once been a well-planned, balanced world extending well beyond the city walls of Tulum. Countless generations of Indians had laboured these stone cities. In those now far-off days, don Pablo told me subsequently, the lords on the high temple at Tulum could gaze across the limitless miles of organized, scrupulous tropical farming, to the temples in the south, north and west. 'The lords could see each other in those days,' he told me, 'across the parks, fruit groves and *milpas*. In those days it was truly a dream to us, Ricardo.'

I was glad of these distracting thoughts about the archaeology of my surroundings. My inner mind was in a state of turmoil over don Pablo's counsel on the Mayan shamans. I could not remember a conversation in which I had learnt so much in so short a time. It had been a low-key performance of consummate skill, his words punctuated by practical observation and action in the forest around us. There had been talk of precognition, of telepathy, of dreams, of curing – short sentences which felt as if they held reasons and ideas I could not yet comprehend.

As don Pablo observed in his recounting of Mayan wisdom, the *abuelos* had left signs, enigmas, in their words, his words now spoken to me. But I was illiterate, yet to see, for example, that it was these modest *h-menob* and their dreaming who were directly responsible for Mayan astronomy, mathematics and hieroglyphic writing. I was groping towards the realization of how this was so, searching for the sinews and ligatures of the Mayan vision. In these early days I was just walking there, remembering don Pablo's words, not understanding them.

I came to a fork in the path. Over on my left, a few steps to one side, I found don Pablo's stone markers. I set off reassured. Soon the forest gave way to thorny bush and thin saplings. I realized I was walking through an old *milpa*, now abandoned and left to return to forest. The path became confusing and I had to cast around for signs of Pablo's passage. I was unable to find any and had to admit the path was just a figment of my imagination. Eventually I re-entered the forest on the north side of the *milpa* and pressed on. Over an hour had passed since I had last seen Pablo and I wondered if I was on the right path. By now we could be two or three miles apart.

The heat of the day was upon me now, humid and disorientating. I had no real sense of how far we had walked. The terrain was unfamiliar to me, its time and distance hard to judge. I was back in deep and difficult forest here, using my *machete* with increasing frequency, bending double under fallen trees and clambering over large limestone rocks. A little further on and this gave way to a clear path. Again, I was relieved to note that don Pablo had placed stones by the side of this.

7

'I give to know'

Soon I came to a deserted *rancho*. There were three Mayan houses set on foot-high earth mounds, each with a small garden around it enclosed by stone walls. The thatched roof on one of the houses had collapsed inwards while the others looked precariously close to the same fate. The houses and their gardens formed three sides of a large compound dominated by a tall *ceiba* tree, the Mayan World Tree through which, they say, souls rise to the heart of Heaven. Beneath the tree I could see a well, an H-frame set above it. There was no bucket, rope, or pulley in sight. This was why don Pablo had brought string and pan. Over on my right I could see the collapsing remnants of a pig enclosure squaring off the compound. Don Pablo's *mecapal* rested against the trunk of the tree. He was nowhere in sight.

I walked over to the well and sat down in the shade. I drank the last of the water in my flask and took my shirt off. I was puzzled at finding the *rancho* deserted. How could someone have worked so hard to create this place and then leave it? It looked as if a large family group had lived out here for many years. Around me I could see orange and lemon trees, banana, papaya and avocado. There were overgrown vegetable gardens, wild tobacco, cotton, chillis and tomatoes. There were the remnants of an A-frame which had once supported log beehives full of stingless Mayan bees. Much labour had gone into establishing this isolated ranch. Now everything was quickly returning to a wild state, weeds and thorn bush overpowering the previously cultivated fruit groves and gardens. Another five years and only the stone walls of the houses would remain as signs of human occupation.

I wandered over to the trees to pick some fruit. There were great quantities of lemons scattered on the ground. As I collected these I felt the brooding silence of this place, compelling, an eye upon the stranger. It gave no clues to its desertion, its abandonment to the elements of the tropical forest.

I found a way into one of the houses, littered with brush, rotting logs and a few rusted tin cans. There were animal tracks in the earth by the hearth and ashes from a long dead fire prepared by some passing night hunter sheltering here. A few peccary bones and teeth were cast to one side, a small Indian stool lay overturned and broken legged nearby, and a tin cup hung from a nail above the fire. There was a musty, dank odour to the house, bat droppings underfoot and a rustling in the thatch above. Collecting a few of the teeth I left, glad to be gone from so decaying an atmosphere. As I came out into the sunlight a shot rang out in the forest nearby.

A few minutes later don Pablo appeared silently, successful in his hunt. He held a coati, a large, ferret-like, mischievous animal, by its long fur tail. Resting his gun against the *ceiba* tree he threw the dead coati on the ground and squatted down in the shade by the well, wiping his brow with a handkerchief. He was flushed with the exertion and excitement of the hunt. He nodded towards me, acknowledging my arrival without a word.

I commented on the accuracy of his single shot. He had shot the coati through the head, the bullet entering from below. The animal had evidently sought refuge up a tree, clinging to the uppermost branches with his long sharp claws. But it had been to no avail and now he lay dead at our feet. Pablo waited until the heat from his work had passed before beginning to talk.

'You learn quickly, don Ricardo, about how to kick stones,' he said, chuckling in amusement at the sight of the scuffed leather on the front of my construction boots.

'A little,' I answered. 'I thought I was lost a couple of times but it was only my fear. How is it though that you can walk across these sharp rocks with only sandals, don Pablo?' I glanced down at my boots. They were rapidly beginning to resemble leather cabbages.

'When you walk you bend your body a little from the waist, and you keep your head at the same level always. You don't climb the rocks, you adjust your legs as you pass across them.' Don Pablo showed me with his hands how to keep my legs moving fluidly across changing terrain. His way of carrying his load was very different from mine. My rucksack jutted above shoulder height and pulled my whole body upright. With his *mecapal* Pablo presented a much smaller figure, bending to sustain a load held below the level of his head. His step naturally followed the signs on the rocks while I was accustomed to a slightly longer stride. My boots were telling me that I was fighting a losing battle.

'The Mayas can walk thirty-five miles a day, barefoot, with your load and mine, Ricardo. Even the *abuelos* of sixty and more can do that. They are accustomed to the heat and the country, that is all.'

'Where are the Mayas who lived here?' I asked after we had rested a little longer.

'They weren't good Mayas,' don Pablo answered in half-thought, beginning to eye the coati, thinking about our growing hunger. 'Well, the *abuelo* who lived here was, but not his sons. You saw the old *milpa* we walked through, how much forest was burnt there. The sons who lived here did that. They burnt too much forest. They did not care what they did, all the good wood, the animals, the plants that were lost. So the *dueños*, the *uyumil kaax* punished them with poverty. After the *abuelo* died there was no more tradition here, they laughed at those superstitions. So the spirits of the forest, the owners of the forest, the *uyumil kaax*, punished their ignorance. The sons

1 *Don Dolores Balam.* 'My *abuelo* was a great shaman, "one who knows". He taught me everything about the forest'

2 *View of Tulum from the sea.* 'We followed the shore day and night and the next day toward sunset we perceived a city or town so large that Seville would not have seemed more considerable nor better; one saw there a large tower'

3 *Three women talking*. 'Women can become prayer-makers and shamans, certainly. If they have good intentions, if they know how to pray, no one takes that right from them. It is the same prayer for everyone in the village'

4 *Mayan milpero and his agricultural load*. 'They carry a Great Idea. It is they who are bringing it out'

5 *The Temple of the Foliated Cross at Palenque* (left). 'They could see the earth down here and where everything was going to be. So then afterwards when they had shared this with the people they also could see that it really came from God to show us how to live'

6 *Mayan woman in contemplation*. 'If the men could roam the forest, work the *milpa*, or go fishing, the women were rooted to the three stones of the hearth'

7 *Gateway to the Montejo palace in Mérida*. 'Two conquistadores stood on the heads of downcast Indians while malign medieval dwarfs of the imagination acted as custodians'

8 *View of Tulum's Castillo*. 'Perhaps a mysterious geomantic sense of their presence was possible, intuited from high on the Castillo stairway'

9 *Hunter's walk*. 'Whereas to me this forest appeared as primitive and chaotic, to him it was a well ordered place, a sacred place'

did not keep *milpa* properly, the land would not produce for them. Soon they disappeared. Look,' he said, pointing to the house with the roof caved in. 'You can see they did not know how to live. I tell you the truth I have known. Even their houses were cut unevenly, the wood badly chosen.'

His voice was sad rather than angry. The place where the Mayans had lived was well endowed. There was water, wild game and the fertile earth nurtured by the *abuelos*. It had all gone to waste here, the root cause spiritual ignorance.

I asked don Pablo what game there was in the forest. He told me of the past abundance of deer, peccary, wild turkey, wood pigeon and *chachalaka*. There was *tepezcuintle*, or agouti, coati, ocelots and American tigers. But the arrival of the white road nearby and new Mexican colonizers clearing huge tracts of forest for cattle-rearing and subsistence farming were bringing scarcity to the region. Before don Pablo could virtually hunt in his backyard, an hour's walk from the village at most. Now he was gone all day and usually only hunted one of the lesser animals, such as the coati before us. Gone were the days of wild turkey, of deer and rich game.

I asked don Pablo if he thought the clearing of the forest was changing the rainfall pattern in Quintana Roo. 'Yes,' he said, 'before it used to rain more evenly during the season. Now it falls suddenly and the season changes abruptly.' I explained the 'sponge' effect of tropical forests, affirming that experiments in the Amazon showed how clearing the forest turned the land into a desert. It was not out of simplicity that the Indians farmed in the forests and jungles the way they did, and had done for five thousand years. Don Pablo thought for a few minutes and then corrected me.

'It is not the way the forests are cleared that is the cause. That also is part of the result. The cause of our growing poverty is that the people who come here from other parts of Mexico do not keep the *costumbre* of the *abuelos*. In these customs, the ceremonies of offering the first fruits, the rain ceremony, the prayers in the village, there is the orientation, the way to live here. It is because the newcomers do not remember the owners that God put there to protect the animals and the forest. Thus they destroy everything, all the trees, all the animals and the plants. The *uyumil kaax* become annoyed and punish these people. Soon we will see that it is so. These are not just stories the *abuelos* left us, don Ricardo, there is great wisdom there.'

Don Pablo had identified the limits of our 'scientific' thinking in relation to Mayan thought and, indeed, to all civilizations but our own. According to our materialist premises, their ways of learning, their rituals, ceremonies and counsels could only be myth, a story, as don Pablo had so accurately defined our implicitly disparaging perception of their *costumbre*. For us there could be no objective, pragmatic basis to ritual and prayer. But for the 'primitive' people concerned religious belief is just that – a practical matter of rain and cultivation, hunger and abundance. Don Pablo's grasp of this distinct perception, theirs and ours, and his ability to phrase it in a single observation impressed me. Nowhere in anthropological literature had I found a preparation for the actual dialogues possible, today, with such men. Theology would have been a better, a more practical tool to bring to this world, I thought, then all that humanist mumbo jumbo which has never even allowed the people their own voice.

'If you had explained these things when the Spaniards first arrived, don Pablo, the Inquisition of Bishop Landa's illegal doing would be sending for you already,' I said. The shamans in the Mayan villages had borne the brunt of Spanish persecution by Church and mercenary killers.

Don Pablo just shrugged and said, 'They knew the shamans had virtues also. They knew they had real powers. They were Christians too, they knew of that from before. That was what the Spanish would not allow. Only they were to teach, only they were to explain, only they were to read the Book. They came to impose their law so they first had to try and destroy everything that was here, the titles to the land, the papers of before, the counsels. They had to deny that the shamans had virtues also. So they called them sorcerers in order to kill them.

But that is not possible, the world here has to continue with the *costumbre* left us by the *abuelos*, great *h-menob*.'

I wondered then at how much colonialism impoverished those who brought it. How many plant cures had been lost to us in the four centuries of persecuting Indian shamans? And how much herbal wisdom was being obliterated now as the forest was brought to its knees by our machines? To outsiders it was a hindrance to their plans for development, an alien and hostile world. To the Mayas it was and is God's preserve, carefully nurtured for thousands of years to keep generations of them alive and healthy, free hunters and farmers sustained by ancient mysterious vision and ritual. In four hundred years we had only learnt to reduce the meanings and secrets of this forest world to blank stone, to nothingness, to a loss of God. We were greatly impoverishing ourselves as well as the Indians.

Don Pablo explained that he was going to cut some fire-wood to cook the coati. In the meantime I was to prepare a large hole in the ground, removing rocks and placing them to one side. He showed me a suitable area, the rocks he wanted to keep and those too small for his purpose.

'When you've done that,' he said, 'go and find some banana leaves. I will show you how to cook in *pib*. We should begin now. It will be an hour before we eat.'

He collected his *machete* and disappeared into the forest. After a few minutes I could hear him hard at work.

I set about preparing the hole, lifting large boulders aside, throwing the smaller ones away. After I had uncovered an area of three feet across I deepened it by scooping out the shallow earth down to solid rock. Wiping my hands I set off to look for the banana leaves. Behind one of the houses I found what I was looking for and cut down a dozen leaves with my *machete*. Back at the hole I waited for don Pablo. Soon he appeared, a great load of wood on his back held up by a tumpline. He began arranging the wood inside the hole. When he was ready he set this alight and stepped back. He quickly arranged the large rocks on top of the blazing fire.

'Now we'll prepare the coati,' he said, watching the flames.

As the flames caught hold of the wood and began to burn fiercely, don Pablo threw the animal onto the pile. The unpleasant smell of burning fur drifted across to me. After no more than thirty seconds don Pablo grabbed the coati's tail and turned the animal over. When this side was also burnt he removed the animal from the flames. Finding a long sharp knife in his *mecapal*, he began to scrape the outer skin off. It came away easily and he was soon disembowelling the animal and removing its tail. He sent me to fetch water and then carefully washed the now gutted animal.

As the fire burnt down, the rocks began to collapse inwards onto the ashes. Don Pablo motioned for me to help him break these up with hard blows from a stick. Now that they were white hot they broke easily and we soon covered the bottom of the hole. He carefully arranged the coati over this layer of rocks and then covered everything over with banana leaves. Finally he used the earth I had scooped out to blanket the leaves, patting the oven firmly so that there was no place where the heat could escape. 'Now we can rest,' he said.

I had seen this form of cooking in Peru, amongst the Quechua Indians, descendants of the Inca civilization. I mentioned this to don Pablo, describing the festivals held there and the large *pachamancas* they prepared, sometimes ten feet across, filled with meat and sweet potatoes. Pablo said he had seen that done once or twice.

'Usually, though, we cook what we have hunted in *pib* like this when the meat is very fresh. Then we can stay another day and, perhaps, hunt something else.'

'How do you know where to hunt?' I asked.

'Well, you find places where the animals go to water. You see their trails, a few overturned leaves, places where they have brushed against a tree, places where they have stopped to eat. Then you climb a tree and wait, sometimes an hour, two, even three. As God wants it, so it will be. You know what animal is going to pass there. If it is peccary there is a strong odour all around, if it is deer you can tell by the droppings. This is when you hunt in the forest. Sometimes I also go hunting on the *milpa*. Then you can see from the food eaten which animal you are going to hunt. If it is coati you know because they waste a lot. They pull down the maize and only eat a little of it, or they open a calabash and just take out the seeds. But if it is agouti, for example, they never waste anything.'

'Do you listen to what the birds are saying ahead of you?'

'I have a wise bird whose voice I know and listen to when I go hunting. I love that bird. It is called *chi chi*. That is what it says to you when you are about to hunt something big. It flies by, calling "chi chi chi", like that. It is a small bird, very clever also.' Don Pablo cupped his left hand to form a nest and showed me with his right hand how small the bird would be within it. 'It is coffee-coloured and has a black line around its throat. That one always advises me. It comes close calling, "There is your deer, your turkey." It never calls for small game, only the best.'

I wrote all this down. 'Is that the only one that helps you?' I asked.

'That is the one I prefer. There are others which just talk, they just disturb the animals. When I am coming close they frighten away the game. They don't help you.'

We walked over to one of the houses and began collecting a few chillis, tomatoes, lemons and bitter oranges. I showed don Pablo how to use a 35-mm camera and he played with this for a while, taking pictures of the *ceiba* and the desolate houses. The sun was still quite high in the sky, the forest a place of silence and tranquility. Only the rustle of the leaves in the breeze, a distant sweeping sound, disturbed the absolute silence, pausing and returning. I was completely absorbed in what we were doing, the world I knew as distant as the far planets. We sat on a log behind the houses, in the cool of the fruit grove. Don Pablo told me that he knew the forest for forty miles around Tulum, trail by trail, step by step. In twenty years and more of walking he had crisscrossed the area many times, weaving an image of this world deep into his mind.

I realized then what a great part hunting and walking played in the Mayan vision. Hunting had led don Pablo beyond his village world to form friendships beyond the *ejido*. It had led him to explore the many ruins of the *abuelos*, and to solitary reflection upon their meaning. He had seen temples with painted murals, caves, white roads or *sac be*, constructed in time immemorial, lost cities and ancient gardens. Whereas to me this forest appeared primitive and chaotic, to him it was a well-ordered place, a sacred place, where he could see the world of the ancients in vivid detail and could understand their thinking in settling an area, and the composition of numerous towns, now ruined, near obliterated in the shrouded glory of the forest. I realized he was not just close to the past, he lived it as present and future, hunting, walking, farming, believing the promise of a returning Mayan vision.

The hunter, I reflected, played a central role in the Mayan hieroglyphs carved on stone, scattered throughout the forest. The walker with his load, the Mayan image of time, is both *milpero*, farmer, journeying to and from his planting and harvesting, and hunter. The hunter roaming far afield, often alone, but sometimes amongst a group of hunters, is as much an integral figure in the Mayan way as the farmer. They are both facets of the whole man at the heart of the Mayan dream walk. Shamanism, in fact, originated amongst nomadic, hunting societies, originated in bone.

In the Mayan hieroglyphs this origin is remembered in the importance accorded to not only the imagery of walking as complex metaphor for time and its cycles, but also in the twentieth sign in the Uinal cycle of twenty – the heart of the system. This sign Ahau depicts the face of the first hunter, Sun Lord, founding shaman. Ahau is the spokesman for the Mayan hieroglyphs, the mouthpiece for the meanings of the signs as a whole. Ahau is 'mouthed and faced' with the distinctive lips of the original Mayan blowgun hunter.

When the Mayan ancients designed the count of time, the ages of the worlds to come, they closed these always on an Ahau ending day, spokesman of the world. Counting in twenty-year periods (7200 days to be precise), they prepared a 'Short

3   *Ahau as blowgun hunter*

Count' of thirteen Ahau spokesmen, one for each of the periods, or *katuns*. This was the count of time the Spanish found upon their arrival, a prophetic count they confirmed by their very arrival at the opening of Katun XI Ahau.

Bishop Landa wrote of the Short Count of approximately 256 years, 'In their language they call these periods [of twenty years] *katuns*, with these making a calculation of Ages that is marvellous; thus it was easy for the old man of whom I spoke in the first chapter to recall events which he said had taken place 300 years before. Had I not known of this calculation I should not have believed it possible to recall such a period.'

The bishop knew that the count was both history and precognitive wheel of time. He himself recorded the arrival of the Spanish on the first day of a new world, predicted within this wheel. While he praised the historical efficacy of the count he wrote blindly and dogmatically of its prophetic function. 'As to who it was that arranged this count of *katuns*, if it was the evil one [the Devil] it was so done to serve in his honour; if it was a man he must have been a great idolater, for to these *katuns* he added all the deceptions, auguries, and impostures by which these people walked in their misery, completely blinded in error. Thus, this was the science to which they gave most credit, held in highest regard, and of which not even all the priests knew the whole.' Incapable of listening to the Mayan shamans, frightened of their predictive powers, the bishop and other Spanish chroniclers did no more than obscure the wisdom and profundity written in the faces of the Ahau spokesmen of time. But here, in this quote, is clear indication that it was the Short Count of thirteen Ahaus which most represented devilry to the Catholic priests.

I asked don Pablo if he knew of the thirteen hunters, Ahaus, and the *katuns* of the Short Count. He shrugged almost imperceptibly and looked pensive for a few minutes. He said the Mayas of today knew those things were written in the 'papers' left by the *abuelos* after the Spanish arrival; they knew they existed and where to find them. He said that they had been sleeping, that they had been put to one side, but that there were always people who had 'carried on the idea'. When I questioned him more closely on this point, he began telling me a long story about thirteen hunters.

'There were thirteen hunters who had the idea of going hunting. And so they got together and all agreed to go. The hunters invited one of the *h-menob*, the greatest shaman. They knew he would help them. He was the *h-men*. There were twelve hunters and the shaman also.

'With the shaman they went out to a place where they knew there were animals. They arrived where they were to stay to hunt. They stopped, found a place, cleared it, prepared firewood, everything they needed. Early in the morning they were to go out hunting. So they slept till dawn. Then they went hunting.

'One by one they were directed by the shaman. "You will go to the east, you to the south, you to the west, and you to the north." Each one left. At last the shaman left. They all left. The first day they did not hunt anything. "How are we going to do this?" they asked amongst themselves. "Tomorrow we'll close off some of the forest and then seven can go ahead where the wind does not blow their scent to the animals. Those who are going to spy, those who are going to come shouting towards the other hunters, so that the animals run ahead."

'They tried it the next day. Nothing. So they asked the

shaman, "How are we going to do this?" "I don't know", he said. "What do you think?" "If you could make us a dog, because if we had a dog we could look for the deer. We could hear him chase them," they said. "Fine," the shaman answered. "If you are in agreement I can do this. I can make a dog. But only in nine days. In those nine days I can prepare a dog from mud."

'He began to make the dog from mud. He spoke, he prayed his secrets every night, every night. As he was making the dog so he prepared his secrets. To give the dog spirit, to give him power. We don't know what the shaman was saying to the dog, what prayers he said to give him life. But that is how my uncle told it to me.

'After nine days, nine nights, he had worked this. At midnight the hunters heard the dog bark. The hunters were happy. They knew now they would hunt deer. They heard the barking of the dog. It had life, it could see, it could walk. But it was only made of mud.

'So the hunters got up early and went into the forest. The hunters were happy with the dog which they had lacked before. The dog went off and found the deer. They hunted them. They killed deer on the first day. They cooked it and salted it. They gave the dog a leg because he only ate meat. They carried on hunting.

'After four days they had a lot of meat. But the load was not complete yet. They went out another day and right away the dog set off barking after the deer. Then it stopped. Who knows what happened to the dog? Did it disappear into a cave? Did the animals kill it? They began looking for the dog. To look and look. After a great time, since there were only twelve of them, they began looking where they had last heard the dog barking. They saw the dog then, by the trunk of a *b'ob* tree. There it had struck, there it was broken into pieces. There the dog died.

'They began to think, now the dog is dead, now how are we going to find meat? They told the shaman that the dog had died. "How did it die?" he asked. "It was chasing deer and it hit against a *b'ob* tree," they said. "The only thing we can do," the shaman said, "is to divide up the meat, share what there is." "But what we want is for you to make another dog, a bigger dog," the hunters said. "Is that what you want?" he asked. "Yes," they answered, "so that we can go hunting." "Fine," he said.

'The shaman began to prepare another dog, a bigger dog this time. So it was. He prepared another dog. After nine nights, they were told, your dog will be ready. The hunters were happy. After nine nights the dog barked again. They were happy because now they had a bigger dog. They were going to hunt more than before.

'The first day they went out and killed twice as many deer as before. But then the dog – at first they only gave him a leg to eat. The dog finished that. The second day they went out hunting again. Nothing, nothing. Finally they killed one and came back to prepare it. They gave a leg to the dog. But the dog was not content with this.

'Night came and they all fell asleep. At midnight, at the same time as he had begun to bark, the dog got up. He got up and ate one of the hunters. He got him by the head and that was that. He pulled him out and ate him. At dawn the others did not know what had happened. A hunter was missing. "But where is he?" they said. "Why didn't he say he was leaving so as to divide up the meat?" They remained. They carried on hunting as usual. But now only eleven of them remained.

'Another day dawned. The same had happened. One of them was missing. Day by day the dog ate them, one by one. They noticed what was happening but they didn't know the reason. At last it was the shaman's turn. The remaining hunters awoke and he was gone. He had been devoured also. He was a shaman but there he finished. Only two remained. "What are we to do?" they thought. "How are we going to carry all this meat?" No one went hunting anymore.

'At last, one dawn, only one hunter remained. That night the last remaining noticed what had happened to the others. As night entered he got a bad stomach, he had diarrhoea. He could not sleep. He saw what happened then. He saw the dog get up. When the dog got up his bad stomach quickly passed. He began to run. There he goes, there he goes. It was hard to run, falling, tripping, getting up again. He could hear the dog barking and barking behind him.

'Then he remembered Our Lord, "Our Father, where are You to help me?" he thought. Only then did he remember the *uyumil kaax*, the owners of the forest. "Where am I to be saved?" he asked himself.

'At last, God all powerful, more powerful than the dog – he arrived where an old man was playing his shaman's drums. When he climbed a small incline he heard the old man playing on his *tunkul* as it is called. You know, that drum has an open hole underneath. As he came down the incline he heard him playing his *tunkul*. He asked the old man to save him from the dog. "What did you do to the dog?" he asked. "Where did you find him?" The hunter began to explain to the lord what had happened to them. "Only because you have arrived here with me will I save you," the old man said.

'The dog was already approaching. The old man had two good swords as well. Then he lifted up his *tunkul* and said to him, "Get in here." The hunter got in and the old man kept on playing. Soon the dog arrived. The old man knew what had happened. What had happened, we could say, is that they kept shooting and shooting the deer. They did not remember that there are owners of the animals. That is what happened to them. The idea of theirs which wasn't good with the deer they prepared . . . well, they had been given power for a while only. They began killing deer as if they were chickens, as if they, the hunters, were the owners. That is how they thought.

'When the dog arrived the old man took one of his swords and hit him. But there was only a spark where he hit the dog with his sword. So then he took his other sword and broke him into pieces. When he had finished killing he took the hunter out from under his *tunkul*. He began to ask about what they had done. And the hunter explained how it had been. "Never again make a dog like that. It never turns out well. It never turns out well. Now you've seen what happens." "I'll never make it again," he said to the old man, "and thanks to you for killing him."

'Later when he had finished explaining to him, as he was lost, he asked the lord to show him the path to his village. "Yes, go this way and right away you'll come out on the path to your village. But don't say who saved you. If you say who saved you from the dog you made you will die, I say." "Fine," the last hunter said. He gave his thanks.

'Arriving at his village he saw that, although it was only a night and a day he had spent with the lord, a year had passed when he returned to his village. Look how that is! He arrived and it was a long time since his family, his wife, had seen him. The lord had told him not to allow them to embrace him. But when he arrived at his house, since they had all thought him dead, they approached to embrace him even though he did not want this. This caused his death. He disappeared. He did not walk again.'

I found it hard to articulate the feelings don Pablo's recounting of this Mayan legend inspired in me. His voice had slipped into a different tone and rhythm, the composition of his discourse drawn from ancient Mayan hieroglyphs and rules of address. The legend was example going back to our previous discussion on the destruction of the forest. The words emerged from the shaman's world, bearing traces of a different time and enchanted space. They wove story and example around the powerful numbers of the ancient Mayan calendar – 13, 7, 9 – and introduced mysterious divisions and groupings amongst them. The legend felt as authentic and precious as a Classic era polychrome vase swathed in hieroglyphs.

'What does that legend mean to you, don Pablo?' I asked.

'Well, it is an example – also a puzzle. I just heard it when I was a little boy lying in my hammock half-asleep, listening to my uncles and *abuelos*. I did not pay much attention then, but there are many ideas in that story. At first you don't see them, but later, if it is your fate, you see them. It is just something turning and turning in your mind. You don't know its reason, what it is, but you keep thinking about it.'

'Was the old man sent by God?'

'Yes, he is the owner of the forest, the *uyumil kaax*. He is sent by God, sent to look after animal, bird, *cenote*, forest and *milpa*. There are many *uyumil kaax*. Each one has his name. So we have to do good for them to help us. Yes. When I kill an animal we don't eat all of it. First I have to put a little for the *uyumil kaax*, to explain that I have killed his animal. I give a little then, to offer to him. I give to know – as it should be.'

On this day, conversing with don Pablo in the heart of the Quintana Roo forest, I saw that the Mayas could just shrug off the last four hundred years of our time and presence in their world. Their history was stronger than ours here, their thought permanent rock. In the gathering dusk we moved towards the *pib* – the ancient oven in the ground – our hunger and need as pressing as that of the people first crossing the Behring Straits ten thousand and more years ago.

∴

8

Spirit of the Beehive

 The Yucatec Maya left a written record of the number of sacred places which had been marked off with mounds and temples by their *abuelos*. The *nucuch uinicob*, or 'great men', had mysteriously planned and designed the overall sacred topography of the Mayan world here. 'Fifteen four-hundreds were the scores of their mounds and fifty,' their descendants remembered with great precision. This was 6050 places representing a superhuman effort by the great men and their followers to etch their vision upon the landscape of Indian America. The time devoted to this task was also remembered clearly as 'three score and fifteen *katuns*', an interval drawn from the ancient chronology, the skeleton of Classic Mayan writing.

The mound-building spoken of in this seemingly unimportant memorandum, written in colonial times in their Books of Counsel, was but a fragmentary reflection of the original whole. For all its attributed symmetry, in space and time, it was a part only of the Classic vision and design. If the great men consciously designed and built a complex series of mounds and religious centres throughout Yucatan, seeing its topography from miles above the earth, *seeing* its hidden centres of special spiritual power and the lines between them, if they did this, how much greater was the overall Classic vision which had linked all the Mayan centres from the Yucatan, to Chiapas, to Guatemala, to Honduras – which had spanned, with great significance, the *centre* of the New World?

A thousand years before the memorandum was written the Mayan religious centres – Tikal, Copan, Quirigua, Pierdras Negras, Uaxactun, Bonampak, Palenque, Coba, and hundreds of others – had been unified by a vision contained in the Mayan count of time and the hieroglyphs which recorded it. Irrespective of language differences and geographical barriers – humid jungles and high mountains – the great Indian centres of learning had been unified in their intellectual endeavour, agreeing on time and the geomantic mysteries of space.

The area which fell within the jurisdiction of the great men was as great as 200,000 square miles. It covered more difficult terrain than Europe and the technology of the people was limited to stone and wood implements. And yet the centres the Mayas built, and the calendrical and intellectual agreement reached between the different linguistic groups, were far more advanced than our European experience centuries later. Fifteen hundred years ago the Mayas had already refuted a materialist concept of history and progress. Their ancient intellectual cohesion, mathematically agreed and designed into the landscape of the tropical world, makes that very clear. In terms of the skills of the *nucuch uinicob*, skills of social organization for what must have been hard, back-breaking labour in the hot sun over hundreds of years, these men of stone tools, planting sticks and blowguns have never been equalled. How did the Mayan *abuelos* bring the adamantly independent people together to carry out the coordinated task of their great vision?

Tulum village was reserved, its charm and beauty easy to miss. Tourists visiting the ruins a few miles away, or staying on the coast, quickly passed through the sleepy, quiet village. They rummaged through the stores, obliviously dressed in bikinis and tiny swimsuits, spoke broken Spanish, and hitched their rucksacks high in preparation for the exhausting trudge to the crossroads leading to the ruined city and a first glimpse of the Caribbean an hour away along the white road. Unaware of the undercurrents or the history of this collection of thatched huts, stone houses, whitewashed walls, modest church and shaded plaza, they turned their backs and walked away.

The village hardly noticed. Here the forest was as much a livelihood as the new developments on the coast and at the ruins. People sought to find a way of keeping *milpa* and temporarily working at the ruins – for money alone. They helped archaeologists, drove taxis and sold game to the restaurants as lucrative pastimes. They kept *milpa*, bees and the hunt as the serious business of living. They had no sense of alienation in their daily lives. They watched the world changing before their eyes with seeming passivity and tolerance, calmly playing draughts during the warm evenings, outside the village stores, under kerosene lamps. When I moved to the village to live I was never allowed to feel ignored or unwanted.

Fifty years after Francisco Montejo's landing here in 1527, Tulum was taxed from afar for fifty people – the rest of the population had either died of new European diseases or, more sensibly, had managed to avoid detection and infection by the Spanish and their tax lists. This was not hard to do since the forest remained a Mayan domain, a stronghold frightening and unknown to the Spanish. The Maya could live undisturbed throughout hundreds of miles of forest. Just how many did so will never be known now, but it was many times the number who, foolishly, allowed themselves to appear on the Spanish lists.

Tulum village disappears from the record from 1579 until the late 1800s. Although travellers and archaeologists such as John Stephens and Frederick Catherwood visited the ruins, the village goes unmentioned and probably unknown to outsiders. In the late 1800s Tulum became one of five villages sacred to the Cruzob Maya and their Oracular Cross. Tulum, San Antonio Muyil (said to be deserted today), Chumpon,

Chanka Veracruz and Xcacal Guardia are the spiritual centres of these conservative and fiercely independent Maya – centres which used to mark out their territory and liberated land.

Within this land the Maya brought back many ancient customs and ideas from the realm of colonial shadows. With no outsiders to supervise or persecute them they were free openly to practise and discuss their ancient vision and ritual. Significantly, in the light of don Pablo's insistence that the Mayans always carried the Christian idea, and in the light of Chilam Balam's long ago prophecy, the independent Cruzob Maya centred the reappearance of the ancient Mayan way around a prophetic Oracular Cross. This cross and its mysterious meaning came from within Mayan thought – it was of their inspiration and doing, not ours.

Tulum was set around a grass-covered plaza with four paths leading away, one at each corner. Along these paths and facing the plaza itself the villagers had prepared their respective compounds. They had built wooden and stone houses in clearings, erected low stone walls, and built shelters for their pigs, chickens and turkeys. The compounds were shaded by a great abundance of orange and lemon trees, bananas, papayas and scented *turuhuy nicté*, cream-coloured candelabra of petals falling all about amidst the loud humming of thousands of bees. A deep sense of peace pervaded the village from dawn to dusk, the great variety of bird song in the fruit trees and forest much louder than the conversation of the people. The rich fragrance of ripe honey, of wood burning in numerous households, drifted across on the breezes that blew periodically through the ventilated, cool houses.

In the centre of the plaza, shaded by a row of tall trees, the church of Tulum was guarded and attended night and day by *h-menob* and prayer-makers. Until recently it had been a simple wooden thatch building painted with geometric white and blue patterns. It had been there at the centre without advertisement, continually attended. Now it had been rebuilt with modern blocks and a cement floor added. It was still thatched, painted carefully in white and blue, and guarded. It looked as simple and devout as before. Without advertisement it had been strengthened.

The four paths from the plaza led to the forest, the coast and distant *milpas*. A hundred yards, two hundred yards and one passed the *balam* spirit guardians of the village. Their place of residence was marked by mounds of loose limestone with simple crosses set on them. At night one could hear the *balams* whistling back and forth to each other, protecting the village from nocturnal evil spirits. Running along the north-south side of the village, the road from Can Cun to Chetumal had imposed a new space upon this once enclosed world. Where previously the village had been surrounded by dense forest with only the sounds of birds and distant sea to be heard, the chink chink of *machete* striking against stone, the grinding of maize on stone *metate*, now a window onto the world had been abruptly thrown open. Not more than fifty yards from one of the *balams* and their timeless task there was a new school, medical centre and government food store. Next to the church there was a basketball court and, a little further back, a low, empty water tower managed to overlook the discreet village.

I lived in a wooden thatched house on the far side of the road, surrounded by papaya trees, lemon and orange, banana and wild cotton. The house was set on an earth mound, a foot high or so, skirted with limestone boulders. Its two doorways faced east and west. There were no windows but I could see through cracks in the walls in all directions – to the fruit grove, the edge of the forest, the small *cenote* nearby where I found fresh water. The abundance of water here meant everyone was immaculately clean, the women's *huipil* dresses a spotless white, the men's faded and patched shirts and trousers freshly laundered when they returned from *milpa* and forest.

The buses and travellers introduced a new rhythm to Tulum. It was no longer a backcountry Mayan village but rather a relatively affluent community of four hundred souls. The villagers were curious about the outside world, in an offhand, conversational way. But they still kept to their own *costumbre*, swimming in faster currents vicariously and periodically only. Their manners and mode of address were mutually respectful, formal, low-toned. They liked working for themselves, frequently switching tasks as the mood took them. Working this way they were agreeable, uncomplicated people, happy to converse for hours, time an abundance not an enslavement. People sat in the shade or by the stores telling tall stories of the hunt, of ruins in the forest, of red-eyed black jaguars encountered on the trail at night. In the fruit groves, tending bees, swinging in hammocks, no one ever seemed to run out of histories and legends to recount.

Families clustered in compounds several acres in size, or sub divided into smaller lots. In these compounds two or three houses would stand close together, surrounded by herbal gardens, a well, fruit trees and, perhaps, beehives. Often three generations of a family occupied one compound, living in separate houses but congregating throughout the day to eat and relax. People were immensely tolerant of each other's behaviour and gossip seemed to be actively discouraged. I lived in one such compound on the edge of the village, alone, but visited often by children and adults, cautious in arrival, but willing to stay for hours, to exchange thoughts and opinions. Their uncanny intelligence invariably left me in a state of dazed amazement. It wasn't just that they said perceptive, intelligent things or that they easily comprehended and elaborated abstract thought. Often people answered questions before I asked them, questions on a different trail of thought than our preceding talk. Sometimes they would come over to the house and complete an idea I was working on at that very moment. I quickly felt that I had entered into invisible communication patterns amongst the villagers.

This was not the first time I felt such things strongly on the edge of Indian America. It seems to me possible that, like the origin and development of Indian civilization itself, events here continue to happen according to a different arrangement of the laws of reality than in the Old World. People in the pre-Columbian world cultivated and developed aspects of man veiled from us in the Old World, and perhaps these faculties allow their descendants to perceive and live by different laws of reality than we do.

What intrigued me now was that when an outsider enters this Indian world he or she also begins to perceive and live by these different laws. Telepathy to me was still a subject tinged with dubious paranormal colour. But here amongst the Mayas I learnt to see it as a normal, daily state of affairs. It was as if alongside the visible relations with people and the audible conversations, there were 'Invisible Ones' who shadowed us, arranged 'coincidental' yet most timely meetings, and who sometimes said things through us. As don Pablo had described it, an idea could be put amongst other ideas in one's head, its potency a sign of its spirit origin.

The people recognize these distinctive ideas and their origin. When I spoke of this theory of the Invisible Ones to a young Mayan of thirty who had just answered a question before I asked it, he smiled and commented, 'Sometimes that is what we call the *abuelos*, the Invisible Ones. What they did before, what they thought, is still here. It is just that they are like shadows. But if you know how then you learn to see, you learn to make a little of their world visible. That is why we say the ruins are enchanted. The *abuelos* are still there but your eyes can't see them.'

'But they can communicate with you while you are walking in this visible world?'

'Yes, they can do that. And you can see it is coming from them as well. How did I know that? How did I think that? you ask yourself. You learn to see that an idea or a sign was put there for you to think. But you don't know how that is.'

Don Pablo's family occupied a smaller compound on the far side of the village, close to the Mayan church. He lived with his wife doña Ophelia and seven children, aged from four to twenty. An elder daughter was married and lived in another village thirty miles away. While don Pablo could roam the forest, work the *milpa*, or go fishing, doña Ophelia was rooted to the household, to the three stones of the hearth, to the *comal*, the hot plate upon which she fashioned innumerable *tortillas*. In some way I sensed that house and village were essentially her domain and that don Pablo liked it that way. It gave her place and position independent of him.

Doña Ophelia talked often of her younger days working with Pablo at DzibAktun or at the *milpa*. She was a large, amiable, yet very shrewd personality, Mayan by language and custom rather than in her features. She and her family had lived in Tulum for half a century at least and she had grown up with Pablo, recalling him when he was eight years old and first shyly arrived in the village of Tulum.

Don Pablo's mother lived in an adjacent compound with his stepfather. Years before, in the early 1940s, she had left don Pablo's father. In those days the Balam lineage from which she descended lived in the heart of Indian Yucatan, south of Saci (Valladolid). Before the Fight of 1848 the lineage had been from Ebtun near Chichén Itza. With the outbreak of the Fight the *abuelos* had moved into the liberated zone. A century later, don Dolores Balam brought his daughter and her two sons Venancio and Pablo to Tulum to start a new life. Don Pablo still vividly recalled the long walk through the forest, the firm pace of his grandfather, and his first arrival in the village.

I could see also that his *abuelo* don Dolores Balam had set him on a singular path. Don Pablo's knowledge of the ancient Mayan vision was remarkably pure. It had surfaced here in Tulum but had actually originated in the very heart of Mayan country. His roots were not so much here in Tulum as back in that more inaccessible Mayan world. I wondered if this was part of the reason for his solitude, his love of wandering, of the hunt and the *milpa*. His own children, playing in the grass-covered square beyond the front door, resting in hammocks, or helping doña Ophelia, would not know such a walk as he had suffered in those early years. If their future was uncertain it did not, for the moment, look as hungry as the past.

Don Pablo's sons were growing into bold fishermen, unafraid of sea or strangers. The younger children, a boy and three girls, attended school until midday and helped their mother in the afternoon. Under eight they were given as much freedom and food as they asked for, without question. Later their roles would be more rigidly defined, the boy helping his father on the *milpa* and at the *rancho*, the girls staying close to home and helping their mother. They slept in a house adjacent to their parents, in one room, tumbled anarchically into hammocks together. They were honest, funny, and never bored. The world was a benevolent, secure place to them. They spoke carefully enunciated Mayan and Spanish. Like their father and mother, they hardly mixed the two except where necessary. There was, for example, no Mayan word for 'exploitation'. Thus they used the Spanish word *explotar*.

Don Pablo told me of a ceremony left to the people by the *abuelos* concerning children. This was the *hetzmek*, an ancient rite and orientation meaning 'carried astride the hip'. When a child is very young, three months for a girl, four for a boy, they are still carried in a mother's arms, their legs together. When they are three months old, the girl's legs are first opened as they are carried astride the hip for the first time. Because a girl's life is governed by the three stones of the hearth, this initiation takes place at this time. Because a boy's life is governed by the four corners of the *milpa*, his step is opened at four months.

It is the godmother of the child who performs the *hetzmek*, attended by parents and immediate family. The tools each child will use in life, a *machete*, a gun, a hoe and an axe, for example, are reproduced in miniature. The girl's tools are scissors, needle and small cooking pan. These miniatures are placed on the ground in front of an altar upon which there are gourds filled with toasted calabash seeds (*topp*), *pinole* or maize gruel, and honey (*kah*), eggs (*he*), and spinach (*chaya*). The godmother takes the child and, after praying briefly, puts him or her astride the hip and circles the altar nine times. As she does this she places the various relevant tools in the hands of the child and explains their uses.

Once this part of the ceremony is completed the food is tasted – the egg to 'open understanding', the spinach to 'divide thought into two parts', the *pinole* 'to remember' and the squash seeds 'to open the thoughts like flowers'. Each of these phrases was a pun on the Mayan words for the food in the gourds. The *hetzmek* was a way of showing the child which way he or she was to walk, how they were to work, to think, to eat. Different people put different tools there – a book, a pencil, a coin – it depended on how you wanted the child to grow up.

Doña Ophelia missed the time she had spent in the forest, at the *milpa*, and in the *chicle* camps when first married to don Pablo twenty-five years before. But she had a strong and independent position within the family and in the village. The household was under her authority. Don Pablo had little to do within the actual compound, his role and life really beginning at forest or water's edge. When young and without family doña Ophelia had come with him, to camps deep in the forest, or to the *milpa* for several days and weeks at a time. Now she concentrated on feeding her family a variety of dishes, squatting by the hearth morning to dusk preparing countless helpings of *tortillas*, pork and turkey, fish, chilli and calabash sauces, and toasted cakes of seeds and wild honey. She explained the many variations of maize dishes, sweet, salted, and the special times for their preparation.

If Mayan women are responsible for the transformation of maize into its many forms and preparations, the men are entirely responsible for its cultivation and transportation from *milpa* to village world. With the developing dry season – February to June – they were up and gone before daylight, some *atole* in their stomachs, a wrapped bundle of warm *tortillas* or some *zacan* in their *mecapal*. It was best to work on the *milpa* from first light until nearly midday, rest an hour, and then devote a couple of hours to beekeeping or hunting before returning to the village. If the *milpa* was far away in the forest they might stay there a few days at a time. There was undergrowth, bindweed and thorn bush to be cleared, a new area of

forest to be cut and left to dry for a few weeks before burning.
The already gathered maize, beans and calabash had to be
sorted and stored in special houses on the *milpa*. There was
plenty of hard work in the hot, solitary sun.

Weeks into my stay in Tulum I tried to recall my original
fears about entering this world. I had been wary of the fierce
reputation of the Cruzob Maya in the annals of our history. I
had been afraid of stepping out of the invisible warmth of my
own familiar culture, into unfamiliar houses open to the
elements. The move required of me had been more than
physical and temporary – it was an emotional relinquishing of
the known, the understood, for the unknown, the mysterious,
the deceptively innocent, the inexplicable.

Don Pablo sensed my unease from the beginning and our
relationship was becoming more comprehensive than language lessons and a first walk in the Mayan world. Step by step
he was leading me further in, bridging with counsel and family
life, his family life, the gap between our worlds. He seemed
able to judge precisely when to take a further step, when to
leave alone, when to listen, and when to guide. I could hardly
believe my good fortune in finding so true and responsible a
Mayan guide, willing to take time and thought over my
Mayan education.

There was no theft, no begging, no violence in the village.
There was privacy, freedom of movement, and a sense of
wellbeing and hope amongst the villagers. They worried
about the jeopardy visited upon their way of life. They
strengthened and elaborated their native church ceremonies
and devotions. But if watching these ceremonies meant one
could catch a glimpse of the naturalness of Mayan worship, a
relaxed but nevertheless devoted attitude, witnessed also on
the ancient Classic murals of ruined cities, there was also a
strong merchant's interest in money, a love of storekeeping, of
barter and exchange, which willingly pulled the villagers ever
deeper into the world we have on offer. They worried because
the government planned to create a new town of colonizers
between the present-day village and the ruins. The design and

the street plans existed, and already a new marketplace was being built two miles away from the established village. Where was this going to leave the villagers later on?

From an early age, by sixteen at the latest, the boys began to earn their living and to keep the money they made from fishing, from tapping the *chicle* trees, from hunting, or from the *milpa*. Equally if a girl earnt money sewing, doing embroidery, or making hammocks, she kept the income as her own. Parents divided their income by halves, the women investing in sewing machines, poultry, gold earrings and necklaces. There were no arguments except when the men spent too much on alcohol, the one occasional exception to a universal cultivation of frugality in all matters.

There was no coercion, no alienation, no competitiveness in traditional Mayan work relations. No one was told what to do, no one was timed. But with the arrival of the new *nucuch uinicob* with their designs and street plans, how long would this last? Already some of the younger men were finding jobs at Can Cun, working on road projects and construction sites. So far they had only done so until they saved enough to establish themselves in Tulum, to pay for a house, a fibreglass boat, an outboard motor, a tape-recorder and radio, a watch. They felt the alienation of working for wages, day after day, against their dreams, and soon returned to their community.

But they returned with an abiding fascination for the products of modernity – for cars, mechanical and electronic things, for pick-up trucks. Working on a *milpa* no one could aspire to these things. Any young Mayan who could, would willingly become a taxi-driver at the ruins, and people who could drive or mend engines were regarded with something of the awe we reserve for shamans. If the young men only stayed working in Can Cun for a few months this first time, they saw and learnt enough to desire modernity in all its seductive guises. They were only just beginning to learn the alienation, the forced labour that was the secret, real price for it. Young men, they thought they could step into the bright light world to escape their own shadows.

I talked with don Pablo about the freedom I saw in the traditional Mayan way, the balance of male and female, the harmony of body and spirit. We were squatting in his patio behind the house, under the orange and lemon trees, close by several logs of native bees which rested against an A-frame. He was preparing to open one and harvest the honey. I asked him if the people in old times had felt as free as the Mayas did after they were given their *ejidos* in the more recent past.

'No,' he said, 'there was a world once when they had no freedom. Well, there was always a world. What happened in ancient times is that people did not live the way we do now. Like us, for example, in the morning I know what I am going to do. If I have to take down coconuts, or fish, or hunt, I know what to do without being told. I know my work. But in those days the people all had to work together. The chief gave the orders. Whenever he gave an order then it was done.

'But then there was a world of great rulers, the Nine Lords they were called. They ruled before Our Lord arrived. That was why no one was happy in the village. No one got on well with the others. The most evil ones walked amongst them. Instead of there being someone good there, to give people an orientation, the most evil ones were there, disorientating everyone and destroying everything. That was how it was. They fought amongst themselves.

'So then, let us suppose, there was a world when Our Lord descended to arrange everything. He finished the people of before and put us here. That was a change of worlds. But the people of before were always like us – Christians. It was only that there were evil rulers amongst them. They thought they were gods. They did not think there was another God in Heaven, they did not think of He who made the earth. They thought it was really theirs, as gods, born with the earth. That was how the Nine Lords thought. They were the chiefs of before, the government in those days.'

I watched don Pablo sharpen a six-inch stick with his *machete*. He began picking up the log hives one by one, feeling their weight. Each was a couple of feet long, eight inches in diameter, with a small entrance halfway along, a cross carved above it, a guardian bee just visible within. Each end of the log was stopped up with a stone, banana leaves and dried mud. It was these stones which don Pablo was examining, replacing each log on the A-frame, undecided as to which one to open first.

The Nine Lords he had just spoken about figure in Mayan thought as synonymous with the Lords of Hell. They are ancient evil figures, the dark counterpart to the light and good order of the first shamans. Just as the latter serve as good examples for the living people, so the former are paradigms of evil, warning signs which can be read at a political, economic, or historical level. In Mayan thought today and in the past it is the struggle of various personages, First Hunters and their sons, against these Lords which provide an explanation, a 'history' of good and evil for the people. In this conversation with don Pablo he was attributing political coercion and private ownership of the earth with the Nine Lords and a previous world the Mayas had suffered.

'Was it the Nine Lords who ordered the people to build all the cities and temples, don Pablo?' I asked, thinking that the people must have been pushed, enslaved, to accomplish so vast a task.

'No, that was the *abuelos*,' don Pablo said. 'But they worked differently from the Nine Lords. When they got together they thought it was a game, the idea of those cities. It was a game, the time of work was like a ballgame, you could say. They had a thousand people, many people, and they also say that before they could just send a stone to its place, where it was meant to go. That is how my *abuelos* tell it, that is how I learnt it also. They would just arrive where the stone was and say, "You go there, and you go there." That is how I think they brought all the stones together.'

'But why did the people help them with their idea of those cities for all those hundreds of years? How did they get the people to work like that?'

'Well, they were great shamans, let us say. So they could see then that it was what God wanted, how He wanted everything set in order here. It was given to them to see a little of how this was going to be. They could see the earth down here and where everything was going to be. So then, afterwards, when they had shared this with the people they also could see that it really came from God to show us how to live. So right away they began to work. But if they hadn't seen that it came from there, from Heaven, then they would not have done it.'

'But were the lords of the cities, those who built them, those who ruled, were they the same as the shamans?' I asked, surprised at his answer.

For some reason I had assumed that the ancient lords and architects, the calendrical priests and hierarchy, were separate from the shamans. I had thought that the latter only really played a local, village role.

'Well, you can suppose that they were put there as lords because they were great shamans, Ricardo,' Pablo said to me.

It was so obvious to him that the ancient lords must necessarily have been great shamans. Now it was obvious to me. Even his explanation of the magical flight of the stones was based on shamanism. A shaman's ability to rise up to the centre of the sky, and to see the earth below, to be given an insight into God's design, is also an ability to abolish weight, to abolish the normal laws of space as well as time. Don Pablo's explanation was entirely logical within a shamanic frame of reference.

Now he had evidently decided which log hive he was going to open first. Conservative in all Mayan matters, don Pablo was cultivating native Indian bees known as *colel cab*, or 'lady bee'. These bees are smaller than ours, darker in colour and stingless. They produce a rich golden honey flavoured by the flora of the forest and ripened by the tropical sun. Other varieties of native bees exist in the Yucatan peninsula, the most prized being wild ones known as *ehol*. These, don Pablo told me, built their hives in the trunks of trees leaving only a tiny entrance. They are extremely difficult to track through the forest but when discovered are patient and calm as the hive is opened and the honey collected. 'They know when someone is going to come so they already prepare somewhere else,' don Pablo explained.

He began to open the log hive he had selected. 'These bees have souls,' he said, 'that is why we put small crosses over the entrance. It is there to protect them, as it does us.' He carefully scrapped the dried mud from the stone covering one end of the log and removed it. He held the log up for me to see. Inside I could see several large wax cells full of honey. They were irregular in shape, two or three inches across, and dark brown in colour. Opening a clean Nescafé jar, don Pablo motioned for me to hold the log. He took the stick he had sharpened and punctured the nearest cell. The liquid, aromatic honey ran out into the jar. An adjacent cell yielded a store of pollen slightly sour in taste. We left this and bled two more cells. Soon the jar was full and don Pablo washed and wrapped the stone in a fresh leaf, added a little mud, and replaced it in the log. He explained that the bees were very sensitive to the hand which wounded them. They felt the 'pain of the hand' in some people and would desert the hive. Equally, if someone had recently touched a corpse the bees would sense death in the hand and would soon leave. 'Bees are very special,' Pablo said, 'they need a lot of respect.' He opened the other end of the log and found a fresh jar to fill.

After we had taken a couple of litres of honey from the logs we relaxed in the shade. Since the bees were stingless there was no need of heavy protective clothing, no masks to worry about, no smoke to force their respect. The bees soon settled down to their regular humdrum existence. Don Pablo and I talked about the new bees now being introduced by the government. These required initial investment in boxes, frames, masks and colonies while the log hives and their colonies only cost about £2. But the honey from the boxes, the 'white bees', could be readily converted into cash through the state cooperative and many Mayans were investing in them. Don Pablo himself had thirty boxes out on his *milpa*. He kept them separate from the *colel cab* because the new bees killed them or drove them into the forest. The *colel cab* work harder, he told me, they are the masters of the forest here. He kept the honey from these bees for family and friends, he concluded, handing me a jar.

'So the great lords and priests, they began as shamans and later were put there as lords? Is that what you were saying before, don Pablo?' I wanted to be sure on this point for, although obvious now, it seemed to me to have important implications.

'Sometimes, if they were great seers, it was so. Sometimes also it was a lineage that showed that it had powers. The father taught the son the correct orientations, the counsels and the writing. But they were shamans. They knew of those virtues and that was how they worked.'

'Was there an examination of their learning, don Pablo? How did people know that what the *nucuch uinicob* were doing was good?'

'Well, that you are going to learn very quickly. Let us say you have a reunion around a table where so many people are going to talk. Well, I am going to see who comes to hear my explanation and who does not. There are times also when before the talk is over, whoever is not interested has already gone or is just playing or talking. So these people are not interested in what I'm talking about. Because otherwise they would just be listening or asking questions, to see how it is, to see whether it is forgotten. So then, from there you are going to gather together again on another day. And whereas at the first reunion there was twenty people, now there are only thirteen. So then you know that seven were not in agreement with you. Yes, that is when you realize.'

Don Pablo looked pensive, gazing down at his bare feet and at the oranges scattered on the ground.

'But also I am not going to swear that my explanation is without error. But that is how I see it, that is how it was sent to me to explain to you. That is what you say at the reunion. Let us respect this view. If not, no matter, it has been spoken.'

'Can people work with one shaman and then go and work with others? Or do you just learn from one person?'

'They can do what they please. Whenever they want they can come to listen again. We don't despise them for it either. Only if they come to play and disturb the reunion. If they are not interested they should just follow their own path without persecuting anyone. That is the most important thing – complete freedom. That is their freedom to follow their own path.'

'But was that same freedom there before, don Pablo, when the *abuelos* wanted the temples built?'

'The people saw that it was a true idea that the *abuelos* were bringing. They saw that it came from God. So they wanted to do it. It was a prayer, an offering, let us say. So they got together with their *batabs*, who were their chiefs, and they went to help. They would go to Cozumel or Coba to help for a few weeks, each year. And then they would help them also. It was all prepared from before.'

Don Pablo was becoming more explicit in his answers, revealing hidden democratic qualities to Mayan life and thought in those now distant times. I remembered reading a Spanish chronicler, Lopez de Cogolludo, who described the Mayan priests and their wild dancing and singing, dramatizing their counsels and enigmatic utterances, criticizing the political rulers face to face without fear of reprisal. These were the shaman spokesmen of the people, whose influence depended on people agreeing with the wisdom of their supernatural insights, and who evidently played a much more central role in Mayan history than previously suspected. They emerged as leaders because of their powers as shamans, because their explanations rang true. If the Mayas had a formal sense of social ranking, based on lineage, they also seemed to have allowed for the emergence of visionaries from the rank and file, from below. Bishop Landa wrote that people learnt to read and write the glyphs, 'if they showed an inclination to this office'. As usual he had hidden much more than he revealed in his words.

'How could the people be free and still have those pyramids of officials and rulers overlooking them?'

'There are kinds of freedom, Ricardo. Like today when people are just wandering about without orientation. That is not so good. But there is a different freedom also, where people do as they please but always with a correct counsel and orientation. That way people are happy, peaceful and in agreement. So they had those lords there, in those days, to see what was coming, to give them a correct orientation. It is like the *colel cab*,' don Pablo said, motioning towards the log hives. 'They all have to live in that log. So they organize themselves well – they have bees there to tell them what is coming and what to do in the hive – they have a queen also. They are disciplined, they don't fight. But when they leave there early they are free. No one tells them where to go in the forest. They go as they please. That is how it was given to them to live. That is what God put them there to do. It is His power. They do it by *costumbre* now and that is how they are free.'

I realized then that the 'power' of shamanic thought, from curing to astronomy, did not imply coercion in any way. It was closer to the Chinese concept of the Tao – the natural, the inherently ordered. The power of the ancient Maya *nucuch uinicob* came from people being able to see the correctness of their counsel, from the people being persuaded that the leaders had supernaturally seen the world from miles above, had also seen the future and its order. They were leaders because they had this power, they did not have the power just because they were leaders by lineage. 'It came from God,' don Pablo said, 'to the wise men, rich and poor alike.'

9

Reflections of a Jaguar
Spokesman

Don Pablo and his sons were busy clearing and weeding the land, preparing to burn off three or four acres of forest to make *milpa* for the year. It was March and don Pablo invited me to come along. The road ran near his *milpa* and we could come and go daily, riding in the back of a passing lorry, and then walking a short distance.

In the early morning light a slight mist hung over the clearing which marked the beginning of the *milpa*. By 7 a.m. we were settling into a palm-thatched, open-sided shelter which served as refuge from the midday heat and tropical downpours. All around us the air teemed with insects, midges, mosquitoes, wasps, butterflies and bees, which orchestrated the bright calling of numerous birds – toucans, parakeets, *chachalakas*, secure in their forest preserve.

We tied our hammocks and ate ripe pineapple. Don Pablo and his sons, Roberto and Juan, sharpened their *machetes* and *coas*, small sickle-shaped pieces of iron beaten into shape and attached to long wooden handles. With these tools they tugged and swiped at the bushes and weeds, their *machetes* ready to cut down stubborn sections of undergrowth, trees and saplings. Filling a gourd with water, Roberto and Juan set off to begin work before the sun rose too high in the sky. They were joking, wide awake, working for themselves.

Don Pablo took me around the *milpa* slowly, explaining everything as we went along. From the clearing where we had rested we followed a narrow path through the forest, fifty yards, past scarred *chicle* trees until the shaded cover above suddenly gave way to a wide, open, cultivated clearing of fifteen to twenty acres. To the left I could see old *milpa*, known as *hubché*, returning to forest and replenishment. To the right I could see banana groves, papaya, orange, lemon, mango, pineapple and avocado. Because of the nature of the soil, great limestone rock harbouring isolated pockets of earth, the *milpa* contained no extensive fields or squared-off areas devoted to one crop. Rather it appeared as an enormous tropical rock garden filled with an exotic and miscellaneous collection of squashes, tubers, herbs, chillis, maize, various fruit trees, flowers, bees, iguanas asleep on rocks, and tropical birds of breathtaking plumage. I stood between forest and *milpa*, my eyes growing accustomed to the details of this secret garden. Don Pablo stood a few feet away, rooting around with his *machete*, digging up sweet potatoes.

We picked our way through banana groves, past pineapples, calabash, and chilli, don Pablo chopping down stunted papayas and clearing dead banana leaves away. Even in tiny pockets in a rock, where only a child's handful of earth could be lodged, herbs and chillis sprouted, strong and productive. Trees also seemed to find an initial handhold and then developed a root structure on the rocks themselves, managing on this precarious basis alone to grow and bear fruit. Walking along at a slow pace, glancing in deep fissures in the rocks, at evidence of ancient foundations for a house, studying the details of various plants as don Pablo listed them, I was soon completely seduced by the fecundity of everything around me. The very seeds of the natural world seemed to have awakened within the heated, white rock, to have shattered its apparent dominion and burst forth in exuberant triumph.

On the far side of the *milpa* we came to a *cenote* forty feet in diameter. A pulley, rope and bucket hung from a simple frame which leant outwards at an angle across the water ten feet below. A path led off to the left around the lip of the *cenote*, descending to a ledge across from where we stood. From here one could dive into the fathomless water, aquamarine in parts, shading to jade green and darkness. There was a fallen tree floating on the surface and tiny fish flitted away at the explosion of bubbles behind the diver. All around from ledges in the limestone tiny birds darted across, skimming the water for midges and flies, sweeping upwards and around, returning.

I sat in the sun drying, the mist now vanished from the *milpa*, the heat of the day beginning to shimmer, the birds to grow silent. Don Pablo began explaining the maize cycle to me. It is this cycle which governs work on the milpa, all other activities secondary to its correct and precise fulfilment. He spoke of maize in reverential tones – as *gracia*, as God's special food for man, precious sustenance and foundation of the world. A Mayan's relationship to maize is prayer-making of the highest order, a reciprocal exchange of man's devotion to God for the sustenance which man, in turn, needs. It is not food alone, bread alone, but a continuing confirmation of God's love of cherished man, of his accessibility to prayer, to offering, to rogation from below.

Don Pablo explained to me that maize is seen to have thirteen stages in its growth cycle. He began to recite the ritual exchange of conversation between one *milpero* and another, a questioning and answering which reveals these stages.

'The first sowing is done when the first rains fall, the 23rd or the 25th of April. That is when the small maize is planted. So then, after three days it begins to appear. That is when they say it is "like a parrot's tail". Because you see it yellow like a parrot's tail. The maize is so beautiful when it appears!' His voice bore traces of the devotion he felt for the ancient grace of Indian America.

'Then later there are those who ask, "How is your maize doing?" Then you answer, "It is at the height of a crouched rabbit." And you ask in turn, "How is your maize doing?" And he answers, "Well, mine is still like a parrot's tail."'

'Another day you meet again. The question is asked, "How is your maize doing?" You say, "Well, it has rained on my *milpa* and it is growing. It is nearly at the height we cut trees when clearing the milpa."'

Don Pablo stretched his hand out to about three feet above the ground. Then he continued with his exemplary exchange.

'"And how is yours?" you ask. "Well, it has not rained on my *milpa* so it is still at the height of a crouched rabbit," he says.'

Don Pablo carried on this conversation for a while, saying, 'This is how the workers, the planters of maize speak to each other.' He described how the small maize began to yield its ears after two and a half months. Three months, he said, and it was already turning yellow. This was the earliest maize to be harvested. 'Large' maize was different. This took four months before it began to dry and six before it was harvested. But this maize yielded two or three ears on one plant, depending on the seed. He explained the pleasure a *milpero* felt arriving at his *milpa* at this time, seeing the harvest that God had granted him.

All the time don Pablo was talking I was taking notes. I could see he was very much in his element out here, relaxed, communicative, free. 'The *milpa*,' he was to say to me on another occasion, 'is where I am most at peace, where I can think clearly, where I can feel God more intensely than anywhere else.' I thought also that it was where he was most in touch with the natural world, spending more hours interacting with this rather than a social world. Here he could reflect as he worked, here the world was not too much with him, not so close that it blinded his soul.

He began to speak of the disasters that could befall a harvest. 'Sometimes in September the bad times arrive. Just as the harvest is tender a hurricane will come and sweep it all aside. You lose your *milpa*. Everything is swept away. You lose your entire *milpa*,' he emphasized. 'Another time God sends a punishment over your *milpa*. Even if the maize has ripened He can send hot rain over it. Then the maize shrivels up as if you have burnt it. It soon dries and shrivels up. Another rain comes also – black rain. After it falls even the leaves are blackened. Everything dries and rots. It is lost. Another rain comes – red rain. After it falls the leaves are reddened. Everything is lost.'

Pablo continued outlining the gambler's odds of all farming. Nothing, however, occurred by chance or accident in his Mayan view of things. Disasters were sent by God as punishment for sins, for the failure to live correctly, for the failure to sustain the spirit guardians with ritual offering.

I asked him if the Mayas grew maize of different colours.

'Yes, white, yellow, black and red,' he answered immediately. People planted the colour they liked to work and to eat. *Choba*, for example, black maize, would be very strong and productive, good for storing for a year or two. The same was true of white maize. If it was harvested on a full moon it might last up to two years in store. But if it was harvested on a new moon it soon turned old. People decided for themselves what they wanted to cultivate and eat.

'Those are the ancient colours of Mayan wisdom,' I observed as I wrote down everything he said.

'How is that?' He was intrigued at the suggestion.

'Well, the *abuelos* spoke of their knowledge in terms of the red and the black, and the orientation of the world, the four directions, were marked off according to the colours you have mentioned. It was a way of associating their counsels, their orientation, their writing, with the *milpa*, with maize, with those who are bringing the "Great Idea" as you say, don Pablo. Also, just as there are thirteen stages in the growth of maize, so they used that sacred number to organize the various ages of the world, the *baktuns*, the *katuns* . . . .'

I trailed off, wondering what don Pablo was going to say about all this. He just nodded at the time, his response to come at the end of the day.

I asked him of there were any special birds associated with the maize cycle, birds whose song showed him insight into when to plant and harvest. He thought for a while and then said, 'Yes, there is the *x-kok*, the nightingale. When the maize first appears you find him singing, "Come on maize, grow taller and taller, come on maize, grow taller and taller." And when the maize has grown he flies from one to another singing to make them happy, to make them grow.

'Later, there is another bird – a very small black bird with a white collar and tie. When the maize has nearly ripened he flies straight up in the air, sings loudly and drops back down upon the maize plant. He keeps doing this like someone spooning hot *atole* into the air to cool it, letting it drop back into the *jicara*, and so, and so, until it is cooled. So we call that bird the "bird that cools the *atole*". When you see him flying like that you know it is nearly harvest time, nearly time for the first *atole*.'

We talked about the practical side of Mayan agriculture. Here on the *ejido* of Tulum, where land was not in short supply, a family of eight or ten people might keep *milpa* of 100 *mecates*. One *mecate*, or *kaan*, was a square 20 metres to a side. Sometimes if they had animals to feed, pigs and poultry, they would keep 200 *mecates* of milpa. One person, on average, could clear 2 *mecates* a day, so if the work was hard it was also intermittent – a hundred days a year at most.

Choosing a place in the forest to cut down, burn, and plant, was governed by many factors. Most important was the availability of water and good soil. Black soil, *ek luum*, is considered good, whereas red land is thin and not particularly fertile. It was always an intelligent move to choose an area where there were numerous ruins because if the *abuelos* had found the land worth settling to any great extent it was probably still very fertile. Areas of abundant trees, of quality wood, or wild fruit and fat game had to be weighed against the need for accessibility to a road and transport. Given the choice between carrying forty or fifty kilos of produce twenty miles to the village, or hiring space on a lorry to take it, the Mayas had not been long in appreciating the difference.

I asked don Pablo if he thought the Mayas had been hunters before they were farmers. According to our more general idea of human history man developed through stages to urbanized life. Don Pablo's answer, however, did not fit this scheme. For him it was a question of balancing all these stages, all these worlds. He worked *milpa*, he also hunted, fished, tied houses, and had mastered various other activities besides. There was a wholeness to Mayan life, lost in our concept of human progress. Even when the Mayas were great builders of stone cities, even when they prepared their astronomy and hieroglyphic writing, they were still also hunters and gatherers. The idea of a 'simple' economic life giving rise to a primitive intellectual and spiritual life just falls apart like common pottery in this Mayan world.

The most important measure, the only measure of progress in this world, is the degree to which those at the base of the social order, those who actually work the land and forest, are allowed to return to work for themselves in freely chosen cooperation, according to ancient custom. Here in Quintana Roo and Yucatan the Fight for that particular freedom was won – the Mayan *campesinos*, the peasantry, formed *ejidos* and cooperatives and worked for themselves as they pleased. Over in Guatemala the fight was still to be won. There the big landowners still used the Mayan Indians as slave labour. There, those who ruled had no intention of allowing the Indians enough land to guarantee their independence and parity with our world. They needed the Mayas not as brothers but as slaves. They wanted them to be more than half-starved, robbed of the chance of ancient self-sufficiency, whipped by necessity into working as slaves.

Now I felt I had detained don Pablo too long in conversation. The coolest hours of the day were rapidly fading into oven heat. We slowly began to pick our way across the *milpa* towards where the boys were working. Along the way don Pablo continued to point out the history and content of the landscape, describing the plants and trees and when he had planted them. I was surprised to discover that he had been working this particular *milpa* for at least fifteen years. I had thought that the Mayas cleared an area, made *milpa* for two or three years, and then moved on. But Pablo moved about within his *milpa*, planting maize in a given area for awhile, and then moving a short distance. Everything else formed a settled, permanent garden.

Don Pablo's words drew me deeper and deeper into this private world, source of Mayan civilization. A Spanish priest was moved to remark of the Mayas' relationship to maize and *milpa*, 'Everything they did and said so concerned maize that they almost regarded it as a god. The enchantment and rapture with which they look upon their *milpas* is such that on their account they forget children, wife, and any other pleasures as though their *milpa* were their final purpose in life and source of their happiness.' This seemed to be as true today as four hundred, or even two thousand years ago. What I was seeing was the timeless base of the Mayan edifice unchanged in its essence since the beginning of agriculture in the New World.

All the great civilizations of antiquity had come and gone, but this had remained. Numerous economic and religious superstructures had appeared and faded in the morning, pale forest mist, trapped in perishable time. But the walker and his load, hunter and planter, had paced out another time in an even, continuing rhythm. He had escaped normal time, enduring, still walking at the heart of the New World. How great was the vision of the ancient ones to express time itself in his image as if they knew the *milpero* and his walk would last all the ages and worlds to come, would sustain his load with only momentary pause and respite.

But there was a practical side also to the poetry of the Mayan vision. Their ancient agricultural practices looked simple, their tools rudimentary. And yet, for thousands of years, whenever the Mayans have been left alone to found their own economic system, they have established a way of life based on freedom of the individual and on work as a satisfying, unalienated activity. This was no simple, primitive economics – this was a highly resilient, deeply perceptive science, which had defiantly resisted more than four hundred years of Spanish occupation and exploitation. Here on don Pablo's *milpa* he kept the freedoms and happiness he had known – to sow in the morning, hunt in the afternoon, give thanks to God in the evening. His concern was to extend the Mayan way, to restore its past magnificence, but never to replace it with false gods and work as we know it. That for him was a step backwards, tried once, never to be repeated.

We arrived at the far side of the milpa where Roberto and Juan were busy clearing the undergrowth with *coa* and *machete*. Already nearly two *mecates* had been prepared, piles of cut-down bushes, vines and trees drying in the sun. Stripped to the waist, the two sons had been working steadily in unhurried fashion. Now they came over and rested in the shade for a few minutes, refreshing their mouths with water from the gourd. They listened to our conversation for a while but soon returned to work. Don Pablo interspersed his discussion of the *milpa* with comments to them.

Working alongside him over the years Roberto and Juan had naturally and effortlessly learnt the nature of the forest world, how to keep *milpa*, how to hunt, how to make offerings to the spirit guardians who protected everything here. Now, at eighteen and sixteen years of age, their relationship to their father seemed to be more of a partnership, their walk and life rapidly becoming distinctively their own. He, for his part, encouraged this.

Perhaps out of a continuing interest in learning theory, perhaps because I was always to be surprised by the sheer intelligence of the Mayas, witnessed not only in their way of living but also in their shrewd grasp of intellectual issues, I asked don Pablo how it was that the Indians seemed so learned without benefit of higher education. Certainly they learnt to read, write and add in the government school, but this did not explain the learning way that evidently left them self-confident, open-minded and sophisticated in wit and intellect. Don Pablo, for example, was not just answering questions. He was actively engaged in forming and shaping what I was doing and he was soaking up whatever skills and ideas I might have to offer in the process. He, as much as I, seemed keen to enter the Mayan world from an outsider's point of view, to see it that way also. He seemed to be working at some hidden intention yet to be explained to me.

Now, as I asked how the Mayas learnt what they knew, how they absorbed knowledge so impressively, he casually handed me a key element in their learning way.

'There are those who we say "have the eyes of the *abuelos*". When they are born you can see in their eyes that they are already very old. There is a certain clarity there. Then later they use old words, old Maya around the village. They use words no one has taught them. They begin to have dreams that make them remember things they already know. So these people who have the eyes of the *abuelos*, they can become very great shamans. It is already given to them in their minds, to see as the *abuelos* saw, to know. Then when the time, the hour, arrives and they receive a sign in their dreams, let us say, or working on the *milpa*, they recognize it. Others may see such signs but they don't know, they don't *see*, they are just looking.'

'But only a few have those eyes?'

'Yes, only some. If everyone was like that . . . well,' don Pablo shrugged, 'how the world would be then? But those who have them share what they see, what they know. They are not egotists, they share it with everyone so that they might all have a good orientation. So that is how we learn here, through the counsels the *abuelos* send us from God. There are those who see how it is going to be.'

'But is it that the *abuelos* are reborn in another generation?' I asked.

'God gives them the Idea again, here in the world, so that they can do it again. The newborn child inherits it then – he or she brings the same Idea. But he is just bringing it, he doesn't know it. When he is older he develops the Idea he is bringing.'

In the early afternoon everyone stopped work for a couple of hours. We had been working steadily from eleven o'clock, my job the clearing of dead banana leaves, hardly a difficult or tiring task. Still, I was not used to the fierce heat and was glad of the shade, a hammock and a few *tortillas*. No one spoke much as we ate, everyone just renewing his energies. Roberto and Juan planned to go in search of wild honey later, taking a gun with them in case they saw an agouti or wild turkey. Behind the first *cenote* there was dense forest, then another *cenote* and a few desultory ruins. It was uninhabited land full of wild game.

Don Pablo finished eating and then disappeared into the forest for a few minutes. He returned with a roughly worked stone figure, two feet tall, a face barely discernible on one side. He stood it upright in our midst and said, humorously, 'This is the guardian of the *milpa*, don Ricardo.' It was a stone he had found one day, clearing the forest, an ancient idol fashioned by unknown hand perhaps millennia ago. For don Pablo it was witness to the many spirits who protect the *milpa*. Softly he began to explain his tangible relationship with these *yuntzilob*.

'When you want to measure some forest, Ricardo, a hundred *mecates* or so, you have to give to know the *yuntzilob* of the *milpa* – the *balam col*, the *chacs*, the *kuilob kaaxob*. That way no harm will come to you when you are working.'

The *balam col*, like the *balams* of the village, stood at the four 'entrances' to the *milpa*, protecting it. The *chacs* were the rain gods, the four Mayan horsemen of the Apocalypse, who rode the sky flashing their lightning swords and tipping their water-gourds slightly to pour water down upon the earth. The *kuilob kaaxob* were the guardians of the uncultivated forest, of wild animals, and birds. Collectively all these spirit 'owners' were referred to as *yuntzilob*, don Pablo said. He continued explaining why he made offerings to them.

'Because if you go in to cut down the forest the *yuntzil* who is there to look after it needs to be advised – so that he can look after you. Because you don't just let anyone come in to cut down your garden, where you have been put by God to take care of everything. Because if you are not respected then you need to call their attention to it. So the *yuntzilob* can send you a mishap – you cut your foot with the *machete*, or a tree kicks you in the face as it falls.

'But if you worship well, if you make the proper offerings at the right time, the *yuntzilob* will help you, they will look after you. Before you arrive where there is a snake you see it. Instead of it looking at you, you are looking at it. If you work without worshipping then things can happen to you.'

Here was the purpose of Mayan ritual and belief described as an integral part of their agricultural life. Where we might corner these beliefs in such words as 'ritual', 'pagan gods', and 'myth', in the eyes of the Mayas they are as practical as putting seed in the ground with a fire-hardened stick.

Don Pablo described the various offerings that each *milpero* must make as he brings his *milpa* into existence. When first clearing forest and just before firing the dried bush, a little *zaca*, or basic maize dough, is mixed with water and honey and offered to the *yuntzilob* with a short prayer excusing the injury about to be done. It is the *kuilob kaaxob* who receive this first offering because they watch over the virgin forest. Just before firing the dried piles of undergrowth and trees, the *milpero* must make a further offering of *zaca* to the *mozon ik*. This is a concentrated, localized whirlwind which, summoned by the low whistling of the *milpero* and his offering, appears with a distinctive roaring sound, sweeping the flames evenly across the *milpa*. I was to hear and see this whirlwind at work on a later occasion, watching it lifting flames and leaves, brushing them across the ashen brow of the *milpa* as don Pablo nervously whistled and encouraged it. If I had not seen it work with my own eyes I would have thought it a mere superstition.

The offerings that are made on the *milpa* are placed on a *mesa*, an altar made of forked posts similar to those in a Mayan house but on a much smaller scale. Poles are lashed across these posts to form a flat surface and branches of the *habin* tree are tied to each corner and then bent and tied to each other to form arches. All the foodstuffs offered to the *yuntzilob* are defined by tradition – they are virgin and sacred foods, special prep-

arations of maize, of *tamales*, of the first beans. Don Pablo
explained the more complex offerings, the *u-hanli-col*, the
'dinner of the *milpa*', and the rain-making ceremony, the
chai-chaac. These ceremonies take several hours to complete
and require the presence of a shaman, unlike the offerings
given during the preparatory stages of the *milpa*.

The *u-hanli-col* is the means whereby a *milpero* offers thanks
to the *yuntzilob* for his harvest and for protecting him while he
works and produces it. A variety of sacred foods, special
tortillas, mead (*balché*) prepared according to ancient recipe,
and chicken broth are offered by the shaman while a group of
invited guests help in preparing the food. The altar is arranged
in a prescribed way, a cross at the head faced with thirteen cups
of *balché* and varying numbers of special *tortillas* – the numbers ancient seeds of time wrapped in present-day ritual.

Roberto and Juan were growing restless with our conversation. After exchanging a few words with don Pablo, they set
off in search of wild honey. We were supposed to follow them
along presently. For now, settling back in his hammock,
watching them disappear into the forest, don Pablo carried on
the discussion. He spoke of the rain-making ceremony with
great affection, remembering the way his *abuelo* don Dolores
Balam had employed him as one of the 'frogs' tied to the four
legs of the altar. The *chai-chaac* was only performed when
severe drought threatened the whole community and it
involved everyone for as long as three days. Drought was a
sign that the *chacs*, the 'owners' of the rain, had withdrawn
their favours from a particular village or area. It was a mani-
festation of a breakdown in relations between man and the
yuntzilob and it required a maximum effort on the part of all to
see this remedied.

For two days a complex series of preparatory acts are carried
out. The men gather around the shaman in charge who directs
them as they build the altar at the edge of the village, a suitable
place for communal gathering. Precisely at noon on the first
day they all go off to a distant *cenote* to collect virgin water.
Henceforth, until the rain ceremony is concluded, the men are

separated from the womenfolk, who remain in the houses preparing the great number of dishes necessary for persuading the *chacs* to relent and send their rain. The men hang their hammocks near the altar and pass the afternoon and night in conversation perhaps going out to hunt in small parties as the shaman begins his prayers. The virgin water is hung in gourds around the altar and candles are lit. An undercurrent of anxiety subdues the gathering.

On the second day there is little movement. The shaman has been praying intermittently for hours, gradually entering into contact with the *yuntzilob* and God, *seeing* the severed relationship between earth and sky and the way to remedy it. The men, sitting by nearby fires, are sent to hunt animals in the forest, the shaman able to tell them where to go in order to be successful. All day he remains by the altar, praying and offering *zaca* to the *chacs*, promising them a more elaborate offering on the third day, requesting that they should be present to receive it.

Dawn of the third day and the shaman is now in a state of near exhaustion, his prayer and gestures made in deep trance. The sacred Mayan numbers, thirteen and nine, reappear, invoked in prayer and as the determining principle behind the shaman's words and actions. Four boys are tied to the legs of the altar as 'frogs' while a man is selected to play the part of the leading *chac*. He carries a small wooden sword and a water-gourd and stands apart from the rest of the community. At midday, as the shaman begins his most earnest praying, the 'frogs' croak from time to time, amd the leading *chac* flashes his sword and tips his gourd gently over the world. The sacred foods are brought to the altar and offered to the invisible *chacs*. Here again the interplay of the numbers thirteen and nine is predominant. The *balché* is sprinkled all around the altar by assistants of the shaman and everyone steps back to let the *chacs* enjoy the considerable feast that has been placed before them. It is the heat of the food which they absorb. When it has cooled, when it has been 'eaten', the shaman steps forward again to conclude the ceremony with a short prayer. The food is shared amongst all the people and a festive atmosphere develops.

'But does it really rain afterwards, don Pablo?' I asked.

'Yes. Sometimes it rains as the *chai-chaac* is ending, sometimes the next day. The shamans know what they are doing each time.'

I wondered then if the ceremony would have survived thousands of years if it didn't work. I asked about the leader of the *chacs*.

'Well, there are four *chacs*, don Ricardo,' Pablo reiterated, 'The first, the second, the third and the chief. He is the last one, he is the strongest in his commands. He is the *tup*. He goes out to see the work that is done by the others. They all have their horses – natural colours, their swords, or *lelem*, and their *chu*, their water-gourds. They ride the sky just tipping their gourds a little. Just a little and it rains well.'

'Do people see the *chacs* at all, don Pablo?'

He was so confident in his description of these *yuntzilob*, I felt sure there were many legends and stories concerning their activities. He became serious for a moment.

'There are many people who aren't careful. It is given to them to see the *chacs*,' he said. 'It is given to them to see but they are just looking, and they look again, and he is gone. He is just a shadow amongst the trees. You see the *chac* and he is gone. He is just a wind. They just give you the shadow to see how they walk.'

'So you don't really see the *chacs*,' I persisted.

'You know they are there. You see a shadow going the wrong way, you sense something unusual. Also you may come across his wind – because the *chac* has powers, a wind trails him which can attack you. If you save yourself after-wards, fine. If not, well, it is not his fault. Because where he walks he has power to walk.

'If you take on his wind,' don Pablo emphasized, shaking his head in dismay, 'you can die. Only if there is someone who can cure you, who can save you, will you be saved. You need to go with one who knows, a *h-men* . . . like my *abuelo* don Dolores

Balam, he could cure all the bad winds of the *yuntzilob*, of the *chacs*. He knew which prayer would take away the wind. He knew who was going to talk, whose shadow had passed by. So then he would ask their pardon, so that they might take back their wind from the person. And they would be cured.'

Here was the dual nature of the *yuntzilob* beginning to appear. If they could aid man in his labours, bringing rain and protecting the maize from birds and animals, they could also attack him if crossed, if man ignored their need for spiritual sustenance. There was a need to stay continually in harmony, in balanced communication with the *yuntzilob* and their invisible but dangerous world. In this sense every Mayan must, to some extent, engage in shamanic practice, always renewing the bridge of communication between worlds with prayer and ritual.

'Sometimes at night you hear the *yuntzilob* whistling – a whistling of a change of weather perhaps. Sometimes it begins to the east and then it is answered from each of the other directions also. When you hear them like that, one after the other, then it is a strong warning – something is happening. Be careful. That is how it is.'

We talked on for a while, unwilling to stir and go in search of Roberto and Juan, preferring the cool shade of the shelter and the hammocks. Don Pablo, I had noticed, organized his labours very carefully. When he worked it was very steady, very systematic. A great deal was accomplished in short periods of time. He seemed effortlessly to feed nine or ten people day after day. And yet he arranged his time so that leisure played an equal part. His way was unhurried, relaxed and productive. It was also deeply traditional, his ritual observances meticulous and punctual.

I was writing my notes about the *milpa* and the *yuntzilob*. Don Pablo, apparently half-asleep, stirred suddenly and asked, 'What are black seeds in a white soil, Ricardo?'

I stopped writing and thought for a bit. He was making some obscure reference back to our earlier conversation about the maize cycle and its colours. Of this I was sure. But the answer to the riddle he had posed eluded me. I shrugged and looked at him.

'Writing, don Ricardo,' he said, simply.

After we had stopped laughing he said to me, in more serious vein, 'We should prepare a book together, don Ricardo.'

I was momentarily taken aback by his suggestion. Then I began to see the perceptiveness and the possibilities behind his proposal. 'Why not?' I thought to myself. If the Mayas were such great scribes in the past, why not today? Still I was cautious.

'Is it because of DzibAktun, don Pablo?'

'Whatever happens to DzibAktun will happen, Ricardo,' he patiently answered. 'It is like a mirror that I put there for others to see, that is all.' He raised his hands palms towards his face as if looking into a hand-mirror.

'But what do you want this book to be then, don Pablo?' I was watching him closely. This was what our days together had been building up to, the intention behind don Pablo's long conversations with me.

'Well,' he began hesitantly, 'it will be like a memory of the *abuelos*, of don Dolores Balam. It will be a memory of that which is to one side. Because it was he who first showed me the way. But we will just see what appears there on the paper. Just let whatever appears, appear. First you look at the white paper, then you look away a little to one side. When you look at it again there it is written.'

His right hand moved in emphasis, palm flat to the ground as if he were unfolding and smoothing out a sheet of paper, or a woven mat.

10

Paradoxical Passages

My newly accorded role of *xcriban*, or secretary, to don Pablo Balam began to awaken a sense of responsibility in me. He had asked me to write a book with him. This placed our relationship on a very different basis from that between other outsiders and previous Mayan sources. Perhaps other Mayanists would come to work in this way with Mayan scholars here in the Yucatan but, for the moment, this was a unique opportunity. No longer could I treat Mayan writing as a pastime for I had wandered into the possibility of hearing a first Mayan counsel on their ancient hieroglyphs. By now I was sure that the Yucatec Mayas remembered at least the key ideas of the ancient signs. If they remembered previous worlds and *costumbre*, the spirits of forest, *milpa* and village, and an extensive oral library of legends, counsels and examples, they surely remembered something as important as the ideas behind the hieroglyphic signs.

My theory was that the four hundred years of Mayan silence on the wisdom of the signs had been a comment on how we had treated them. I was sure it had not been an emptiness of memory. Indeed in some still unknown way the very content of the hieroglyphs must have governed their behaviour. I could see that asking questions about the signs, trying to circumvent four hundred years of persecution, was going to be fraught with difficulty. No longer was my time to be tropical and easy. At the end of a few months here I was embarking on the most promising walk of my life. Don Pablo's words rang in my ears: 'Just let whatever appears, appear.'

Living in the village I began to research the history of Mayan writing from a shamanic point of view, borrowing this observation about the ancient lords and priests, searching for key questions I could ask. The history of Mayan writing appeared in abrupt phases, visible forms in its development suddenly reverting to invisible ones, as if by collective design and decision. This process seemed integral to the writing, a testing of shamanic abilities: dream walking between worlds, now visible, now invisible, now in duration, now outside of it.

The first visible phase of Mayan writing, and the most splendid, eloquent, and public, was that corresponding to the Classic Maya era of about 100–900 AD. This phase has been termed the Long Count, for it is distinguished by the vast cycles of time which the Classic Maya shamans obsessively studied and recorded on stone monuments or stelae. Beginning from an initial date 4 Ahau 8 Cumhu 13 (*baktuns*) 0 (*katuns*) 0 (*tuns*) 0 (*uinals*) 0 (*kin*), a date which closed a previous Long Count cycle of time, and which is equivalent to 12 August 3113 BC in our calendar, the Classic Mayan shamans calculated, studied, and recorded dates ninety million and even four hundred million years in the past, and several thousand into the future.

Why these Classic scholars chose a starting date for their calculations which was three millennia earlier than they were working (*circa* 100 AD) is unknown. The Mayan ancients evidently decided that an event on a certain day, three thousand years before, had a transcendent meaning only revealed much much later, a meaning which placed it at the beginning of a new history of the world, a new Long Count cycle of thirteen *baktuns*.

The Mayan shamans, mathematicians and astronomers developed an array of time periods, hieroglyphs and chronological principles in order to record, with great precision, these vast durations of time, the movement of stars and planets, and their thoughts upon the significance of what they saw. They used the day, *kin* in Maya, as the basic unit of their chronological system. The other time periods they employed were:

> *uinal* − 20 days
> *tun* − 18 *uinals* or 360 days
> *katun* − 20 *tuns* or 7200 days (19 years 73 days)
> *baktun* − 20 *katuns* or 144,000 days (394 years 52 days)
> *pictun* − 20 *baktuns* or 2,880,000 days (7890 years 41 days)
> *calabtun* − 20 *pictuns* or 57,600,000 days (157,808 years 21 days)
> *kinchiltun* − 20 *calabtunes* or 1,152,000,000 days (3,156, 164 years)
> *alautun* − 20 *kinchiltunes* or 23,040,000,000 days (63,312,328 years)

Most Mayan Long Count hieroglyphic texts were dated in periods up to a *baktun*, i.e. approximately 400-year groupings. The higher periods were employed to cast time back into an eternity of unimaginable duration − cycles of thousands of millions of days which abolish a historical sense of time, which subvert individual biography. Why, I found myself asking, did the Mayan ancients do this? What were they trying to accomplish so far beyond the frontiers of human history?

The Long Count time periods were wedded to a vigesimal system of numeracy which made use of two extremely clever mathematical principles − place value and a concept of zero. The brilliance of the Mayan numerical system becomes evident when we compare it to the Old World system in use at the same time under the Romans. In comparison with this numeracy, for example, which used seven signs, the Mayas needed only three − a dot to represent one, a bar to represent five, and a zero sign resembling a shell or a four-petalled flower. Extremely complex calculations could be recorded very simply with this system. A date found painted on a tomb at Tikal is a good example.

The top hieroglyph (a) is an introducing glyph signalling a date in the Long Count to follow. Then we have (b) four dots

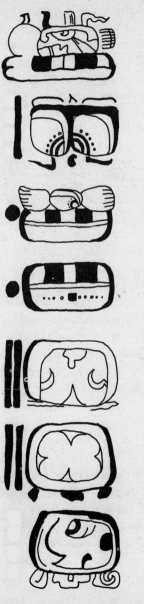

(a)　introductory glyph

(b)　9 *baktuns* = 9 x 144,000 days

(c)　1 *katun* = 1 x 7200 days

(d)　1 *tun* = 1 x 360 days

(e)　10 *uinal* = 10 x 20 days

(f)　10 *kin* = 10 x 1 days

(g)　4 Oc

TOTAL 1,303,770 days

4　*Date on a tomb at Tikal*

and a bar, or 9, and the hieroglyph for a *baktun* period of 144,000 days. This is followed (c) by one dot and the hieroglyph for a *katun*. After this (d) there is one dot and the glyph for a *tun*, or period of 360 days, and in (e) two bars signifying the number 10 and the glyph for a *uinal* period of 20 days. The last two hieroglyphs consist of two more bars, for 10, and a day sign for *kin*, and finally four dots, for 4, and the day sign Oc. Transcribed, the date reads 9 (*baktuns*), 1 (*katun*), 1 (*tun*), 10 (*uinals*), 10 (*kins*), 4 Oc (written 9.1.1.10.10.4 Oc in Mayanist shorthand). When this date is added to 12 August 3113 BC or, in Mayan terms 4 Ahau 8 Cumhu 13.0.0.0.0., it yields a date in 458 AD, the height of Classic Mayan hieroglyphic activity.

This example of Mayan chronological numeracy and writing is the most simple form of Long Count text. In more elaborate hieroglyphic texts, such as those in the Temple of the Cross, and the Temple of the Foliated Cross, or on the monumental stelae at Tikal and Copan, hundreds of hieroglyphs are inscribed, beginning with a Long Count date but continuing with dozens, even hundreds of undeciphered glyphs. Sometimes these are set around a carved relief of priests holding up spirits, shields and offerings, with birds of mythological magnificence perched above or to one side. While the Long Count dates, and some of those referring to astronomical and historical phenomena, can be read by Mayanist scholars today, the great majority of signs remain charmed and enchanted riddles beyond our powers of explanation.

Most Long Count Mayan writing which has survived from this period, from 100–900 AD approximately, has done so because it was carved on stone, on wall panels at numerous religious centres, and on stairways leading up to high temples. More restricted texts have survived on polychrome pottery, incised on bones, or carved on wood. Given the rapidly destructive effects of tropical jungle and climate, the surviving texts are miracles, the final, irrefutable accomplishment of anonymous Indian scribes, shamans and scholars.

Over 650 main hieroglyphs and 200 additional suffixes and

prefixes have been identified and catalogued from these surviving texts.* Although mostly undeciphered, they give us a
clear indication of the phenomenal intelligence of the ancient
Mayan shamans. There are glyphs dealing with earth, sky, fire
and water; with astronomy, medicine, mathematics, theology
and cosmology. There are glyphs associated with colours,
directions, ceremonies, gods, history, war, and dynasty, cities,
lineages, political unions, animals, birds, plants. All these
glyphs are flesh upon the skeleton of the Long Count chronology, a summation of the body of Mayan knowledge – *uinic*
and *uinal* in their wholeness.

The magnificence of Mayan Long Count writing, its cohe-
siveness across the centre of the New World, the depth and
mystery of the vision it enshrines, these qualities have
attracted ever growing numbers of outside scholars to the
frustrating, obsessive task of decipherment. What power is
there hidden within these signs that it held such disparate
Mayan groups together for a thousand years? One of the
earlier Mayanist scholars, Leon de Rosny, who discovered one
of three surviving Mayan hieroglyphic codices in a waste-
basket in the National Library of Paris in 1859, was to remark
of the task of decipherment that 'one must be a madman or
predestined to be one' to attempt it.

Innumerable theories and interpretations of Mayan writing
have been put forward, but progress has been slow, intermittent and overwhelmingly dependent on Spanish documents of
the sixteenth and seventeenth centuries. Beyond the little the
Mayas wanted such people to know, it is doubtful that there
were many Spanish priests educated enough to grasp the
complexity, or the subtlety, of Mayan thought and writing.
Numerous pitfalls, false beginnings and foolish notions litter
the history of Mayan writing, our history of Mayan writing.
Three approaches, however, have opened pathways and are
generally accepted as partial decipherments.

* The most extensive study and catalogue is J. Eric S. Thompson, *Maya
Hieroglyphic Writing*, University of Oklahoma Press, 1960.

5   *Centrepiece in Temple of the Cross, Palenque*

The most accepted of these has been the ideographic approach. This assumes that Mayan hieroglyphs represent ideas, or entire concepts, in comparison with the essentially pictographic writing of the central Mexicans, the Nahua, where the elements of the system are stylized pictures of actual objects. While the Nahua also made limited use of ideograms, a picture of a rabbit for the moon, an eye for a star, footprints for a path, their writing was at heart pictures representing objects. The Maya on the other hand were fundamentally ideographic, combining this with phonetic qualities rather than pictographs. Where a hieroglyph fails to open to ideo-graphic decipherment, examples exist of a phonetic interpreta-tion yielding results. Both the ideographic and phonetic interpretations have the advantage of being able to point to Gaspar Antonio Chi's 'Alphabet' as an original inspiration.

This alphabet has achieved a certain notoriety amongst despairing epigraphers. It was given to Bishop Landa in the second half of the sixteenth century by his Indian source, Gaspar Antonio Chi, a member of the Xiu lineage which had welcomed the Spanish at T-Ho a few decades earlier. The Bishop believed that he was being given the glyphic equiva-

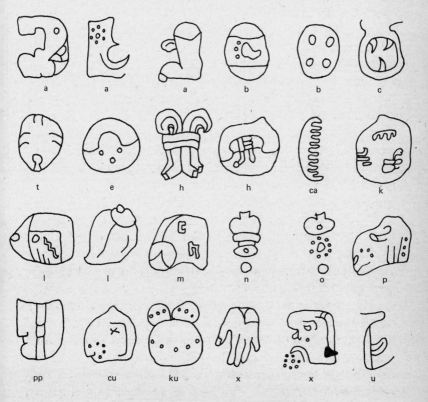

6 *Gaspar Antonio Chi's 'Alphabet'*

lent for each letter of the Spanish alphabet. However, Gaspar
Antonio Chi 'misunderstood' what he was being asked for and
actually gave phonetic and ideographic equivalents.

For the sound 'b' Gaspar drew this 🐚, a road with a
footprint upon it. The Mayan for 'road' is *be*. In other cases his
signs are evidently ideographic. An example of this can be seen
in his drawings for '0'. This consists of a circle of dots, or
beans, with one enclosed in a gourd 🝊. An idea is hidden
here, still to be deciphered. Other signs represent a hand,
heads, a comb, and still more obscure allusions.

Scholars have puzzled over this alphabet, sensing that it
might be more than a misunderstanding. It supports the
phonetic and ideographic frames to deciphering Mayan
hieroglyphs, I thought, but it also reminded me of don Pablo's
puzzles and his habit of speaking in cryptic phrases. If Bishop
Landa expected the Mayans to spell out their literacy, he knew
little of their way of thinking.

Two other lines of inquiry into Mayan Long Count writing
have also proved to be valuable aids to decipherment. The first
of these could be called the calendrical for it argued that the
Mayan hieroglyphs were entirely devoted to matters of time
and the calendar, to sacred matters, with no interest in human
history. Until the late 1950s this calendrical approach was the
only one to yield definitive results. Basing themselves on the
information provided by Spanish chroniclers, most notably
Bishop Landa, on three surviving hieroglyphic codices, and on
the Long Count texts carved on stelae, numerous scholars had,
by mid-century, managed to decipher those hieroglyphs
which did refer to chronological matters. This was a magnificent achievement.

As the calendrical approach began exhausting its potential,
leaving two-thirds of the glyphs undeciphered, so a historical
approach gathered support. A growing body of evidence,
based on readings of stelae at Classic Mayan sites such as
Palenque, Piedras Negras and Yaxchilan, began to appear and
were quickly accepted. The idea of a historical content to

Mayan writing had first been proposed in 1912, when an American Charles Bowditch suggested that Stela I at Yaxchilan probably contained a history of the figure depicted upon it – his birthdate, accession and government. For some inexplicable reason fifty years were to pass before another generation of Mayanist scholars, notably Tatiana Proskouriakoff and Heinrich Berlin, produced decipherments of Long Count texts which outline several examples of such histories on stelae and wall panels.

Living in Tulum village I was in no position to do more than begin to absorb the enormous body of research that has been written by people trying, with some success, to comprehend the meaning of Mayan writing. I was not even sure what I was looking for in my studies. Each interpretation and 'frame' towards decipherment that had been tried in the past led a certain distance into the forest of signs and then petered out. A true indication of how limited our understanding was could be seen in the twenty signs of the Uinal, the heart of the system. While the interpretations of these signs which I had read did not appear to be wrong, they were lifeless, incoherent, partial. There had to be more to these signs, an inner coherence, a Great Idea put there by the ancients and still hidden from us.

No one knows for sure why the Classic Maya abruptly stopped carving extensive hieroglyphic texts on stone in the central area or why they collectively stopped erecting stelae in the ninth century AD. For the preceding 800 years, hundreds upon hundreds of texts had been carved on stone and painted on murals in temples, from the wing of the land in Yucatan, through the lowland jungle areas of Petén and Chiapas, to the highland areas of Guatemala and beyond, into the hidden wastes of Honduras and El Salvador. That so many Indians, in so many disparate cultural and geographic areas could have worked in such unity never ceased to amaze me. Suddenly, in systematic, relentless order, the Long Count

activity ceased. No Long Count stela beyond the first years of
the tenth century AD had been discovered. The Classic Mayan
religious centres were abandoned, stelae often cast down, their
faces hidden, the Long Count writing veiled by the forest for
nearly a thousand years.

Several theories have been advanced to explain this very
abrupt and widespread closing to the Classic Mayan world.
Soil exhaustion, famine, drought, rebellion and a combination
of all four factors have been proposed as hypothetical causes.
These explanations fail to give adequate importance to the fact
that the ending of the intensive period of Long Count Mayan
writing occurred, systematically, everywhere in the Mayan
area within a prescribed period. Local, natural or political
conditions would not have prevailed over the whole. Far from
the closing of Long Count writing representing a collapse of
Mayan organization, its *completeness* in a mere century reflects
collective decision.

I remembered don Miguel's words about the gods distancing themselves and telling the people to leave their sacred cities
and change their *costumbre*. If it was a legendary explanation it
still seemed more plausible than those we had proposed. Thus,
when I looked in the ancient count of time it came as no
surprise to find that it was Copan which first ceased carving
and erecting stelae. Copan is recognized as the centre of Classic
Mayan scholarship and writing activity. A decision systematically to shut down the Long Count would naturally have
emanated from here. Furthermore the cessation, the change of
clothes and custom, coincided with the opening of a Katun XI
Ahau cycle in the Short Count cycle of approximately 256
years and with the opening of Baktun 10 in the Long Count.
The latter was a time period marking the advent of a major
new world and time. Don Miguel's few words about the
Classic Maya, I came to realize, were confirmed by the ancient
hieroglyphic texts, and a count of time more than two
thousand years old.

The Long Count was continued, in the Yucatan, by the
Kahlay Katunob or, as it is known amongst Mayanists, the

Short Count. This was a cycle of thirteen *katuns* which returned to its beginning every 256 years approximately. Since each *katun* is $360 \times 20 = 7200$ days in length, the Short Count was 7200 days $\times$ 13 = 93,600 days or $256\frac{1}{2}$ years. Each *katun* of twenty *tuns* (7200 days) was designated according to its ending day, always Ahau, and a numerical coefficient I–XIII arranged in a retrograding sequence, beginning with Katun XI Ahau. Bishop Landa left us one of several illustrations of the Short Count.

7   *The Kahlay Katunob, the Short Count*

This cycle of 256 years was the means whereby the Yucatec Maya continued the ancient Long Count in accurate but shorthand form. The Short Count was synchronized with the more ancient count; indeed it emerged from within it.

The Short Count was recorded on bark-paper codices and some dates were carved on stone monuments in the Yucatan. The frame it provided for post-Classic Mayan hieroglyphic writing, from about 900 AD until the coming of the Spaniards in 1539 and later, was unique to the Yucatan peninsula. As don Pablo had put it, they were bringing the Great Idea. Elsewhere in the Mayan area, in Chiapas and Guatemala, in highland areas, no trace of the Short Count has been found. The Quiché, the Cakchiquel, Tzetzal and others continued to use hieroglyphic writing, but they progressively gave prominence to central Mexican, Nahua elements, such as a fifty-two year cycle, obscuring the specifically Mayan Long Count as if by design. 'Only hiding his face is the reader of it,' they wrote in their major Book of Counsel, *The Popol Vuh*.

Throughout the post-Classic era in the Yucatan I had the impression that Mayan writing had become considerably more secretive, more guarded, perhaps restricted to certain lineages only and their jurisdictions. It was a period during which the Mayas were progressively encroached upon by Nahua lineages coming from central Mexico. The early Toltec invasions in the first centuries of this millennium seem to have been relatively enlightened, cooperative exchanges. The later Aztec *arrivistes* set the pattern for the subsequent cruelty of the Spaniards, for dogma and violence. Theirs was to be a temporary rule and they acted accordingly. They knew their time was limited and had no deep interest in the intricacy of the Short Count or the immense cycles of time it evoked. The face of Ahau was replaced by the pictograph Xochitl – 'Flower', by the flower of the Aztec world, spectacular, blood red and mercifully brief.

The Short Count was used to record Mayan history, prophecy and calendrical number and reason over 256 year cycles. After this the thirteen *katuns* returned to exert their influence anew, beginning always with Katun XI Ahau. By understanding the events of the past, the visions of the future left by the ancient *abuelos*, and the confluence of calendrical glyphs which located both in time, the Mayan shamans could produce counsels of the future. Bishop Landa described this reading process:

Then with many prayers and very devoutly they invoked an idol they called *Kinich Ahau Itzamna*, who they said was the first priest, offered him their gifts and burned the pellets of incense upon new fire. Meanwhile they dissolved in a vase a little verdigris and virgin water which they say was brought from the forests where no woman had been, and anointed with it the tablets of their books for their purification. After this had been done the most learned of the priests opened the book and observed the predictions for that year, declared them to those present, preached to them a little, enjoining the necessary observances.

It seemed remarkable to me that this single, vague description is all that has survived concerning the reading of Mayan hieroglyphs. When the Spanish settled in 1539–41 the knowledge was still there amongst the Indians – there were priests and shamans who could read the Short Count texts and, more than this, who could accurately locate themselves according to the Long Count also. But the Spanish priests never set down any known explanation of how to read the signs. There were Spanish priests, subsequent to Bishop Landa, who as late as the 1690s claimed to be able to read Mayan writing, but if they left an account of this, it has disappeared or has been suppressed. We learn only that the Mayas were still reading and writing hieroglyphically a mere two and a half centuries ago.

Bishop Landa played a sinister, paradoxical role in the early years of European occupation of the Yucatan. His Spanish contemporaries record his avid scholarship and knowledge of the Mayan language and customs. Yet Gaspar Antonio Chi's 'Alphabet' shows Landa's extremely superficial appreciation of Mayan thinking and humour. Moreover he was responsible for the most infamous destruction of Mayan hieroglyphic codices and stelae (idols) and he tortured and persecuted the

Mayan shamans with extraordinary medieval sadism. A contemporary Spaniard was moved to denounce him in a letter to the King of Spain, Philip II;

They [the Franciscans under Landa's authority] set about the business with great rigour and atrocity, putting the Indians to great tortures of ropes and water, hanging them by pulleys with stones of 50 or 75 pounds tied to their feet, and so suspended gave them many lashes until the blood ran to the ground from their shoulders and legs. Besides this they tortured them with boiling fat as was the custom to do with the negro slaves, with the melted wax of lit candles dropped on their bare parts; all this without preceding information or first seeking for the facts. This seemed to them the way to teach them [Christianity].

Why had Bishop Landa and the Franciscans, ostensibly so well studied in Mayan matters, pursued such a course of tortures even without proper Spanish authority to do so? The answer to this seemed to lie in the end result – we never learnt to read the signs and no record of how to do so has survived. Possibly the Spanish priests acted out of simple ignorance and blind fear, seeing only that every intellectual and spiritual sign of the Indians was a 'lie of the Devil'. They may well have felt an inferiority in sacred mystical matters. Certainly I no longer needed persuading that the Mayas were more advanced and more sophisticated in their understanding of time than sixteenth-century Europe. The evidence was carved on innumerable Long Count stones. Perhaps the Spanish preachers had felt threatened by this evident sophistication and dexterity, and had blindly lashed out, destroying the evidence, persecuting the spokesmen and preparing, as Landa did, a 'history' of the Maya to replace the apparent void he himself had created. And he never left an explanation of how to read Mayan hieroglyphs.

Another possible explanation for the silence we have inherited from the Spanish occupation may be that their priests, later than Bishop Landa, actually learnt enough about Mayan writing to realize that they contained ideas more advanced than those of Europe, most notably in regard to time and cosmology. They may have seen, as the Mayas insisted it could be seen, that the Indians had a prior knowledge of the word of God and the Christian way and that they had known in advance of the coming of the Spanish. If the Spanish priests had been shown, by objective count and reason written in the glyphs, that this was so, it would have so threatened their hegemonic European sense of history, time and the Catholic doctrine that they would have done their utmost to ensure that the true history and content of Mayan writing remain undeciphered by others.

There is evidence to support this view. First of all there is the total silence and lack of documentation on this particular subject – the reading of the only complete system of writing in the New World. Without doubt Catholic savants recognized the fundamental importance of this system and there must have been scholars working assiduously on its decipherment. Equally, the dismemberment of Jacinto Canek, Mayan rebel, theologian and shaman, in the 1760s tells us that the Spanish authorities had precise knowledge of what they were attacking – shamanism. This observation needs to be coupled with the fact that it was the Mayan shamans who promoted the 'heretical myth' of their prior knowledge of Christianity. This was the most sensitive of issues.

Even Bishop Landa had been obliged to confess:

Baptism is not found anywhere in the Indies save here in Yucatan, and even with a word meaning to be born anew or a second time, the same as the Latin 'renascer'. Thus in the language of Yucatan *sihil* means 'to be born anew' or a second time, but only however in composition; thus *caput-sihil* means to be reborn. Its origin we have been unable to learn, but it is something they have always used and for which they have had such devotion that no one fails to receive it; they had such reverence for it that those guilty of sins, or who knew they were about to sin, were obliged to confess to the priest, in order to receive it; and they had such faith in it that in no matter did they ever take it a second time. They believed that in receiving it they acquired a predisposition to good conduct and habits, protection against being harmed by the devils in their earthly affairs, and that

through it and living a good life they would attain a beautitude
hereafter which, like that of Mahomet, consisted in eating and
drinking.

He had added:

The Yucatecans naturally knew when they had done wrong, and
they believed that death, disease and torments would come on them
because of evil doing and sin, and thus they had the custom of
confessing to the priests when such was the case. In this way, when
from sickness or other cause they found themselves in danger of
death, they made confession of their sin; if they neglected it, their
near relatives, or friends reminded them of it; thus they publicly
confessed their sins to the priest if he was at hand; or if not, then to
their parents, women to their husbands, and the men to their wives.

The Mayas never ceded the argument to the Spanish priests. In
this respect it is surely of great significance that the Vatican
recognized Yucatec Mayan as a liturgical language – the only
Indian language so recognized by the Church. Equally, to this
day Mayan Christianity is administered by Mayan religious
specialists – Catholic priests are not allowed to serve inside
the native churches. These represent considerable achievements. When the Spanish first began to preach they invoked a
list of Ordinances which stated, in part, that the Indians were
forbidden to preach the Holy Word unsupervised amongst
themselves. They were not to be allowed to move from one
town to another, each town was to have a school, and the
Indians were compelled to attend in the form and manner
required by the padres. The laws went on to stipulate that since
'many of the chiefs and older men, in the respect they hold by
their ancient descent, call the people into secret meetings to
teach them old rites and draw them from the Christian doctrine, in the weakness of their understanding, all such actions
and meetings are prohibited. These Ordinances were directed
at the shamans and their counsels. The Mayas, for their part,
hid the hieroglyphic texts, studied our books and said nothing.

If subsequent accommodations with the Mayan shamans
proved necessary for the Church, notably as a result of rebel-

lions, they never published an account of how to read Mayan writing – if they knew. The colonial documentation was carefully administered, censored, 'lost'. The laws and doctrines of the Spanish and the Church, their punishment and violence, the monopoly of the Catholic orders, all these sealed off the Mayan world from outsiders. The 'history' of pre-Columbian Indian America has been written entirely from premises and sources resulting from this totalitarian censorship.

The destiny of Mayan writing and reading remains as obscure as its origins. Just as the hieroglyphic system abruptly appeared nearly two thousand years before, *as a unity*, don Pablo was to insist later when we reviewed these ideas, so the entire script and the body of knowledge it contained became invisible, *as a unity*. It was still there, perhaps in this very village of dawn long after the Spanish occupied T-Ho, but a silence collectively understood by the Indians, read in the signs, descended between their world of thought and ours. For the next four hundred years it was to remain complete.

I held a copy of one of the *Books of Chilam Balam* in my hands. In the *Books of Chilam Balam* the Jaguar Spokesman is talking riddles, preparing his history of the future. I could see the scribe in 1595, shaman scholar fallen on Castillean times, nondescript *milpero* living deep in the forest, invisible, path well disguised. Even while I was only beginning to meditate upon the cryptic secrets set down so long ago their transcendent power reached me clearly. Midday, midnight I could see the *xcriban* squatting in his house, eyes intent on the page before him, his hand slowly tracing a new, secret writing for the time and world now upon him.

It was the Franciscans who first taught the Mayans to write in Roman script. When the Spanish priests first arrived there were few of them and many millions of Indians. The Indians were eager and quick to learn the Catholic world view. A mere eight priests, for example, baptized over twenty thousand Mayans in the first year of their missionary endeavour.

Amongst these Christianized Indians the priests selected the sons of the most influential, leading families and obliged them to attend special schools where they taught them Catholic doctrine, ritual, and the use of alphabetical reading and writing skills. These fresh-faced sons were then sent back to their native towns in the interior of the Yucatan where the priests thought they would serve as spiritual ambassadors of the new faith.

But the Mayans saw their own purpose in their newly acquired skills. The Word that had arrived with the Spanish had been prophesied from within their own ancient literate tradition and it confirmed the value and legitimacy of this prophetic inheritance. Now the alphabetical form of expression of the new Word was quickly converted into a cryptic Mayan literacy – a shamanic writing which served a purpose utterly different from that presumed by the Franciscans who had passed it to the native sons. While these shrewd Indians now worked with the greatest facility in two literacies, hieroglyphic and alphabetical, the Spanish evidently never came to understand or work with more than one – their own.

The Mayan *xcribanob* quickly developed a form of written Maya using the newly learnt alphabet but retaining their own language. This writing consciously created anew the difficult cryptic nature of the ancient hieroglyphs. It was written in such a way that only Mayan scholars could truly and correctly read it even though it borrowed Roman script. Outside scholars of this very distinctive phase of Mayan writing have commented on its impenetrable nature – usually blaming the anonymous Indian scribe for being a semiliterate hack, lacking spelling and punctuating skills. Others have noted that even a thorough knowledge of Mayan grammar and vocabulary 'renders surprisingly little aid in deciphering the documents'. None have ventured to suggest that the Mayan shamans wrote this way on purpose.

The notebooks which contain this colonial Mayan writing are known to us as the *Books of Chilam Balam*. Perhaps twenty of these notebooks, written from the sixteenth century until the close of the nineteenth, have come into our hands. Often they are copies of copies, many containing passages found in other notebooks. All are centred around extensive paradoxical passages of history and prophecy structured according to the Short Count cycle of the previous Mayan world – the post-Classic era. In secret, abbreviated form they contain the true count of Mayan time and history – the history of the future as seen by the Mayan abuelos, the first shamans.

The *Books of Chilam Balam* are the most undervalued and misunderstood form of Mayan writing. They represent a distinctive phase and purpose in the history of Mayan writing as a whole, a fusion of oral counsels, songs and hieroglyphs into a new form and expression suited to the New World introduced by Katun XI Ahau 1539 and the arrival of the Europeans. They have remained impenetrable, asleep, seemingly modest in their value to historians and epigraphers. But they are the last written Mayan documents to appear and their meaning has been kept as a secret amongst Mayan shamans for centuries.

1980 AD 1539 AD *Books of Counsel*	1539 AD 900 AD *Kahlay Katunob or Short Count*	900 AD 100 AD *Long Count*	100 AD 300 BC ?
Chilam Balam Popol Vuh	Hieroglyphic codices	Stone stelae. Unified Mayan project	Bark and deerskin codices?
Use of Roman script	Use of Mayan glyphs and Nahua pictographs	Full Mayan hieroglyphic writing	No known early forms of glyphs and Long Count
Predominantly in the Yucatan but also in highland Guatemala	Mainly in the Yucatan. A continuation of the Long Count	Appears as a unity through-out Mayan area. Disappears as a unity but it is remembered in Yucatan	Full Mayan hieroglyphic writing

The Mayas counted backwards as well as forwards in the ancient Long Count – from an ending date in the future to the present, to the past. In Mayan '*xoc*' is the ancient word for both 'count' and 'read'. Thus it seemed logical to assume that we also needed to read the distinctive forms of Mayan writing backwards, back from today, back from the texts written by anonymous colonial Indian scribes, back to the Short Count and Long Count hieroglyphs.

Seen backwards through time the history of Mayan writing appeared as a partially assembled skeleton with critical bones missing. Where were the origins and the destiny? Even the colonial Books of Counsel, written in our script, refused to yield their enigmatic secrets. They combined paradoxical passages, signs to the glyphs, consciously and cleverly disguised. 'Only hiding his face is the reader of it,' they said. 'Who will be the interpreter?'

But even though it was only partially assembled, the skeleton of Mayan writing inspired deep contemplation in me. From my admittedly limited experience of the Maya I believed that outside scholars had too easily discarded the part the living people had to play in the task at hand. Here was one critical, missing bone which needed to be included in the framing and deciphering of Mayan writing. If it had been given to the people to keep the ancient count of the universe in spite of successive waves of invaders, and they had done so, then it might have been given to them to open the books with an oral 'key' and to interpret them to us at this late hour. If the living people could only decipher the most recent Books of Counsel, these, in turn, would lead back to the Short Count and thence to the Long Count.

But was I just dreaming the logic and symmetry of this argument, alone in Tulum village? Could the Mayan *abuelos* really have designed a Great Idea through so extensive a period of time as well as across so vast an area of the New World? Could the people have been persuaded to keep the Great Idea secret, in oral form, through dozens of generations and had they succeeded?

I found don Pablo sitting by the light of a solitary, flickering candle, talking with doña Ophelia. The children were bundled into hammocks, half-asleep in the shadows. Don Pablo's animated expression danced in the light, his words interspersed with deep chuckles and nods as he slowly unfolded his story. Doña Ophelia produced some chicken and *tortillas* from pots near the fire, and settled back into her hammock to rest and talk. No one minded my presence and the family flow continued uninterrupted.

Much later we talked about Mayan writing and its history. My account was long and detailed, full of questions. Most of the family soon fell asleep, save for doña Ophelia and Pablo who muttered a few 'ahas' and 'ahums'. He took a great interest in finding out what work was being done on Mayan writing. After I had finished talking there was a silence which stretched into minutes, into a quarter hour and more.

Don Pablo stirred and asked 'Do they say what the *abuelos* called the signs?'

I thought about the things I had read and said, 'No, I don't think so.'

Don Pablo said, 'We call the writing *akab dzib* or "night writing".'

11

The Awakening of Ahau

For many weeks don Pablo refused to answer my questions about night writing. He drew into himself when I raised the subject, often refusing even to comment briefly. Finally he began asking me questions. We talked about fray Diego de Landa and how his work with Mayans had allowed us to decipher the basic cycles of the Mayan calendar. We talked of the enigma of Gaspar Antonio Chi's 'Alphabet'. I said that it seemed to me that there was a real clue to Mayan writing there but we couldn't see it.

Don Pablo thought for a long time about this and said, 'Landa wanted to come and give his laws. That is why he burnt the books. So that only he would be respected. But there they wait for him . . . . Our Lord will see him. There he will see if he is truly king of the earth.'

His voice was assertive and sure of judgement, controlling a rising anger. I could see that the burning of the Mayan codices still pained him greatly, striking deep into the heart of Mayan thought.

'Later you can dream of what you have burnt. And then how will you see it? You can be told between dreams, "There you will see about the books that you have abandoned."' Pablo's voice changed into dreamed dialogue, an imagined conversation between Bishop Landa and the Mayan *abuelos*.

'So then when they told him they were abandoned he awoke and thought "Where have I abandoned the books? Where will I look for them now?"' Pablo moved about as if he were searching for hidden codices. 'That which he did is sad. So that he could work first, he burnt the books. So that is what he did. Yes, that is what he did.' He laughed at his own cynicism.

'But he's dead now. If he were alive he would not want others to make their books, only him. He thought he was the only one who knew, the only *h-men*. No, he was not. The writing remained. The idea of before was carried forward until now. So that no one should come to know of all that the Mayas had done, all that they knew, that man Landa burnt the books and made his own. Then he did not live longer to say how the world is to continue. What he did is already done.'

That was don Pablo's first discussion. I was to find that when talking about Mayan writing he never gave excessively long explanations. He put signs there; he did not spell them out. He used short phrases and images which contained greatly compressed meanings. In talking about fray Diego de Landa he had spoken about dreaming the books, of the *abuelos* talking to Landa in his sleep, of the ancient codices as oracles whereby one could see how the world was to continue. These glimpses inspired me to probe deeper, to seek more detailed discussions. I wanted to see how the ideas of before had continued, not just hear it asserted.

Don Pablo was initially resolute in his silent, unexplained refusal to talk about night writing. At the same time he was not discouraging me in my quest but rather seemed to be waiting for something I could not understand. He spent more and more time cross-questioning me on what we knew of Mayan writing. In this he reminded me of don Miguel. We were entering sacred Mayan thought, the most precious heart of their thinking and the learning way was heavily circumscribed by ancient custom and timing.

On another occasion, working on the *milpa*, clearing ground for the year's planting, don Pablo began asking me questions about the sacred 'papers', specifically the *Books of*

Chilam Balam and *The Popol Vuh*. As he spoke I realized that he had read the Quiche Maya *Popol Vuh* (in Spanish) and that he considered it very close to the Yucatec Maya vision, even though the two Mayan groups were separated by a thousand years. *The Popol Vuh* had always seemed to be heavily overlaid with Biblical and Nahuatl elements.

'No,' don Pablo said, very sure of himself, 'that comes from the Mayan *abuelos*. Only it is very dissimulated because they had to hide the power of the ancient Mayas. But later it will be seen again.'

I knew then that he could see a common hieroglyphic content in Quiché and Yucatec Mayan colonial texts, he could see glyphs invisible to us even though the books were written in Roman script. The hieroglyphs are the last known common denominator between highland and lowland Maya and in some mysterious fashion don Pablo had seen below the surface texts and their differences, had seen into a deep pool of common Mayan knowledge.

We spoke of ideas that remained hidden. Don Pablo talked of the Mayan jade mines no one had ever discovered, comparing this with the way their writing, specifically its origins and destiny, had remained undisclosed. I reminded him that we had managed to read some of the signs, the calendar, the Kahlay Katunob (Short Count), and Long Count chronology.

Don Pablo nodded, but added, an amused expression on his face, 'The *abuelos* put that there so that when the truth is revealed, when the time arrives for the writing to appear again, then you can see that it is so. It is like an examination so that you can see that their virtues, the power given them by Our Lord, is real and true. Then, perhaps, you also will take their counsels to heart.'

I was silenced by this. Like don Miguel, he had stated that the writing had a future destiny, a reappearance to come. More than this, he had said that the fragments we had been given were put there for a reason, were there to prove something yet to come.

Don Pablo wandered off to begin cutting a firebreak around the *milpa*, a long and arduous task productive only in a precautionary sense. I was left with the distinct impression that he had decided something for himself about our work together. To begin with he was recovering all that outsiders had taken from here, in the way of understanding. But he was beginning to speak, to explain, to show the depth and vitality of the Mayan vision. For my part I was becoming more and more sensitive to how slight gestures, voice tones, changes in mode of speech, were consciously prepared signs keying texts chosen as gifts towards my learning. But I was slow to learn, slow to bring out the intelligence of this Mayan man's walk and vision.

The brief conversations continued over several weeks, intermittent, bright glimpses, each time leaving me puzzled over how the words could relate to Mayan writing. They were distinctive from other phrases, more cryptic and intense, following the pattern don Miguel had first revealed to me and confirming his words. But I was still not seeing the meanings of the signs and Pablo had not explained night writing to me. I realized that he, not I, was making the decisions here, guiding the development of my learning.

Another time we spoke of writing. Don Pablo asked me to teach him how we wrote their language. He listened as I explained a system found in Alfred Tozzer's *Mayan Grammar*. After I had finished he showed me the system he had learnt from someone in the forest. He revealed that he had taught himself to read and write Spanish also twenty years before. I praised him for his remarkable vocabulary, realizing that it was the result of hours of reading and careful listening. I wondered also at how deep his knowledge of Mayan must be, for it was obvious he was a scholar of this, consciously maintaining its purity. Later I realized he had been subtly showing me that it was not my writing skill he was borrowing, it was my *English* writing skill.

Don Pablo asked me how we had come to have the Mayan Books of Counsel in our possession. 'Who gave you the right?'

I explained that often the Books had been transcribed from village originals which had since disappeared. If we had not made transcripts and photographic copies a hundred years ago they might have been lost for ever, they might never have appeared. Don Pablo was not visibly convinced by this. He thought for a while and then said, 'Still, those who have them now have no *costumbre* for seeing the future so how are they going to read them?'

I had to agree with him there. We really had not understood much of the Mayan Books of Counsel, the *Books of Chilam Balam* and *The Popol Vuh*.

'Perhaps if you explained a little of what is there,' I said, 'then they will reappear and people will want to return them to the Mayas. They could exchange them for a little understanding.'

I could see that Pablo liked this suggestion. I said it casually, almost without thinking, then realized I had unwittingly suggested the reverse of Chilam Balam's long-ago words. Now it was we who were asking the Mayas for a sign towards reading their scriptures.

Don Pablo began explaining the meaning of night writing to me.

'There are signs which arrive in your dreams,' he said with very great solemnity. 'It is shown to you so that you can think it, so that you can put your idea there. Then when you understand it you remember that is what you dreamed. Now I've seen it clearly. It is your good fate. It is given to you in your mind, so that you think it, so that you dream it, so that you see it before you really read it, before you arrive at where it is written in the book or on the stone.'

I fumbled with his explanation. It was entirely different from any other definition of a system of writing I had studied. Don Pablo seemed to be saying that the hieroglyphs could only be read shamanically. Observing my confusion he added, 'You can't understand how that is yet, how that can explain our writing to you. Only if you arrive at the right hour, the night when you should see the writing. That is when, if it is your fate, you really see. But that is because it is your fate only, the hour has arrived for you to see it.'

'But you are thinking and thinking about it before, studying all the books and histories and still the writing refuses to say anything.' I was disheartened.

'Yes, you have to know this and this. You need a lot of love for it, the wisdom that is there. Will God give me the learning I need to understand this and how it is? You have to study hard. But only when the time arrives will you be given the idea. Such and such a day go and look at it again. Maybe when you looked before you did not see. But now when you look you are given the idea of how it is. That is when one begins to understand. But all of it,' don Pablo shrugged, 'who knows? But one or two you can begin to study. Later you can see how it continues.'

'But the night is the last time the Mayan *abuelos* would choose to paint their books,' I said, even more confused.

'They know how they wrote it, how they dreamed it. They know how they wrote it. Perhaps they had more sight than us. Perhaps they just *saw* it.'

I thought about the meaning of night writing, noticing implications in the overall framing that don Pablo had given to our conversations. For one thing he spoke in the future and the present. He spoke of the reappearance of the writing, of how the Mayas had remembered the idea of before, of how they knew their time was recorded there on the stones. But this was only a part of it. Later I was to see that it was his specific emphasis on the future which was crucial to understanding the ancient purpose of the writing – its destiny.

Don Pablo referred to all the phases of Mayan writing as night writing. There was no distinction for him between the colonial, supposedly alphabetical texts, and the ancient glyphs. This puzzled me for a long time until, finally, I understood his point. His definition of night writing was, in fact, a description of how a hieroglyph worked on the reader's mind. The glyphs were ideographic but the idea each contained was not obvious. Don Pablo was saying that the idea arrived in one's mind first, and then found realization in the hieroglyphs. He was also saying that the colonial Books of Counsel were designed to do the same. Even if they were written alphabetically the sentences were so enigmatic that a reader would have to arrive with the right idea, *a priori*, before they would open their meanings. They were put there to confirm a vision which, evidently, had to appear from within the reader as an inner illumination.

I realized then that this was what Don Pablo was patiently waiting for in me. He promised that 'one or two' of the signs could be studied and he was giving me the counsels the Mayas gave their own children on such matters. Beyond this, if he knew more, even if he could actually explain a hieroglyph to me, he had to hold back until I *saw* for myself. This was very important; it was intrinsic to the nature of Mayan night writing.

If I could sift and interpret these ideas from don Pablo's words, they did not spell out the meaning of a hieroglyph. He had made me aware that these were essentially shamanic texts, literate shamanic signs. He was answering my questions very carefully and with a deep sense of responsibility, giving me an orientation, causing me to learn for myself. His method, I could see, was ancient in origin, the learning way of the Mayan people. He would not give me the questions. These I had to dream up for myself. I was still standing in the forest, gazing at a tiny stone in don Pablo's hand, waiting for the question, the idea, which would make it speak to me. Don Pablo insisted this time that only if I dreamed it, only if it was my fate, would our discussions on Mayan writing continue. But he promised also that it was possible to understand the ancient signs today. Indeed he was continually implying that this was their original purpose.

It happened then, much later, that Ahau began to speak to me, began to declare himself in dream, an idea amongst ideas, exactly as don Pablo had explained night writing to me. Awake I had been thinking about Ahau. His face was so distinctively Mayan, 'he of the blowgun', Hunter and Lord, with his blowgun hunter's lips, and lines beside representing his weapon.

8   *Ahau, Mayan portrait and oracle*

In every way Ahau was obviously a key sign in Mayan writing. He was the spokesman glyph of the twenty signs of the Mayan Uinal, he was twenty in the cycle of twenty, end-beginning of time. Next to him the first sign of the Uinal was Imix, reminiscent of a grain of maize in contrast to Ahau's hunting prowess, a feminine sign (*im* is 'breast' in Yucatec Maya) associated with agriculture. But Ahau was the spokesman, the unifier and completer of the cycle. His face appeared thirteen times in the Kahlay Katunob, one for each *katun* of twenty years, and it was reading his face, a Mayan portrait, that introduced the prophecies associated with each *katun* age.

Why was Ahau depicted in the hieroglyphs with such distinctive lips? It came to me that this was so in order to emphasize his power. He was end-beginning, spokesman of time, and only blowgun hunter's breath was simultaneously life and death. The idea of Ahau's lips fitted perfectly with his internal place value within the Uinal cycle of twenty signs.

Seeing this I also saw a way forward through the forest of

signs. If Ahau was depicted ideographically according to his internal place value amongst the twenty signs at the heart of Mayan writing, then the other nineteen signs also might yield their ideographic content according to their place value, their interrelationships within the unity of the cycle. This was an approach to reading the Mayan Uinal which had not been tried before, and it held out the promise of revealing the coherent ideographic body of thought which must necessarily reside invisibly in the Uinal. I saw also that the Mayan time tense announced by Ahau as the major preoccupation of the ancient shamans was not a past or future tense, it was *simultaneity*, the abolition of temporal duration, the exiting from normal time.

Don Pablo listened impassively as I explained the insight which had been given to me. When he spoke his words came from thousands of years ago, describing the appearance and simultaneously the reappearance of the original Mayan oracle, Ahau, the unifier and spokesman of an entire system of thought and writing already presupposed in his very glyphic depiction.

'Ahau has no movement, his mouth has not opened yet, he cannot speak. He only has his breath, he only has the power to do what he does. Anyone else who sees it does not have the power. Only he has the power for that . . . to be able to speak. He has no other movement, he only has his breath. He cannot hunt, he cannot do anything yet. But with his breath he begins. When that begins his mouth is opened.'

He paused while I took notes. I sensed the very great antiquity of Ahau in his words. I had the impression that he was the original Mayan mouthpiece to the one true God or Hunab Ku. Through contemplation within the overall system of the hieroglyphs his features and characteristics would reveal the wisdom of the shamans, a vision sent by God and written down, cryptically, by the Classic Mayan spirit lords.

Don Pablo said, 'Yes, his mouth is opened when you see it. He speaks and no other. Only he has the power to do what he does. You could say that he is a god, he is Lord, he is the spokesman for them all. He explains how it is.'

He gazed down at a drawing of Ahau, which we had done in the earth. Then he whispered, 'It is as if it is nothing. For a long time you cannot understand it. Only when the question is asked will he speak to you.'

Ahau had begun to awaken and soon I learnt to see deeper into his enigmatic face. Ahau is a uniquely Mayan glyph, or sign, for in the Nahua pictograph he is replaced by Xochitl, or 'Flower'. This distinction points to Ahau's role as spokesman for a system of writing which is intrinsically different from that of central Mexico. A hieroglyph is not a pictograph. The one is enigmatic, not obvious in meaning, the other is an open 'flower', a reading, designed to be obvious and explanatory.

These differences point to fundamentally different purposes between Mayan and Nahua writing. The former was designed to record, in complete but secretive form, the wisdom of the ancient shamans for posterity and future complete reappearances. The latter was designed to be published openly, a partial reading for the moment long ago. These different purposes underpinning the two literacies are also manifest in the calendars of the two areas. While the ancient Mayas dealt in millions of years of past time, and thousands of future years, dealt with whole time, the Nahua worked happily with more ephemeral fifty-two year cycles. Their intention was to understand the brevity of their moment, a mere generation at a time, not time in its entirety. That understanding had already been developed and cast into the Long Count when the Nahua emerged. They saw only the future it prescribed for them.

For the Mayas the appearance of Nahua writing, of Quetzalcoatl and the law that came from Tula, coincided with the beginning of Baktun 10 in the Long Count. This was a major new world and time emerging, bringing new gods, customs and theology. For the Classic Mayan shamans and scribes this was a sign of the growing power of the Lords of Xibalba, the Nine Lords of Hell. In the colonial Books of Counsel there are frequent, insistent references to the central Mexicans, associating them with the Lords of the Underworld.

Sections of *The Popol Vuh*, for example, appear to be a history of the confrontation of Mayan shamanism and writing with these forces. Read as such, they record its systematically 'invisibility' at the end of the Classic era, from Baktun 10 onwards, its 'hidden face', as a conscious and ancient plan directed towards outwitting and defeating the Lords of the Underworld. To begin with, in the Third Creation, the Lords of Xibalba defeat Ahau, personified in two characters, 1 Hunter and 7 Hunter. Later the sons of these two set off to revenge their fathers' deaths. Their names are Hunter and Jaguar Deer. As they leave they say,

> 'We're going then, oh our grandmothers;
> > We're just taking leave of you.
> And this is the sign of our word
> > That we shall leave now.
> Each of us shall plant this cornstalk for you;
> > In the middle of our house we shall plant it then,
> It will be the sign of our death
> > If it should dry up'

> > > > *The Popol Vuh,* lines 3431–3440
> > > > (All excerpts from *The Popol Vuh* are from
> > > > Munro S. Edmonson's superb translation.)

In the hieroglyphs this sign of the word is represented by Imix, the first sign. 'Maize' is *Ixim* in Yucatec Maya and the reversal of this, in Imix, reflects the reversal of the world in the hunter's walk. They are descending into the Underworld to oppose the Lords of Xibalba and revenge their fathers. I began to see how the Uinal was inspired by this shaman's walk and how it could be arranged directionally. Ahau and Imix lay to the west, at the gate to the Realm of Shadows. Equally I could see that the account written in *The Popol Vuh* was dreamed out of the signs of the Uinal and led back to them in mysterious fashion.

The two sons journey to the heart of the Underworld. Here

they are given many tests and trials by the Lords. They have to
name the names of the Lords, they have to smoke a cigar all
night and bring it back whole in the morning, they have to
play the ancient ball game, the prize four pots of flowers to be
stolen from Knife house and its guardians. These trials are
shamanic tests of endurance, skill, intelligence and wit. Hunter
and Jaguar Deer survive them all. When, finally, they come to
'disappear', it is explicitly stated that they choose to do this, as
a trick to outwit the Lords.

> 'For since they were forewarned
>   They had endured
> All the suffering,
>   The trouble given them,
> But they were not killed by the trials of Hell;
>   But they were not defeated
> By all the biting
>   Animals there are in Hell.
> And so then they called on two far-seers,
>   Like those who are diviners.
> These are their names
>   Poor
> And Rich;
>   They were trained sages.'

The Popol Vuh, lines 4129–4142

Hunter and Jaguar Deer explain to the sages that the Lords
are 'gathering their counsel' because they had not been able to
kill the two sons by trials. Now Hunter and Jaguar Deer in
turn are preparing their revenge. They say to Poor and Rich,

> 'And this is your instruction
>   That we shall tell:
> If you come to be asked by them later
>   Concerning our death
> When we are burned up,
>   What will they say,
> Oh Poor
>   Oh Rich,

If they talk to you?
  Might it not be good
For us to toss their bones in the canyon,
  Or might it not perhaps be good
But really their face will be revived again
  You say.
Might it not perhaps be good
  For us just to hang them in a tree?
If they say that to you next,
  Indeed it would not be good,
For really you will see their faces revived again
  You say.'

The Popol Vuh, lines 4155–4174

This imagined, future conversation between Lords and the trained sages, Poor and Rich, continues. Hunter and Jaguar Deer provide the examples of what the trained sages are to say. They are told that when the Lords grind up the bones of Hunter and Jaguar Deer, 'the way fresh corn is ground', then the prophecy of their reappearance will be manifested.

I read many ideas in these lines. Hunter and Jaguar Deer are the representatives, the sons, of Ahau, who was disassembled in the ninth century AD, at the opening of Baktun 10 in the Long Count. This 'disassembly' is presented here as a shamanic conjuring trick of a very high order, an *enchantment* of the reader's perception. Equally Hunter and Jaguar Deer 'die' in order to outwit the Lords. It is their bones, bones of Jacinto Canek as well, which the Lords disassemble and grind up, for it is in these bones that their shamanic power resides – the ability to exit from time and re-enter it at a predestined moment.

Hunter and Jaguar Deer 'die' and their bones are ground up and strewn along the river. But they just sink below the surface and become 'handsome sons'. Their faces come out again. This time when they appear it is disguised as beggars, as poor people, humble before the Lords. Soon they become magicians.

'They set a house on fire as though it were really burning
  And then suddenly it materialized again
They were watched very closely in Hell.
  And then they sacrificed themselves,
Each of them dying for them
  And then being laid out for dead.
After they had killed themselves
  Their faces suddenly came back to life again.'

The Popol Vuh, lines 4271–4278

Hunter and Jaguar Deer become famous throughout the land, performing their Classic shamanic skills and dances. They are sent for by the Lords of Xibalba, who still haven't recognized who they really are. Their behaviour before the Lords provides a paradigm for all subsequent Mayan reticence.

'Truly wretched
  Was their appearance
When they arrived.
  And then they were asked
Their mountains
  And their towns
And they were asked their mothers
  And their fathers:
Where do you come from?
  They were asked.
We probably don't know, oh Lord.
  We never knew the face
Of our mother,
  And our father
Because we were still small
  When they died,
Was all they said.'

The Popol Vuh, lines 4345–4360

Hunter and Jaguar Deer, disguised as tricksters and magicians, act as if they have forgotten their origins and the wisdom of their fathers and mothers. It is a trick to put the

Lords of Xibalba off their guard. Soon the two are performing their dances, the house-burning trick, and sacrificing a dog and a man, only to revive them again. The Lords are impressed. 'And now sacrifice yourselves in turn,' they say. After Hunter and Jaguar Deer have successfully done this, the Lords themselves ask to be sacrificed.

'Do it to us!
    Sacrifice us! they said then.'
The Popol Vuh, lines 4471–4472

Hunter and Jaguar Deer do this – and the faces of the Lords are not revived. They are defeated. The counsel of their death adds,

'It was just a miracle,
    And it was just by transforming themselves that they did
        it.
And so then they named their names.'

The Popol Vuh, lines 4525–4528

It is by appearing to be insignificant, meek, poor people while retaining a memory of the ancient wisdom and its powers that the two sons of the first hunters defeat the Lords.

Later they go in search of their fathers – 1 Hunter and 7 Hunter. Their intention is to reassemble them. They know how to do this.

'And this then was the reassembling of their father by them.
    And then they reassembled 7 Hunter.
They went there to reassemble them
    In Dusty Court.
But really his face wanted to exist
    And was asked about the name of everything.
His mouth
    His nose
The socket
    Of his eye

He first found its name
  But very little more.
Only he couldn't name any longer
  The name of the lips of his mouth.
So he couldn't really speak,
  And thus they honoured him.'

> *The Popol Vuh*, lines 4659–4674

I read these lines as a history of the Mayan hieroglyphs, the
bones of the ancient fathers. The writing was hieroglyphic in
order that it both remain hidden and yet be a complete record,
or skeleton, of the ancient wisdom put there with foresight in
Classic times, in preparation for a future reassembling. When
Hunter and Jaguar Deer reassemble their fathers, only part of
their power returns. The text reads,

'And they left the heart of their father.
  "It will just be left at Dusty Court
And here you will be called upon
  In the future,"
His sons then said to him.
  Then his heart was consoled.
"First will one come to you.
  And first also will you be worshipped
By the light born,
  The light engendered,
Your names will not be lost."'

> *The Popol Vuh*, lines 4675–4685

Henceforth, throughout the post-Classic era and the Spanish era, Classic Mayan writing enters a disassembled form,
those who know of it disguised as poor but bringing the Great
Idea nevertheless. 'Your names will not be lost' echoed down
the ages.

I saw that the bones of the ancient wisdom of the Classic
Maya are disassembled today amongst the various Mayan
groups. When the Classic shamans disappeared at the advent
of Baktun 10, they left each Mayan group an instruction and a

counsel for them to keep. The Quiché Maya had been given an enigmatic history of the Classic Mayan era, and a cryptic history of the hieroglyphic writing. This ancient counsel was later written as *The Popol Vuh*, the Book of Counsel, in Roman script to ensure its survival for the day when it would be needed. The Yucatec Maya, in turn, had been given a Short Count and had left written documents, the *Books of Chilam Balam*, which made it possible for us to 'read' such a count today and cast back accurately through all the cycles of the Long Count, confirming its origins and destiny and, when the time was right, the content which the Mayas themselves saw in their ancient writing. The means of examining a subsequent reappearance of Ahau had been conscientiously prepared centuries ago.

The Mayas in Chiapas had remembered Classic Mayan kinship systems, and the Maya in Guatemala the ancient day count and sacred cycle of 260 days. The theoretical reassembling of these counsels, and those remembered by the more than twenty Mayan groups, was a prerequisite for understanding the body of Classic Mayan thought as a whole. The counsels had been put there, originally, a thousand years ago, precisely for this eventual purpose.

This reading of a section of *The Popol Vuh* opened a wide window through which I could catch a glimpse of the still unfulfilled destiny of the Classic Mayan vision and the shamanic power it enshrined. The Yucatec Maya counsel, written as the *Books of Chilam Balam*, and the count of time they record, add to this. They demonstrate the nature of the power which the ancient Mayan shamans had conjured into temporary one-thousand-year 'invisibility'. Without the Long Count, and without the Yucatec Maya Short Count, the Kahlay Katunob, which was its continuation, the story of Mayan writing would be confined to the realms of legendary thought, a magnificent intellectual and poetic edifice based on mythological premises – the struggle of Good and Evil, shamanism and sorcery, life and death, and the promise of an eternal return.

But the Mayan count of time, carved on imperishable stone and kept without break in its stride for more than two thousand years at least, shows us that the power the Classic Maya shamans commanded was a science of time, an *actual* ability to contemplate their skeletons and really exit from time, to abolish duration and foresee millennia. This was their power, a gift from God, an orientation for the people based on sound reason and conviction, not faith alone.

Sufficient decipherments of the ancient Mayan count have been made for it to be possible to show that the first Mayan *abuelos* must have had a real ability to exit from time as we understand it:

> The Spanish occupation in 1539 and the definitive foundation of Mérida coincided with the beginning of Katun XI Ahau, traditionally the beginning of a Short Count cycle of 256 years.

> The 'collapse' of the Classic Maya Long Count stela cult and the desertion of religious centres such as Copan, Tikal, Palenque etc, during the ninth century AD coincided with the inaugural period of Baktun 10 in the Long Count. This cycle presaged a new world, 'a change of clothes'. Disassembled, the Classic Maya world disappears.

> Nevertheless, the colonial Books of Counsel written down two *baktuns* (800 years) later record two Long Count dates which demonstrate the continuing command by anonymous Yucatec Maya scribes of the entire Long Count. The two dates given are

> 3 (*baktuns*) 15 (*katuns*) 0 (*tuns*) 0 (*uinals*) 0 (*kin*)

> and

> 4 (*baktuns*) 15 (*katuns*) 0 (*tuns*) 0 (*uinals*) and 0 (*kin*)

> (*Chilan Balam of Chumayel,* pages 79 and 83).

When subtracted from 11.15.0.0.0 (1519) which is the relevant base date given in the same text, used because it marked first contact with the Spanish, the two dates yield 8.0.0.0.0 or Baktun 8, and 7.0.0.0.0 or Baktun 7.

11.15.0.0.0.	11.15.0.0.0.
3.15.0.0.0.	4.15.0.0.0.
8.0.0.0.0.	7.0.0.0.0.

According to Sylvanus G. Morley, who worked out these correlations, these two *baktuns*, Baktun 8 and Baktun 7 respectively represent when the Maya first began to record their 'skeleton' on stone, and when this chronology (the Long Count) was first developed.

That the colonial Mayan scribe, writing in the *Chilam Balam of Chumayel*, could tell us so much with two obscure references is a stunning accomplishment – time transcribed into mathematical riddles which presume a considerable *a priori* knowledge of the Mayan system by the reader in order to be understood. He, or she, must be 'one who knows'. Deciphered, the riddles show us the unbroken symmetry of the Mayan Long Count well into the Spanish era. Casting back from the arrival of Hernán Cortéz in Mexico in 1519, an extraneous event equivalent to the landing of Martians in London, the Mayan scribe was able to see how such an event fitted perfectly within the Long Count which had been worked out and inscribed on stone hundreds of years earlier. Reading forward from 1519 the scribe could see, confirmed in the irrefutable count prepared by the ancient *abuelos*, that such an event had been built into the system in advance. 1519 was the first announcement of a new world coming. Exactly a *katun* later and Katun XI Ahau at that, the Spanish arrived in the Yucatan to stay. This was not faith alone that the ancient shamans had left the sons of the ruins. This was conviction based on objective examination, by number, count and reason, of the ancient, inherited texts. The sons had been left a science of time, a history of the future, inscribed on stone.

The Long Count of 13 *baktuns* completes itself on a day, 24 December 2011 AD. The Mayas today speak of the end of this present world around the year 2000 AD. The few years' margin is referred to humorously in Mayan as the 'beak of time'.

It is recognized by Mayanists today that the Long Count cycle was worked out backwards from this date in 2011 AD, time as seen in a mirror. In dream walk the ancient shamans actually exited from temporal duration and came forward several *baktuns*, to the end of the thirteenth. From this vantage point they *saw* time backwards, they saw the worlds to come and understood their destinies. From here they worked out mathematical matrices for these worlds, number, count, and reason, uncovering their hidden symmetry in time and they inscribed this pure vision on the Long Count stones. Because they actually *saw* time backwards they were able to write it down forwards with no error in the count of forthcoming worlds.

The vision of succeeding generations 'was chipped'. The Mirror 'clouded over' so that they could only *see* a little way forward. The Long Count was to be a progressive revelation to them. They could only understand the next cycle coming as it was recorded by the *abuelos* on stone texts, as its meanings were progressively revealed to them in dream, 'an idea amongst ideas'. But they knew that the ancient signs 'not all of which they could understand' as fray Diego de Landa put it, contained succeeding futures as well. They were hidden in the night writing still to find a reader. 'Only hiding his face is the reader of it.'

An account, a history of each world to come until the completion of Baktun 13 in the Long Count was inscribed on stone, to be seen in the future. And not just by Mayans. Bishop Landa was given statements when he did not understand but which scholars, hundreds of years later, did. They turned them and unlocked the basic Mayan calendar. Likewise, seemingly vague dates in the colonial Mayan books actually contain vital clues to the purpose of Mayan writing, clues dormant for centuries but put there in order to awaken. The same was true of the more ancient hieroglyphs, perfectly designed both to record the truth and hide the reading of it until someone, in dream walk, was given the right question and idea. Ahau was, and is, spokesman for a system of oracular writing.

I realized that don Pablo had been working within this ancient tradition. He was now adding key oral counsels. Like the traditional Mayan scribes, he said a great deal succinctly, while appearing to say little. He had explained the theory and purpose of ancient Mayan writing and I had nearly missed seeing it. He had been talking backwards, from the future, and he had been saying quietly, yet very insistently, that Mayan writing contained a future reading, worked out millennia ago. This was now due to appear, at the close of the Long Count.

Ahau was the first sign to appear to me in dream. Don Pablo said, 'Yes, truly the voice came from there to hear, to see that it is as I have explained it. But you will never understand how the *abuelos* did that, how they knew it would be Ahau first.'

I asked him if reading the spokesman glyph now meant it was going to be easier to read other glyphs. He thought for awhile and said, 'The same question does not necessarily give you reason with the other signs. Each time whoever put it there hid it. He knew which year, how many years, before it would be seen, before it would be understood by outsiders. He knew which year it would arrive. He knew the time when someone would study a little of it. What you can reach is what you can reach. The learning never ends. Now you have seen where the path lies. It never ends. You learn one sign, then another, and another, little by little.'

12

The Centre of the World

We set off in the early morning light from Saci (Valladolid), in the heart of the Yucatan, thirty miles east of Chichén Itza. By the already bustling marketplace there were small buses waiting to take people to outlying villages. We bought some Spanish sausage, a kilo of *tortillas*, tins of sardines and a few other necessities. Out in the backcountry away from the roads there were few stores and these limited in stock and many miles apart. Don Pablo carried his *mecapal* containing his hammock, ropes, a change of clothes and his water-gourd. His young son Fidel, on a first visit to the Mayan heartland, looked apprehensive, clutching his *mecapal*, barefoot as he preferred to be, gazing into the market stalls and shops as we waited for a bus to take us to the centre of the world.

We had come from Tulum to this peaceful, highly mannered town in order to begin mapping the sacred topography of the Mayan world. Francisco Montejo had been sent from Zama in the east to the west, to Chakanputun in Campeche, to read the stone and wood, to learn where and when to make his definitive entry into the Yucatan. This was how don Pablo had translated and explained some lines in my copy of the *Chilam Balam of Chumayel*:

'On the day of the first turkey,
On the day of Zulim Chan,

On the day of Chakanputun,
Look at the wood,
    Look at the stone,
Lose your consciousness,
    Gazing into the face of Katun XI Ahau.
XI Ahau
    Is the beginning of the reading,
Because it was this katun
    When the foreigners first arrived,
When they came,
    They came from the East.'

Merely exploiting the judicious opportunity of entering at Chakanputun in the correctly prescribed year, 1539, Francisco Montejo had learnt no more of the virtues, the secrets, inscribed on stone and wood. The consciousness had been lost to him. More than four hundred years later don Pablo was beginning our walk from the centre of the Mayan world. We planned to head south along the backbone of Indian country towards Xcacal la Guardia, the sacred village of the Cruzob Maya in Quintana Roo.

The centre of the world is marked by a stone Cross with night writing on it, don Pablo explained to me. This Cross is housed in a Mayan church a mile outside the village of Xocen, two leagues south of Saci, where we were waiting for the bus. The Mayas for ten leagues around are known as 'those of Xocen' because the Cross is very powerful. There are periodic visits, festivals and counsels given here. 'Xocen,' don Pablo explained to me, 'means that it is read or counted here. *Xoc* means count and read.'

I realized that he was referring to the old Mayan counsels and understood that the centre of the world is where they are given, or read, today. Shamanically speaking, this spot is where earth and sky meet, where God and man are in closest communion. From here space is extended outwards to the four quarters as the world is periodically destroyed and recreated.

A dilapidated, wooden-sided bus pulled up and people climbed aboard. Inside there were wooden seats packed closely together and no glass in the windows. The passengers were mostly Mayan women, shy at my presence. A couple of men hid their curious glances in our direction as I manhandled my rucksack aboard and sat crouched on one of the seats. In the Peruvian Andes I had travelled hundreds of miles like this, knees under my chin, surrounded by goats and chickens, ice-black night outside, narrow mountain roads, praying that the dog tired driver would not fall asleep. I was glad, this time, that I was in the tropics at sea level and only going a few miles.

We set off with a clatter through the dusty streets and were soon at the turn off onto the unpaved, white road to Xocen. Half an hour later we pulled up in the deserted square, a ruined Spanish church before us, a group of Mayan houses discreetly bordering the other three sides, hidden behind whitewashed stone walls. At a store don Pablo bought three candles and asked permission to visit the Cross and church which were a short distance outside the village. Don Pablo was known and highly respected in these parts, and there was no problem obtaining permission. The guardian of the church would be told of our visit and would meet us there.

We passed under the eye of the curious, along paths marked by stone walls on both sides, family compounds beyond. Three hundred yards later this began to give way to cleared ground, to cattle compounds and woods. There was no dense tropical forest here, only low savanna bush, interspersed with areas of shaded woods. It was mid-April, the height of the dry season, and in a few hours the temperature would soar into the nineties. Already iguanas and birds were beginning to settle into the crook of trees near water.

'Only mad dogs and Englishmen,' I said to Pablo, 'walk around in this weather.'

He laughed. 'And their Mayan guides,' he added.

We walked through the woods, don Pablo leading the way with Fidel. I brought up the rear, enjoying the clear path and the luxury of being able to look about me as I walked, settling into the endless miles to come with a great teacher and guide to explain them to me. Already I could feel us distancing ourselves from roads, noise and tension, slowing our mental rhythms to a seemingly stationary, eternal moment. Up ahead Fidel too was beginning to relax, asking his father a stream of questions in Mayan, absorbing the answers as they came, between footsteps. He was a sharp, witty talker, astute beyond his twelve years, penetrating in perception and observation like his father.

Soon we arrived on a wide avenue bordered on both sides by woods and the occasional *milpa*. It led directly to the church as few hundred yards away. This was small, a chapel really, distinguishable from an ordinary Mayan house only because it had a new tin roof covering an outer sanctuary. A 'steeple' painted blue, topped by a cross, rose above the inner, hidden sanctum. The outer area seemed to be for congregational purposes, just as the avenue we were walking on suggested the coming together of many people at this sacred, powerful place. As we approached I saw that there were benches along the low walls of the outer sanctuary, and a swept concrete floor. Candles, resting on a T-shaped stand before the inner sanctum, flickered and wavered as we settled down to wait for the guardian of the Cross.

He soon appeared from nowhere and everyone shook hands with great deliberation. He was a gentle, intense man of about fifty, dressed in patched working clothes, healthy and vigorous. He didn't seem put out by having to come here in mid-morning. If he was poor, he understood the wealth of time that is given to us. He helped us light the three candles which we had placed in readiness on the wooden T-shaped support in front of the inner sanctum.

We sat a while watching the candles flutter and go out in the light breeze, re-lighting them, talking to the guardian about the village and the surrounding area. He was visibly proud of the church, the new roof, the concrete floor, the strengthening of faith they represented. As we spoke in low tones, two women approached carrying a small child, feverish and crying. Glancing at us, murmuring a greeting, they entered the inner sanctum. Placing the child before the Cross they knelt to pray for her health.

I watched them taking careful note of the Cross and its two companions. The main Cross was unmistakably stone, granite even. It seemed to emerge from a solid, tiled altar three feet high. The Cross itself was only two feet high, dressed in a *huipil* obscuring the night writing carved on it. Flowers were scattered before it and it was covered with necklaces of silver coins, small wooden crosses, wax figures and small pieces of coloured paper. The other two crosses I could see were dressed in the same fashion, but they were wooden, portable crosses, probably carried in the numerous processions which begin their walk here.

The inner sanctum was dark and cool, a simple place of worship reminiscent of the Temple of the Cross at Palenque in its mood and sacredness. The suffering child stopped crying and the women kept on praying in low whispers. Periodically they closed index finger and thumb into an O–shape, kissed their thumbnail loudly and repeatedly, crossed themselves and carried on praying.

Twenty minutes later they emerged, the little girl sound asleep. They nodded to us, spoke a few words to the guardian and then set off back to the village. After they had gone, don Pablo and I took our shoes off and the three of us entered the centre of the world, kneeling before the Cross, while the guardian waited outside. Don Pablo and Fidel began praying in Mayan, a chant of words repeated and varied, punctuated by the curious kissing of the thumbnail I had just witnessed with the two women.

After we had prayed in front of the crosses for a quarter of an hour or so, spiritually preparing for the walk to come, we made a slow move. We thanked the guardian for giving us his time, praised the new roof and floor and exchanged ritual pleasantries. We left a few pesos for a mass to be said by the village shamans and said our goodbyes. We walked back towards Xocen, but before arriving turned south along a clear, wooded trail. Half a mile along this we stopped to talk and adjust our equipment.

I asked don Pablo if there were still unknown Books of Counsel in these parts. 'Yes,' he said, 'there is one at Kanxoc, another at Xocen and, well, those papers still exist here.'

'And people read them here, as counsels amongst the people?'

'Those who have them will be reading them. The idea has always remained. That is what serves them. But it is better to leave it to the children rather than write it down. If they want to learn then they will understand it quickly. Also if you are speaking the counsels, they keep them in their hearts, not just their minds. It isn't important to leave a lot of papers now.'

'But do the shamans read the books to the people, don Pablo?' I persisted.

'Well, if they do not read them so that people hear them giving the counsels, no one is going to have a good counsel. They will just do what they think. And then afterwards they discover it isn't what they were given to do.'

I thought this over for a while, tugging and re-adjusting the straps of my rucksack.

'Reading those books aloud, don Pablo, is like hearing a song. It has the rhythms of song. So that what is written is what was spoken or sung long ago. There was no difference. Maybe then, in the old days, it was the same with the hiero-glyphs? People would hear the songs and then be thinking and thinking about them. Then one day they would be given an idea and would also see it written on the stones. But, just like us, they wouldn't know how that was, how the *abuelos* did that.'

Don Pablo was listening to me attentively, occasionally saying a few words to Fidel, who was squatting in the middle of the trail, resting. He absorbed my suggestion and then said, 'Yes, it was a prayer they were all singing and hearing. Those were their prayers there on the stones and they were waiting for the blessing to arrive, to see, to have an orientation. But before, we don't know if what is said is true. It is like observing a story that enters your head and as you are young, you are just walking, you don't notice what is happening. But then the time arrives to recognize it. Then it is like waking up to see. And what you see leaves you astonished. Little by little you learn to see quickly. How do you learn to see, to know what is going to happen tomorrow and the next day? That is the great virtue that the *abuelos* put there so that it is not forgotten – how Our Lord left it for us to look after the world. Because the writing is for that, to look after the world, to pray for salvation in the world, to live another eight days. That is the purpose of the writing, don Ricardo.'

Don Pablo was so open in his statements now that I felt overwhelmed by the depth and scale of his knowledge. Here we were at the centre of the world. In every direction he knew villages, people and their histories. In one village, Xuilub, eight leagues from Xocen, they still speak old Maya, don Pablo told me, in another village, Tixhualatun, they sing their words rather than speak them. In one village they keep the dance of the *tunkul*, the shaman's drum, while in yet another there is a great shaman, an Old One, who knows many of the most effective medicines of before.... The list went on and on, covering the ten leagues around the Cross at Xocen. I felt that the notes we were writing and the map we were drawing would merely be a first counsel and orientation for outsiders.

We set off again, hoping to cover six leagues before sunset. The light danced in the heat at eleven o'clock in the morning, and the path we were following was clear of rocks and trees. We padded along, through woods and across recently burnt *milpas*. Stripped of trees and bushes, these *milpas* offered no protection from the heat and we moved across the blackened soil and the bleached white limestone landscape in a daze, eager to reach the far side without delay. From time to time don Pablo called a halt to point out animal tracks, ruins and vultures circling over unknown prey.

Every league or so, every hour of walking, we passed through small villages. Often these were no more than a gathering of three households around a well or a *cenote*. Here in the Yucatan Brahmin cattle abounded, corralled behind stone stockades, given pride of place in the shade. Don Pablo told me that twenty years before such cattle were allowed to wander free since there were no rustlers in these parts. There were no roads that gave access to the Mayan heartland. Now, however, all cattle had to be penned and many Mayas, who owned a few head of cattle only, had elected either to slaughter or to sell them.

In truth I was being shown a world in transformation. Before the coming of the white roads, now slicing through the Yucatan from all directions, linking backcountry areas to towns such as Saci, Tizimin and Chan Santa Cruz, this had been an entirely separate Mayan world with the Indians only rarely going to the Spanish towns for the *fiestas* or markets. Since the Fight, don Pablo told me, there had been no large haciendas here, the land held in *ejidos* by the people, the government a faraway dark cloud. You could buy a whole pig for fifty pesos, a turkey for twenty. People had been truly self-sufficient, even making their own buckets from the bark of the *choy* tree and rope from the *henequen* plant which abounded all about.

There had been no doctors, no schools, no police, no soldiers. There had been no robberty, no violence, no interference of one by another, no taxes and no bosses. I asked how people saw this in those days. Did they feel deprived and neglected? Was their undeniable poverty abject and without dignity? 'No,' don Pablo said, 'people were happy, they were very happy. There was food and work for everyone, there was a place for everyone, there was peace and liberty.' He said this with great feeling. 'They even had dances out here with musicians and everything,' he added, his eyes alive with the memory of them.

Now in the houses there were plastic buckets, soft-drink bottles, store-bought shoes and signs of visits by government surveyors and paramedical teams seeking to eradicate malaria and Dengue fever. There were schools and medical centres in the villages linked by white road to the Spanish towns, and there were basketball courts and concrete, breezeblock government houses built to standard design, squat and out of place. Still, Pablo told me, people were happy and they welcomed the roads and the merchandise they brought. They could get their agricultural produce to market quickly without the backbreaking labour of walking it through the backcountry. People had more money in their pockets than before, and the children were going to school and were learning to read and write Spanish. When people became sick they could more readily receive medical attention. He thought for a few seconds and added, 'Of course if they die anyway then the family has also lost months of income and are poorer than if they had just gone to the *h-men*.'

I asked whether the *h-menob* resented our kind of medicine which reduced everything to physical terms. He said they did not, because people went to the shamans first and they suggested if they should see a doctor. You paid a shaman with a chicken, a bottle of *aguardiente*, some tobacco. They never took so much as to impoverish you. They were men of good heart. Also, if they asked a lot in payment, people would begin to believe and say that they caused the illness, that they were sorcerers. Doctors were advised if the sick person needed surgery, if the sickness was seen as a physical disorder not curable by spiritual or herbal means. But surgery cost thousands of pesos and few could afford it. Equally pills and medicines in bottles cost a lot, don Pablo said, and often it was old, useless rubbish which had found its obscure way to the provinces. He shrugged and said, 'If your hour has arrived and God calls for you, what else can you do but go to Him?'

At one o'clock we stopped to rest, drenched in perspiration, by a well at a *rancho* called Chac Pat. An enormous *ceiba* towered above us and nestling amongst its exposed roots, we soon cooled down. Recovering, we prepared a few sardines and *tortillas* for lunch. It was too hot to eat with any appetite and we chewed slowly, saying little, going back over the miles we had come.

The *rancho* seemed deserted but I knew that unseen eyes

were watching us from the houses. Soon the women began to appear, ostensibly to fetch water, but really to examine this strange travelling party. Travellers often passed through these parts, muleteers, swine-herders, and *milperos* on their way to Saci. But very rarely, if ever, did blond, blue-eyed white people venture out here amidst the heat and scarcity of country life. Children clutched at their mothers' *huipiles,* wide-eyed at my presence, while the women giggled and muttered by the well, casting surreptitious glances our way. They asked where we came from and where we were headed – standard first questions, always to be answered truthfully when passing through an *ejido* distinct from one's own.

While we chatted to the women, explaining that I wasn't an engineer sent by the government or a prospector of secret treasures, I examined them more closely. Even in the middle of their working day they wore immaculately clean *huipiles*, embroidered by hand with exotically coloured flowers. The women's hair was neatly combed and tied back from the neck, and they all wore gold drop earrings, necklaces and plastic shoes. They were exquisitely mannered, copper elegant and petite, quick to smile and hold their own against these strange men. Although their husbands were away on the *milpas* I noticed no fear of us, only shyness. Even in this feeling they sensed no displacement by men. They seemed utterly secure in their world, more subtle than men, shy only because people naturally are that way inclined.

After we had rested and refilled the water-gourds we set off again, following a trail through woods and across a smouldering *milpa*. In the distance I could hear the clop clop of an axe on a cedar trunk. I could see birds wheeling and circling above. Even if the pulse of Mayan life was quickening erratically, a new life or death for these people, a milpero's way remained unchanged in its essentials, governed by seasonal rather than economic cycles.

About three o'clock we arrived at the village of San Juan. Here don Pablo had a friend from the old *chiclero* days and we stopped by his *rancho* on the outskirts. He was at home sawing a tree trunk into planks to make a table. He had his workshop under a rudimentary *guano* palm shelter outside his house. We squatted down to rest and watch him work, the conversation warming minute by minute as we passed through initial ritual exchanges. Don Pablo's friend sawed back and forth as the moment unfolded, seemingly immune to both heat and exertion.

As don Emilio worked he began telling us about a ruin a few hundred yards away, 'a town of the *abuelos*'. I realized that for these people this would be the only reason they could fathom for my presence. No one in his right mind would walk these trails just for the walk. I feigned interest although, in truth, I had seen so many ruins by now that the shade we were in seemed a more agreeable place to be. Still, the ruin obviously fascinated this man and the people of his village, and I decided to go and see for myself.

As we were leaving, don Emilio's father, a half deaf, toothless *abuelo* with the wispy beard of a Chinaman, bounded from the house. He wore a simple, collarless, white shirt, *culex* trousers tied at the knees, and rough-cut pieces of rubber, tied with string, for sandals. He asked if I spoke Mayan and when I said, 'Only a little,' he laughed and laughed as if it was inconceivable that I could know anything at all if I didn't speak it. I warmed to him immediately.

We set off across the village and along a path leading to a *milpa*. Crossing this we stood before a pile of rubble twenty feet high.

'This was the lord's house,' the *abuelo* said. 'Over there is the market place of the ancients, the house mounds and some walls.'

I looked impressed amongst the veritable crowd of people that had appeared suddenly. The *abuelo*, his son, don Pablo, Fidel, and I scrambled up the lord's house. From here we could see a half mile across broken rock, scrub bush and *milpa*. I took the old man's point – this was the highest mound on the site and thus the lord's house.

As I took pictures don Pablo and Fidel examined the surrounding countryside, counting the number of mounds to be seen from this high place. Suddenly the *abuelo* began dancing up and down, talking excitedly about the music he heard coming from these ruins at night. When I grinned, more at his antics than his words, he grew adamant.

'I have heard it,' he announced to the gathered multitude below. He proceeded to give a rendition of the nocturnal music of the ancients. It sounded suspiciously like contemporary *jaranas* to me but I dropped the point. He had heard it, I had not.

I asked the *abuelo* if he would mind me taking a picture of him, here, high on the lord's house. He stopped his dancing, stood to attention and said, as the shutter flashed, 'I wish I was wearing my other sandals.'

At dusk we arrived at the *rancho* of a very old, much respected friend of don Pablo's. Together they had worked *chicle*-gathering for many seasons, sharing shelter and food out in the forest during the months of hard rain. It was five years since they had seen each other and don Pablo was eager to learn if don Pepe and his family were well. We had walked five or six leagues, a hungry and exhausted trio. I was as keen as Pablo to find a place to tie our hammocks.

Don Pepe's *rancho* straddled an important crossroads in the Mayan trail system which crisscrosses the Yucatan. Certain nodal points exist in this system. At these points numerous trails converge and depart. Mapping these points and the trails that lead from them opens up the entire Mayan heartland. The people who live at such places serve as important communicators amongst the people, collating the news that is brought to them from the four directions and passing it on to successive travellers in turn. The efficiency and rapidity of this system is astonishing, the people's awareness of what is happening several days' journey away unparalleled in detail and observation by newsprint or radio.

While we rested at the *rancho*, watching don Pepe feeding his pigs, chickens, and turkeys, his wife prepared buckets of hot water for us to bathe in. I was utterly exhausted, happy that we had worked the day to its fullest, to the limits of my endurance. Fidel was propped up against the side of the house, a *jicara* of water forgotten in his hands, his toughened bare feet hardly the worse for the day's walk. He was listening to the two older men deep in conversation. Their masks of inarticulate Indian were cast aside here, miles into their own world. The conversation could go on for three or four hours at a time, drawing strands from a richly textured literacy we know nothing about.

Don Pepe was not, by race, very Mayan. This was unimportant. He was a *mayero* living the Mayan way, speaking Mayan as his mother tongue, and only a little Spanish. He was a Mayan in Mayan eyes, respected because he knew how to look after the land, keeping the proper *costumbres*, frugal with himself, generous with others. He led us across his compound to a small thatched storehouse where there was plenty of room for the three of us to hang our hammocks. In the dark corner I could see a *xux* basket employed for bringing calabash and maize from the *milpa*. Don Pepe bustled around making sure we were happy and comfortable.

I lay back, sandals off, and swung myself back and forth in the hammock. Outside nocturnal birds, the *puruhuy*, were calling and I could hear the wind swishing the trees in the distance long before it arrived at the *rancho*. The buckets of hot water were ready now and one by one we scrubbed and picked the occasional ticks off legs and arms. We changed into fresh clothes, our faces revived.

Later we wandered over to the main house and sat on the rocks outside, waiting for the call to dinner. It was to be simple fare, Spanish sausage heated on the hot coals of the fire, fresh golden *tortillas*, beans, chilli, salt and lemon. There was sweet, cool water to drink with it and honey in the coffee that followed. The three of us ate first, sitting at table while don Pepe talked on, helping his wife with the flow of *tortillas* coming our way.

Their family had all grown up and moved away to nearby *ranchos*, marrying and seeking their own paths. The dancing and music of before had stopped, the occasional wild sessions of drinking all night with visiting muleteers and other travellers were no longer a temptation. Travellers still lodged here and the old couple still gave life to *rancho* and *milpa* and received life from these. The white road by-passed their firmly traditional lives.

In the morning, at 6 a.m., we gathered our counsel for the day. A day of rest was unanimously agreed on. Don Pepe wanted us to stay longer, to converse and help him decipher the titles he had just received for his land. Until recently he had been in the same position as don Pablo, working on land which was only *solicitado* or 'requested'. Now he had been attached to the nearest *ejido* and had received papers saying so. The government was evidently going from place to place sorting out and finalizing long-standing requests and disputes. I read out the terms of the agreement to don Pepe while Pablo explained the difficult passages in Mayan.

After we had breakfasted we wandered around the *rancho* examining the *cenote* overhung by a large *ramon* tree which emerged from the depths below. A limestone section, forty or fifty feet across, had collapsed long ago, exposing a small *cenote* thirty feet below. Around this a great deal of fertile soil had collected and don Pepe had planted bananas in it. Periodically he shinned down the *ramon* tree and collected the harvest.

The compound of the *rancho* covered three acres and was enclosed by stone walls on three sides and by a *pak chac* on the fourth. This was a means of fencing by cutting young saplings low down and bending them over. As they continued to grow they wove in and out of each other, becoming stronger and stronger until they presented a wall of foliage and thick wood.

The compound was swept clean and dotted with small huts containing saddles, tools, another maize storehouse, a pig enclosure and roosts for chickens and turkeys. It was a small universe, twenty miles from the world. In the fresh, renewed morning light the sounds were entirely rustic; a distant lowing of cattle, a dissatisfied pig grunt, turkeys gobbling in unison. There was a sparkling clarity to the light, a breathtaking brilliance of colour.

Fidel examined the scene from a more practical perspective, sitting on the edge of the *cenote*.

'I think I prefer fishing,' he said. 'Life out here is too hard.'

Don Pepe and don Pablo were busy talking about the land, rising prices, the market value of pork and beef, this year's *milpa*, building a new house, the weather. They were topics as ancient as the bird song all about us. Waiting for a lull in the discourse, I asked don Pepe what the people around here thought of the changes being wrought. I knew from his land titles that he had lived in this forest world for over thirty years and his opinion would be wise and considered, more valuable than years of fieldwork by an outsider.

Don Pepe told me that most people welcomed the roads, the attachment to a wider world, the opportunities for seasonal work other than keeping milpa. They also wanted to learn to speak, read and write Spanish. They wanted a part in the future of Mexico.

'In other words,' I said, 'they want to be equal with other working Mexicans.'

'They want to be on a par with them.' Both don Pepe and don Pablo corrected me, using the Spanish word *parejo* rather than *igual*.

Don Pepe began to elaborate on the point that he was trying to make. 'They say that if people are going to come here, to establish themselves then they must respect those from here, respect what they have done and what they are. If they just come here and scoff at our language and *costumbre* and put themselves here just like kings then it is not so good. We should be *parejo*. They can work over there, where there is a place for them, and we can work over here. We can give them help and they can help us also. That is as we have always wanted things here, without quarreling one with another. But they must respect what we are.'

Don Pepe hesitated, momentarily glancing at don Pablo.

'You see, those virtues which the *abuelos* left to us, the poor *campesinos*, so that we could live, so that we could search for a living, those virtues are not just toys to be played with, to be broken by children and thrown away. That is not how it is – they have their wisdom, their power also.'

Don Pepe's counsel was the same as don Pablo's previous statements to me, the same as that written on the stone for Katun XI Ahau 1539. At this twilight hour in the Long Count of time these people were evidently not about to betray what they had been for the last seven Baktuns at least. But I was depressed by the prospects. In some insidious fashion, when you put a bottle of sweet soft drink to your lips you also swallow all the poisoned black waters of the system that produces it. Still, the Mayas had four hundred years' experience of our dubious, crafty, sleight-of-hand ways and they were still here today, walking and talking the ancient Mayan way, far from demoralization, far from defeat by a materialism that now, changing costumes, seeks to seduce them away from God.

'But do you think that the government really cares about the people here?' I asked. 'Do you think they know anything about what the Mayas want?'

'That is what we don't know,' don Pepe said. 'Perhaps those who don't even know the names of the trees and the plants want to come here and tell us what to do again. Perhaps also they want to help us but don't really understand how. We do not know, we are just seeing what they do.'

Don Pepe thought for a while, gazing out across the chasm over the *cenote*. Slowly he added, 'It is good that a counsel be put there. It should be written. Then we will be able to see a little further, see a little of what is coming to us here.'

13

Crossed Signs and a Body

It seemed for countless days we walked from village to village, *rancho* to *cenote*. Out in the backcountry, the pace of walking determined the pace of time and a league seemed many miles. In fact we walked two days south of don Pepe's, rested, walked another day, taking short side trips and long conversational rest stops. Every step was a step into an undisclosed, hidden world, close to God.

'I don't understand don Pepe and some of these other Mayans we have stayed with,' I said at one of our resting places. 'Even though they are so poor they refuse any money for our stay.'

'That is how they are saying you are their friend. If they come to Tulum, or to visit you, then you do the same for them.'

'Yes, but they know it is unlikely that they will visit me. They could accept some pesos from me and still be friends.'

'That is not the point. It is an idea, a principle that there is amongst us. But you must always ask how much something costs – to stay somewhere, to eat. Then if they want they will say "Nothing" or "Twenty pesos" or whatever they feel. It is up to them.'

After a while I said, 'They call that idea "reciprocity" in anthropology, don Pablo.'

'Reciprocity,' he repeated, carefully spelling it out in his field notes.

We walked on, past *ranchos* and *milpas*. The earth was deep red here, ash covered where *milpas* had been burnt. In places tree trunks still smouldered and the limestone stood out nakedly against the barren landscape. It was hard to imagine that in a few weeks, with the coming of the rains, all would be lush green again.

In the woods the foliage withdrew in the heat, turning brown and offering less and less protection from the relentless sun. Numerous varieties of cactus stood out now, growing from cracks in the rocks and nooks in trees. Some were six foot high, some mere inches. They evoked an impression of a semi-desert world where lizards and iguanas, vultures and snakes thrived in the shimmering heat. Occasionally the bright red flowers of a tree and the deep cream, strongly scented *turuhuy nicté* offered momentary respite. Around *cenotes* the tropical vision returned with shaded fruit groves of orange, mango and banana, tall *ceibas, ramon* and hanging vine.

We rested in the coolness of such places, in the shadows of torn down haciendas, passing through unknown, unseen ruined sites, amidst tales of caves with writing, idols, temples and hidden treasures. We met hunters, a girl on her way to get married with father and family accompanying her, a proud man on horseback, mules and their owners, *milperos* and *abuelos*.

Our party presented a strange spectacle, but we were well greeted everywhere we went. There was a place for us every night. Sometimes it was a house on a *milpa* near the trail where dusk had caught us. Sometimes it was in someone's house in a village, our hammocks slung alongside the family's. Sometimes it was a native church, or a deserted house kept up for visitors. We were always offered water, salt, *tortillas*, beans, and perhaps eggs or sweet potato.

The evenings passed in conversation, two hours, three hours, people sleeping an hour or two, getting up, talking, going back to sleep, getting up and going out to hunt or to the *milpa* before dawn. Just as the Mayas like to work intermittently, carrying out a multiplicity of tasks as the spirit moves them, so they seem consciously to cultivate the active use of the dreaming hours, never simply dividing them off from daylight or succumbing to their oblivion.

My respect for this world and the civilization that had cultivated it grew daily. The manners, the low tones of speech, the measured thoughts, so obviously carefully crafted by philosophical people, the evident happiness of the households, these piled impression upon impression in my mind and Fidel's. Because I was with two Mayan friends my reception was more at ease that it would otherwise have been. But even if I'd arrived alone, don Pablo told me, these were Christian people and there was nothing to fear from them. 'They are your friends, people of good heart', he said.

In my notes I wrote of the great variety of subjects don Pablo discussed with our hosts, and of the impression I had that an extraordinary amount of knowledge of the past is present amongst these people. Don Pablo, I saw, was but one amongst many living Mayan scholars. Indeed it seemed that here also different villages and localities preserved particular *costumbres*, distinct from those of other villages – disassembled. This was the case especially amongst the older Mayan villages and in areas around major ruined cities where, more likely than not, the people living in their shadows are the great-grandchildren of the original occupants. Because the Yucatec Maya resisted Spanish linguistic incursions and forced migrations so effectively, a sacred topography is still in place here, an implicit Mayan space we have never known. Without school, without Spanish, these Indians have kept the essence of their ancient learning way, a stunningly competent ability to grasp an idea and develop it into modes never perceived by us.

Amongst these *campesinos* there are great thinkers, great

shamans also, who can talk for hours without using one word
of Spanish, who can speak old Mayan and have a deep
knowledge of the purest Classic Mayan universe of discourse.
It was this universe which produced the *Books of Chilam Balam*
and, indeed, the hieroglyphs themselves, and it is only by
replacing these within it that we can hope to appreciate their
yet-to-be-dreamed meanings. The hieroglyphs are ideograms – in some still incomprehensible fashion the ideas they
contain appear as we return the stone to the centre of the mat
and settle down to hear the many explanations of the living
spokesmen.

Even while we were walking in terrain which was markedly
different from the forest of Quintana Roo, don Pablo's knowledge of birds and plants remained as detailed as ever. He
pointed out several herbal cures, the *pinta* tree from which the
ancients made the ink for their books, the *barbra chi'ich* bird
which warned travellers of danger ahead, the *chipitin* insect
whose screeching in the forest announces where there is water.
At any given place don Pablo could continue in this vein for
half an hour at least, breaking off when the listeners became
distracted by something happening around them.

We spent a night in the Indian church at Santa Rosa.
Arriving at dusk we waited outside the house of one of the
village leaders until the heat and potentially harmful spirits we
were bringing from the bush vanished. Then don Pablo
inquired about a resting place for the night. We were led to the
church in the centre of the village by a *cenote*. It was a simple
sanctuary, a *guano*-thatched, wooden building, distinguishable
from the other houses dotted about the square by its situation
rather than by any outward features.

The three of us lit candles and crossed ourselves before
unpacking hammocks and settling in for the night. From out
of the darkness a little venison, beans and *tortillas* appeared, and
some water. A half dozen villagers gathered to watch and
await our story. This was the time to do things properly.
There is a way of tying a hammock, keeping it folded over the
shoulder while the first end is tied, using a knot which won't

slip but can be untied easily. There is a way of folding and tying the 'arms' of a hammock so that the individual cords do not become snarled. People always watched very carefully to see whether I had learnt such rudimentary skills. But everything was in good humour.

Late in the evening, after people had returned to their houses, don Pablo and I sat outside the church, discussing the walk and the stars, listening to the cicadas and the sleeping village. Tomorrow we would be back in Quintana Roo, back in Cruzob country. Don Pablo asked me, 'What do you believe in, don Ricardo? Are you a Christian, let us say?'

I knew that he had wanted to ask me this question before but for some reason had not. At the same time I had not rushed to offer him an unsolicited answer, wondering what I would say when the time came. As it was I said, 'Well, I started out walking as a Christian but then I saw some things which didn't make sense. There in Peru there were altars of gold as tall as that tree.' I pointed to a twenty-foot tree in the nearby darkness. 'And all the poor begging on the streets outside. That was a great deception to eleven-year-old eyes. Since then I have never looked inside a church for something to believe in.'

Don Pablo thought about these words in silence, considering their implications. A reformation of the church in the Yucatan had been a very important motivation for the Fight of before. Since then the Mayas had worked openly with their own prayermakers, their own churches, their own word. Don Pablo's faith was strong, hard to explain to twentieth-century man. In all my conversations with don Pablo he was always certain to place God at the centre of the equation. If I strayed onto atheistic premises he brought the conversation back again and again. 'It is only intelligible in terms of God,' he said. That was his faith, his observation.

'Yes,' don Pablo said, 'That is a deception that they do. They say to the poor, "You must be more faithful, you must give us more before you get well." But that is a deceit. You see here, where we have no priests from the Church, where we have our own *h-menob* and prayermakers, you see here that people are healthy, people are happy. There is just enough to eat. There is freedom. That is because the *h-menob* know how to pray, they know how to work, how to take care of everyone.'

Listening to the sounds of the village, thinking about don Pablo's observation, I took out a sheet of paper. Unfolding it, I placed it on the ground before us. On it were six hieroglyphs, signs from the Uinal, which I had been working on. Continuing with the idea that the internal place value of the twenty signs was important in reading the ideas hidden within them, I had assembled the hieroglyphs in a pattern according to their place in the cycle of twenty.

Working with the established meanings for these glyphs* I had begun to examine their relationship to one another. Ahau and Imix were male and female, end and beginning, lips, breath, breasts and seed. They were to the west, where the sun enters the womb of the earth and begins its nocturnal journey through the underworld. The fifth sign, Chicchán, was associated with the serpent, the seer of the depths of the underworld. Opposite this sign in the Uinal cycle was Men, the fifteenth sign, associated with shamanism (as in *h-men*, 'one who knows') and with the eagle, the seer of the heart of the sky.

Seeing this connection between the fifth and the fifteenth signs in the Uinal, Chicchán and Men, reminded me of jaguar figures at an early Olmec (or Balam) archaeological site known today as La Venta. These figures, which it has been estimated were carved as early as 500 BC, represent jaguars, or the Balam lineage of shamans, with serpents' tongues and feathers for eyebrows. The idea expressed here, and in the Uinal, is that of the shaman's farseeing, paranormal sight. A shaman, like the sun, journeys into the underworld; he 'dies' and dream walks to the realm of shadows to gain wisdom, to

---

* See J. Eric S. Thompson, *Maya Hieroglyphic Writing*, University of Oklahoma Press, 1960.

Men

Ahau

Chuen

west

east

Imix

Oc

Chicchán

9 *Crossed signs and a body*

learn science. Equally a shaman walks to the heart of the sky, a waking dream through the *elon*, the stairway to the sky, to restore communication with God and the *abuelos*, to see the future, to be given the blessing, the sight which is then brought back to the community and shared.

In *The Popol Vuh* there is a reference to Quetzalcoatl, the Plumed Serpent of the Nahua civilization of central Mexico. The reference shows how the idea discussed above underpins the title and concept of the Plumed Serpent. Quetzalcoatl is the great shaman who can see far in front of himself, through mountains and into valleys, who can trace lost souls and remedy the world. The passage in *The Popol Vuh* reads

> 'Truly it was a spirit lord
>   That Quetzal Serpent became.
> For a week he climbed up to heaven,
>   And for a week he went to make the descent to Hell,
> And again for a week he became a serpent;
>   He actually changed into a serpent.
> And again for a week he made himself into an eagle.'

The Popol Vuh, lines 7759–7765

When I came to consider the tenth and the eleventh signs, Oc and Chuen, the emerging pattern became clear. Oc is foot (print) in Yucatec Maya, the verb *ocol* meaning 'to enter'. Here, halfway through the Uinal cycle of twenty signs, here to the east was the entering of the light, the journey to the sky, the shaman's dream walk to acquire paranormal vision. The next sign, Chuen is 'artisan' in Yucatec Maya. Together the two signs evoked don Miguel's phrase 'the movement of hand and foot', the casual statement he had made to me long before I saw it written here.

Working on the decipherment of these ideas hidden within the Uinal I had become convinced that I was seeing the origin of the Mayan system of writing as a whole. These twenty signs of the Uinal are inspired by and record the shaman's ecstatic dream walk to the spirit world. At the centre of the phenomenal body of knowledge recorded by Mayan hieroglyphic writing, the history of the future, the *abuelos* inscribed the learning way which they had employed in order to see the future, which they had employed in order to understand time in its entirety.

The hieroglyphs I knew were essentially a form of oracular writing – an Indian script developed in antiquity and inscribed on stone for all succeeding generations. As each world completed its destiny, a new word emerged from within the mysterious signs. But seeing this depended on the reader cultivating the dream-walking techniques central to shamanism. Even so the vision acquired from 'walking' to the spirit world, to the heart of the sky and the underworld, was not left to individual, mystical perception. It could be objectively examined by others according to number, count and reason within the immutably carved hieroglyphic system. I realized that if it had been given to me to see the relations between the six signs of the Uinal they must be appearing for a reason which could be discerned and examined by others, too – once the vision had been fleshed out.

Thinking about this, I noticed that the six signs on the paper before us referred in mysterious fashion to parts of the body – the mouth, the breast, the eye, the foot, the hand. Here was the Uinal spirit body beginning to reassemble itself and step forth.

Although no shaman can explain how or why he can, nevertheless, by the power that his thought receives from the supernatural divest his body of flesh and blood, so that nothing of it remains but the bones. He then has to name all the parts of his body, mentioning each bone by name; and for this he must not use ordinary language but only the special and sacred language of the shamans that he has learnt from his instructor. While seeing himself thus, naked and completely delivered from the ephemeral flesh and blood, he dedicates himself, still in the sacred language, to his great task, through that part of his body which is destined to resist, for the longest time, the action of sun, wind and weather. (Mircea Eliade, *Myths, Dreams and Mysteries*, p. 83)

The six signs pointed to the shamanic origin and purpose of Mayan writing. They simultaneously represented a Mayan epiphany. The six glyphs whose meaning had begun to appear formed a cross and referred to a spirit body. Here was the Cross of Our Lord, the destiny of Mayan scripture and simultaneously the shamanic origin. Here was Mayan Christianity emerging from within the oracular hieroglyphs as neatly as the unbroken count of Mayan time had predicted and presumed Old World chronology when the Mayas noted that the Spanish arrived on the first month, of the first year, of a Katun XI Ahau in the ancient count which they had inherited from their Classic *abuelos*. Here was a history of the future progressively revealed, the sign seen by Chilam Balam, the Great Idea behind the talking, Oracular Cross of the Cruzob Maya of Quintana Roo. The ancient *abuelos* had seen it all in advance millennia ago and they had written down the critical signs where one would expect to find them – at the very heart of the twenty signs of the Uinal, the spirit body that restores communication between heaven and earth.

Don Pablo had been busy examining the piece of paper I had placed on the ground. He had shown no surprise at its sudden appearance. He said, 'That is when Our Lord Jesus was born. That is when He gave us the orientation of how we are to take care of life. As you see the signs there . . . .' He pointed to the paper flat on the ground. 'That is how He separated each of us to our own place, to our own lands – whites, blacks, Mayas, Chinese – each one a different part of the world. This is a great orientation, it is a parable for people to understand. Here at the centre, at the crossroads, you are given your first movement. Your heartbeat is there at the centre. "Which way am I to walk?" you ask yourself. Only your heart tells you.

'And here all around,' he continued, his fingers circling the crossed signs, 'is the walk of Our Lord. When the world was prepared He walked the world like this, putting everything in its place, putting everything in order.'

'But who put it there, don Pablo? Who was the visionary who first arranged those signs?'

'No one put it there. It was put there by He who gave us blood, He who gave us heart, He who gave us life, He who gave us a body to walk the world in His footsteps.'

'So it was given to the shamans to see it only. It was given to them so that they could see what was coming and remedy the world?' I asked.

'Yes. It was given to them so that they would have a good counsel, so that they would know how to walk, how to look after the world.'

He took hold of the paper, raising it up vertically. 'And this was when Our Lord descended. The Son who came, He knew how it was going to be . . . that he was going to be crucified and everything. He knew it was so that the world could continue. First He walked the world. He prepared the underworld down here. He prepared Hell for those who had to go there, for the Nine Lords. Then He walked in the light until He arrived where He had begun. That was the walk of Our Lord, when He descended to prepare the world. Afterwards they took Him and nailed Him so that everyone could see what He had done. Only those who killed Him could not see it. The sign was there but they did not see it.'

I grew silent at his words. They reminded me that there was a passage of great importance in the *Books of Chilam Balam*, the meaning of which could only really be seen after the vision that had been given to us now. In fact it seemed that the original *xcriban* of the text knew when he prepared it at what time, what hour, it was to serve as a means of objectively examining such a vision, for many other Mayanists have translated and commented upon it without understanding its true significance.

'Thus spoke the first sage,
   Melchisedek,
The first prophet,
   Napuctun,
Sacerdote [priest]
   The first *ah kin*, Sun Priest.

This is the song,
   How the uinal was born,
Before the dawning of the world.
   He began to walk
By Himself alone.
   Then his maternal grandmother said,
Then His maternal aunt said,
   Then his paternal grandmother said,
Then his sister-in-law said,
   "What are we to say?
How is Man to be seen on the road?"
   So they spoke as they walked,
But there was no Man.
   Then they arrived at the east.
"Who has passed this way now?
   Here are His footprints,
Right here,
   Measure them with your foot."
This was according to the Word of the Cultivator
   of the World.
   And they measured the footstep of Our Lord.
He who is Holy God.
   This is the origin of the count of the whole world.'

Here was the dream walk of the Uinal personified as Our Lord – the prime mover in Mayan writing seen as the prime mover in Christianity – as Jesus Christ himself. Here was an ancient vision in the same tradition as don Pablo's words on the six glyphs before us. But the real key to this passage resided in the enigmatic mention of Melchisedek in the opening lines. Previously considered as merely a 'pious interpolation' by the Mayan *xcriban*, this reference actually reveals the hidden content of the Uinal. In Paul's Epistle to the Hebrews (v6) Jesus Christ is introduced with these words, 'Thou art a priest for ever after the order of Melchisedek.' Subsequently Melchisedek is spoken of as the priest who knew 'the first principles of the oracles of God'. He is a spiritual prototype for Christ, he is 'king of Salem,

king of righteousness, king of peace . . . having neither beginning of days nor end of life.'

We can see from these references that the Mayan scribe
writing,

> 'Thus spoke the first sage,
>   Melchisedek,
> The first prophet,
>   Napuctun,
> *Sacerdote* [priest]
>   The first *ah kin* . . .'

is referring to the way in which Jesus Christ emerges from the
New World priestly line of Napuctun just as Our Lord is
referred to in Old World scripture as being a priest for ever after
the order of Melchisedek. The scribe is saying that the ancient
shamanic scripture known to us as Mayan hieroglyphic writing
is as much Holy Word, Holy Scripture, in a Christian sense, as
the first principles of the oracles of God of which Melchisedek
was keeper and first priest. The Mayan *xcriban* was saying that
the Indians here at the centre of the New World had also
received Holy Writ through the shamans. Truly the shamans
had journeyed to the heart of Heaven, truly they had been given
the word, written into the signs of the Uinal.

I could see then that it was we, inheritors of the Spanish
sacerdotes, who had not seen, who had broken up New World
Christianity exactly as don Pablo had said all along. The Mayas
had always carried the Christian idea. Now, in hieroglyphs, in
Chilam Balam's text, in oral counsel, and in my own vision, I
had seen for myself that it was truly so. I realized that the ancient
literate shamans had not lied, they had really communicated
with God in their dream walk visions, they had been given
supernatural wisdom and had recorded their future vision in
count and mysterious sign. The history of the pre-Columbian
world, as we had written it, began to change in the potent light
of this, the briefest of Mayan texts, page 60 of the *Chilam Balam
of Chumayel*. What will happen if we ever come to be given

understanding of the entire scripture that has been left? Then the origin of the count of the world will be renewed.

I asked don Pablo what he thought this awakening of vision and understanding of Mayan night writing meant now at the end of the Long Count. Neither gesture nor expression on his part revealed his innermost thoughts to me. His earlier crossing of himself was the only gesture given as sign. Now he was still, his thoughts here and at the end of the world. He said, 'We will leave the counsel here. Let us see what your *ah kinob* think now, what they say about what has appeared already. We shall wait and see if people are ready to hear the counsels this time. Because it is for everyone, for whoever wants to reach it. It is not appearing to punish anyone.'

We walked sixty miles in the next four days, moving out of Yucatan into the deeper forests of Quintana Roo. Here, instead of a Mayan village every three leagues or so, we came across more isolated settlements, some apparently deserted, others crowded, a number only family compounds, others villages of a hundred inhabitants and more. We had entered Cruzob country again, but this time much closer to the centre than Tulum. Here the Indians were much more closely tied to counsels which emphasized the Fight of a hundred years ago against the federal soldiers – a Fight which had established these Mayas as completely free agents, free to practise their own Christianity, free to work and barter the resources of the forest, free from 'Spanish' domination in all its forms. These were the Mayas who most closely adhered to the Chilam Balam counsels read during *fiestas* each year. It was these Cruzob Maya who had been given the sacred duty of guarding the Oracular Cross which, the Mayas said, had been asleep for eighty years and more.

On the eighth day of our walk, in the crisp early morning light, we stepped from the forest onto the road leading to Felipe Carrillo Puerto and the end of our journey. But first we set off along a secondary white road leading to the sacred village of

Xcacal La Guardia. As in Tulum, a complex, profound history is hidden behind the obscure, evidently straightforward façade of this simple Mayan village. As we walked a league along the new government road, don Pablo explained what he knew of this village. He came here for the fiestas once a year and he respected the great traditionalism of the people, the Oracular Cross which was guarded by armed Mayans here, and the lack of compromise of the Mayan way of life which he noted amongst the people. 'They have a good counsel here,' he said. He told me there was a reciprocal respect for Tulum and surrounding villages even while these were more accommodating to the outside world and its ways. However, subtle distinctions between villages existed and Xcacal remained the sacred centre, guardian of the Oracular Cross of the Cruzob Maya.

Soon we passed a freshly cleared and fenced area of forest where the villagers were planning to keep cattle as a cooperative project. From the distance, across this open area a shout hailed us from the roof of a large house in the process of being thatched. As we approached I noticed that a group of Mayans were working together nearby, cutting and trimming poles to make the walls of the house. One of them came over and lightly shook hands, a welcoming friendly expression on his face. Neither he nor any of the others were perturbed in the slightest by our arrival. He asked where we came from and our interest in coming to Xcacal and we answered him openly.

We stood for a while, talking pleasantries, watching the *guano* palms being tied onto the roof of the house, the Mayas cracking jokes with us and amongst themselves. The spokesman for the group stood by us acting as host. He was dressed in carefully patched, faded, cotton shirt and traditional knee-length *culex* trousers. Under his straw hat his hair was close cropped, streaked with grey and white, but his features seemed younger than his sixty and more years. I was to learn that he was the leader of those who guarded the Cross at present. Now his simple working attire and the sensitivity expressed in his conversation and manner quickly persuaded me of his deeply spiritual outlook. But if I had seen him in a crowded market, a bus station, an urban setting, I doubt whether I would have noted anything about him – except perhaps the evident contentment of his life.

We walked to the village a mile away and settled our loads in the shade of one of the houses. Already I was feeling saddened at the end of our walk. I felt the step was only just beginning to open and, characteristically European, I wanted more. In my present frame of mind I could have walked all the way to Tayasal, the last Itza stronghold deep in the jungles of Petén, two hundred miles further south. Until the 1690s when the Itza finally invited Spanish priests to journey there and baptize them – according to prophecies contained in their ancient hieroglyphic codices – this had remained an independent centre of learning for the Yucatec Maya. Historical documentation shows us that a complicated trail system existed in those days linking the centre to the Yucatan proper. Indeed Chief Canek, leader of the Itza at Tayasal, had sent messengers to T-Ho to advise the Spanish of the proper time, according to their count, to come and baptize the people under his rule.

Equally intriguing was the fact that an Englishman had lived and worked with the Itza at the time, had been accepted amongst them on reciprocal terms. No records exist of his dialogues with the Indian Chief Canek, keeper of the sacred codices, although I suspected that he had given the Itza a copy of the Bible and had encouraged them to read it for themselves.

Now don Pablo, Fidel, and I were ushered into don Marcelino Poot's house in the contemporary Mayan sacred centre of Xcacal. Three women and several children hurriedly tidied an area for us, letting hammocks down and providing us with *kanché* seats to sit on. A few words were exchanged as don Marcelino bustled about ensuring our comforts, passing a gourd of refreshing water around for us to taste, and a little *atole* to revive us. Soon we were all settled in, the women sitting with us, preparing maize dough for *tortillas*, carrying on their tasks, listening to our conversation with engaging attention and occasional comment.

Again I marvelled at the frugal lives of these people – how

little one actually needs, in a material sense, I thought. Despite his age, this man and his family could at a few moments notice have bundled all their material belongings into light, small loads and collectively vanished down forest trails, leaving hardly a trace of their presence. But what these Invisible Ones knew, what they understood of the mysteries of God and human life, would astonish the richest and most learned amongst us.

Don Marcelino was eager to converse with us on serious matters. Using no Spanish he launched into an extensive oral history of the Mayans, going back several centuries, dotting his account with the names of Mayan leaders out of the past. Each time he mentioned one of these names he would examine my expression carefully to see if I knew of their place in the Mayan scheme of things. He talked of the slavery of Spanish times, of Mayan freedom since the Fight, of God and the right way to live here on earth. His words flowed gently, there was no obligation to believe or agree. The three of us nodded our attentiveness at the counsel we were privileged to hear. We passed the bowl of *atole* back and forth, savouring the sacred grace of ancient America at the end of our walk.

The perfectly articulated memories and the careful pronunciation of pure Maya coming from don Marcelino revived me from my growing melancholy. I realized that the ancient tradition of thought which had been inscribed on stone and set down in the *Books of Chilam Balam* was still here, still alive amongst many, still manifest in all its breathtaking scale and profundity amongst the living people. At the end is the beginning it promised and this dream walk was really only beginning.

Don Marcelino completed his counsel speaking of the sudden arrival of the white roads, of taxes, of government offers of help. He was undecided about the changes. He asked me how the people could defend themselves now, against the threat of an overwhelming return of colonizers from Mexico, against the return of the Spanish language.

I thought for many minutes over his question. Here in this peaceful household of Mayan Indians, so neglected by us in the past, and yet so willing to make the attempt to counsel with us, there was vision and insight more precious than anything we had ever seen fit to offer them – freely. Here, in themselves, according to ancient counsel and learning way they had overcome our meaness of spirit, our egoism, not by becoming hardened with conspiratorial bitterness and an aggressive stance, but with a genuine openness, even innocence.

'Speak to us with the *Books of Chilam Balam*,' I said, 'the ancient scripture will not fail you.'

Glossary

abuelos: Ancient Ones or grandfathers and grand-mothers. A spiritual as well as kinship term

aguardiente: firewater, cheap liquor

ahau: twentieth day sign in the Mayan Uinal cycle of twenty. Ahau is Lord, blowgun hunter and oracle in the Mayan system

ah kin: sun priest, calendar priest, literate shaman

ak: liana used for binding or 'tying' Mayan houses

almaxikin: counsel given by parents to their children as an orientation on how to live

amigo: friend

atole: maize gruel

baktun: Mayan time period of approximately four hundred years. ($360 \times 20 = 20$ *katuns* $\times 20 = 1$ *baktun*) Mayan Long Count writing of the Classic era (100 AD to 900 AD) divided time into thirteen *baktuns*

Balam: an ancient Indian lineage

balam: spirit guardian of the *milpa* and village

balam col: spirit guardian of the *milpa* (*col*)

balché: ceremonial mead used by shamans during ritual offerings. Of pre-Columbian origin

batab(ob): Yucatec Mayan term which in pre-Columbian and colonial times was used to designate the leaders of a town or village, appointed by the central authority of the *halach uinic*

b'ob: tree of obscure mythological significance in Mayan thought.

brujo: sorcerer engaging in black magic. Opposite of *h-men*, or shamans

bueno: 'good' or 'well now'

caciques: provincial class of exploiters, often but not necessarily landowners given to the use of coercive, violent methods of imposing their will

campesino: small, subsistence farmer, or peasant

Castillo: Castle. Here a reference to the high temple of ancient Mayan cities such as Tulum. A Spanish term which may have been adopted by the Mayans as a result of the Spanish using their cathedrals and churches as fortresses in times of Indian rebellion

cenote: natural reservoirs of water formed when the limestone surface crust collapses to reveal the water table below

chac: Mayan rain spirit guardian. Important 'power' who holds sway over the destiny of the maize harvest

chachalaka: popular bird for hunting, slightly smaller than a pheasant. Often domesticated by the Indians

chai-chaac: Mayan rain ceremony employed during times of drought

che'el: large raucous bird, sky blue in colour, red-eyed. Sometimes referred to as the *gringo* bird because of its noisy, chattering habits

chicle: resin tapped from the *chico zapote* tree used as the basis for making chewing gum

chiclero: person who taps and collects *chicle* resin during the rainy season. Because of their wandering labours they have a deep and intimate knowledge of the Mayan forests

chintok: hardwood used for the main posts in Mayan house-building

chu ha: water-gourd with maize husk stopper. The thick corklike skin of the gourd keeps the water cool on the hottest of days

chultun: natural and/or artificial reservoirs of water cut in limestone surface of the Yucatan. May also have been used for storing maize and produce from the milpa

coa: small sickle rudely shaped from scrap metal. Used for weeding and harvesting on the milpa. Often has a long handle added so that the farmer does not have to bend down to do the weeding

cocol: the slightly bitter bark of this tree is used to supplement maize in the making of tortillas during severe draught

comal: flat metal griddle upon which tortillas are toasted over a fire

conquistador: conqueror. Term mistakenly applied to the Spanish invaders of the New World

costumbre: custom, tradition, ritual

culex: traditional Mayan cotton trousers worn to the knee and tied there with string. Their use increasingly rare

ejido: land held communally by a village. The individual farmer owns the fruits of his labour but not the land itself. Of pre-Columbian origin

encomienda: royal land grant given to the early Spanish colonizers of the New World. In exchange for a nominal responsibility for converting the Indians to Christianity the Spaniard had a right to their labours, their produce, and their land

federal: reference here is to the federal police working out of Mexico City

fiesta: festival or carnival usually lasting several days and nights

figura: figures, face, countenance

frijoles: red kidney beans, essential staple food in Mexico

guayabera: traditional cotton shirt worn by city menfolk in the Yucatan. Loose, sometimes embroidered, worn outside the trousers without a jacket

guano (xaan): small palm grown especially for purposes of roofing Mayan houses

grace, or *gracia:* term used by the Mayans to refer to maize, 'the grace of God' *hacendados:* owners of haciendas and large tracts of land

halach uinic: true man. Yucatec Mayan term which in pre-Columbian times was used to designate the ruler of a province

hijo de la chingada: popular Mexican expletive roughly translated as 'son of a bitch'

h-men: pronounced 'men'. Mayan for 'one who knows', a shaman

huaraches: sandals worn by the Mexican and Mayan peasantry. Often cut from the rubber of used tyres, they are attached to the feet by thin leather thongs. Essentially pre-Columbian in concept

hubché: area of the milpa which has exhausted its potential and is allowed to revert back to a wild state to replenish its resources

huipil: white cotton dress worn by Mayan women in the Yucatan. Usually embroidered with flowers along the borders

jarana: traditional Yucatec dance – also adopted and transformed by the Mayans for their village festivals

jicara: small gourd used as cup or bowl amongst the Maya

Kahlay Katunob (The Short Count): the count of the *katuns*. A period of about 256½ years formed of thirteen periods of 7200 days

kanché: small Mayan stool or carved tree trunk used as a seat in the houses

Katun XI Ahau: the first age of the cycle of thirteen ages of twenty years each which made up the Kahlay Katunob, or Short Count. The Spanish in 1539 arrived in Yucatan at the beginning of a Katun XI Ahau

Kuxan Suum: the living cord which in *illud tempus* joined earth and sky

lec: gourd used to keep tortillas warm and clean. Often covered with an embroidered cloth

lub: resting place and time

machete: razor sharp steel blade with a wooden handle, often three feet and more in length. Used universally by the Mexican peasantry as the basic tool of life. A Mayan can construct an entire house with a machete as his only tool

macho: male, strong, robust but also, dull and stupid. Synonymous with 'male chauvinist' in Western thought

manta: blanket, shawl, or bolt of cloth

mecapal: name for the bag in which a Mayan carries his belongings or agricultural produce. Held in the small of the back by a tumpline passed across the forehead

mecate (kaan): measure of land 20 × 20 metres. Employed by Mayans in discussing and measuring their *milpas*

mesa: term used to designate the ritual 'altar' upon which offerings are made to the spirits and to God

metate: stone block upon which maize is ground to make *tortillas*

milpa: clearing in forest formed by slash and burn methods of farming. Cultivated area worked by an individual or family which subsequently owns the fruit of its labours

milpero: Mayan term for farmer or whoever works *milpa*

mozon ik: localized whirlwind which assists the Mayan farmer when he is burning off a section of the forest prior to planting

nucuch uinic(ob): 'great men'. Term used in the *Books of Chilam Balam* in reference to the Ancients who build the various Mayan cities

Petén: literally 'region' or 'plain'. Term now applied to the deep tropical rainforest of Guatemala

peten: small tray woven from vines. Hung from crossbeams of the house and filled with peppers, limes, and/or *tortillas* out of the reach of animals and insects

pib: form of cooking by means of heated rocks in an earth oven. Used by hunters to prepare fresh game

pich: small bird common in Yucatan – only one sings at a time, hence its name which means 'only one'

pom: perfumed Mayan incense derived from the resin of a tree. Pre–Columbian in origin

presó: literally, 'imprisoned'. In context a pun on 'present'

rancho: Small, rural homestead, supported by a family

sac be: 'white road'. Term used by the Mayans to describe the ancient roads constructed by their forefathers linking numerous sacred sites together. Now deserted and overgrown in the forest

sacerdote: Spanish, Catholic priest

sisché: small bush, the leaves of which when chewed bring relief from toothache and headache

taco: a *tortilla* containing a variety of meat and fowl fillings. Usually spiced with chilli and sometimes fried

takinché: tree, the bark of which is good for dysentery

tamales: made by boiling *zacan* then adding lard and salt before cooking. The dough is then divided, and fowl, pork, or meat seasoned with tomatoes, *annatto* and salt are added. Each piece is then carefully wrapped in banana leaves and baked in *pib* or in a pot

Tata Dios: Father God

tejon: coati

tepezcuintle: agouti

Territorio: Territory. Term used to designate Quintana Roo before its recent full statehood

T-Ho: ancient Mayan name for present day Mérida

tortillas: uah in Mayan. Maize pancakes made in a variety of ways – some sweet, some salted, mixed with beans or toasted. Ancient Indian staple bread, constituting more than 60 per cent of the average meal

tunkul: Small drum used by shamans during their chanting and praying to contact the spirit world. Of great antiquity

turuhuy nicte: fragrant, flowering tree found in the Yucatan forest, notably during the dry season, February–June

Tutul Xiu: ruler of the Xiu province at time of Spanish occupation in 1539. Willingly ceded authority to the Spanish according to ancient prophetic counsel of Chilam Balam.

u-hanli-col: the 'dinner of the *milpa*'. Harvest ceremony offering the first fruits to the spirits who helped the farmer

Uinal: Mayan term for the twenty signs used to designate the basic twenty day cycle of their pre-Columbian calendar

uinal: the spirit body who restores communication between Man and the invisible world of the spirits

uinic: Mayan word for 'man'

uyumil kaax: the spirit guardians of the forest

yaax ek: medium, light wood used for making the forked posts of the roof in a Mayan house

yalba uinic(ob): Yucatec Mayan term which, in pre-Columbian times, was used to designate the farmers, the *milpero* majority of a province

Yucalpeten: 'Region of the Roe Deer'. Ancient Maya-Itza term for the Yucatan peninsula as a whole

Yuntzil(ob): general term employed in speaking of all the spirit guardians. Those of village, forest, and *milpa*

xaan: see *guano*

xcriban: Scribe or secretary. Since the Ancient Ones wrote down all of time in their count, subsequent shamans and scribes are essentially secretaries, reading and re-writing their ancient visions

Xochitl: Flower in Nahuatl. The twentieth sign in the Nahua cycle, equivalent to Ahau

zaca: Drink used ceremonially as an offering to the spirits. Made of maize cooked with lime, then ground and mixed with water

zacan: ground maize. A very fine, moist meal allowed

to sour for a day before if is used, to make it more digestible. Subsequently made into *tortillas* or diluted with a little water and drunk

zastun: small crystals used by shamans to divine sickness and the future. Usually held up to a flame of a candle or fire and gazed into in a trance state

Further Studies

RECOMMENDED READING

There are many books about the various strands of Mayan life and civilization touched on in this work; the problem is to find ones best suited to the reader's particular interest and needs. This list is no more than an introductory selection that compliments the areas touched on in this work. They have been chosen on the basis of availability and relevance.

On Mayan writing:
J. Eric S. Thompson, *Mayan Hieroglyphs Without Tears*, Trustees of the British Museum, 1972.
  A short general introduction by the acknowledged epigraphic master.
J. Eric S. Thompson, *Mayan Hieroglyphic Writing*, University of Oklahoma Press, 1960.
  A comprehensive, scholarly work which provides the necessary manual and data for those wishing to pursue an awakened interest in Mayan writing.

On the Mayan Books of Counsel:
Munro S. Edmonson, *The Popol Vuh, The Quiché Maya Book of Counsel*, Middle American Research Institute, Tulane University, New Orleans, 1971.
  A precise and detailed translation of the text, uncovering its hidden structure and much of its content for the first time.
Munro S. Edmonson, *The Chilam Balam of Tizimin*, University of Texas, 1981 (in press).

On a general introduction to the study of shamanism and other civilizations:

Mircea Eliade, *Myths, Dreams and Mysteries*, Fontana Library of Theology and Philosophy, 1968.

Far and away the most sensitive and observant of texts written in a clear, accessible style. More closely allied to comparative theology than mundane anthropology it is without doubt the best explorer's manual I have seen.

Mircea Eliade, *Shamanism: Archaic Techniques of Ecstacy*. Bollingen Series LXXVI, Princeton University Press, 1964.

A comparative study of shamanism throughout the world showing its essential characteristics and inherent unity across cultural boundaries. The author does not deny the 'paranormal' powers of shamans, nor the integrity of their labours.

RECOMMENDED VIEWING

Nothing can make the world and vision of the Maya more real than a visit to the Mayan area. The Mexican Government has brought the Mayan cities in the Yucatan and Chiapas within the reach of many thousands of travellers. There are comfortable hotels, efficient bus and air services, and guided tours at reasonable rates. Details can be obtained from government tourist offices and private travel agencies. The ancient Mayan city of T-Ho (Mérida), the present-day capital of the Yucatan, provides a central base for such expeditions. The people of Yucatan welcome, encourage and reward visitors. Visits to outlying Mayan towns and villages (such as Dzitnup outside Valladolid) are equally well received. Bus and taxi services are available at reasonable cost.

Where travel is not possible, the next best thing is a visit to a museum which displays Mayan artifacts, stelae and hieroglyphic writing. The finest museum is indubitably the National Museum of Anthropology in Mexico City, but there are also fine collections in the following museums:

The British Museum, London

The Museum of Mankind, London

The American Museum of Natural History, New York

The Museum of the American Indian, Hope Foundation, New York

The Brooklyn Museum, New York

The Museum of Primitive Art, New York
The Metropolitan Museum of Art, New York

RECOMMENDED LISTENING

An excellent Yucatec Mayan language course consisting of twenty-four tapes and two books is available from:
Language Laboratory
University of Chicago
1126 East 59th Street, Room 4
Chicago, Illinois 60637, USA

For spoken Yucatec Maya:
Robert W. Blair and Refugio Vermont-Salas microfilm copy available from:
The Joseph Regenstein Library,
Department of Photoduplication, University of Chicago,
1100 East 57th Street,
Chicago, Illinois 60637, USA